THE BOOK OF
MONKS ORCHARD
AND EDEN PARK

Park Farm
and stables

Walled garden

Dower House,
one-time site of
Wickham Park

IAN MUIR AND PAT MANNING

HALSGROVE

First published in Great Britain in 2004

British Library Cataloguing-in-Publication Data.
A CIP record for this title is available from the British Library.

ISBN 1 84114 338 3

HALSGROVE

Halsgrove House
Lower Moor Way
Tiverton, Devon EX16 6SS
Tel: 01884 243242
Fax: 01884 243325
E-mail: sales@halsgrove.com
Website: www.halsgrove.com

Frontispiece photograph: *An aerial view of the Bethlem Royal Hospital grounds, 1991.*
(By Courtesy of English Heritage)

Printed and bound in Great Britain by CPI Bath Press.

Dale Bealby, 1953–1992.

There was a time when meadow, grove and stream,
The earth and every common sight,
To me did seem
Apparelled in celestial light,
The glory and the freshness of a dream.

It is not now as it hath been of yore:-
Turn whereso'er I may,
By night or day,
The things which I have seen I now can see no more.

from *Recollections of Early Childhood*
(WILLIAM WORDSWORTH)

St David's class of youngsters, c.1940/41. **Left to right:** *?, Shirley Malkin,*
David Malkin, ?, Janet Hutchinson, ?, ?, Mary Smythe, Barry Jackson. (STD)

Foreword

This is a wonderful book. A combination of history, researched as impeccably as ever by Pat Manning, and the more recent recollections of people who grew up loving where they lived.

As the memories of local residents tumble forth, so what they are telling us really comes alive, and we are back with them enjoying life in a world so similar to and yet so different from the one we take for granted today.

In Ian Muir's recollections of 40 years ago, for example, Saturday afternoons were synonymous with soccer. Today, football has been taken over by the media and players are celebrities in their own right. At that time it was a participation sport and players built lasting friendships both with team-mates and with players from opposing teams. In those days youngsters kicked a ball around a park rather than kicking each other after closing time.

Cliff Watkins, 2004

Bill Bailey with the Marian Vian football team. (JH)

CONTENTS

Acknowledgements

We are very grateful to all those who let us use their images and for all help received. We are particularly grateful for the Century Photos of S.A.J. Quilter of 301 Upper Elmers End Road, whose images were supplied by St David's College and the 1955/56 Mayor William Duncan's family.

We thank Howard Smith for the information and photographs used in Chapter 5, not forgetting Paul Faires' Beckenham Town scrapbook.

Photographs and progress reports of the construction from 1928–30 of the Bethlem Royal Hospital are held by the Bethlem Royal Museum and we gratefully acknowledge the archivists' assistance.

AB	Ann Bartlett with photos from Diana Garratt (née Tonkin)	JHU	Jim Hurley
AC	Audrey Conway	JL	Janet Lambert
AH	Allen Horsley	JS	Janet Starr
AL	Alwyne Loyd	JSU	John Surtees
AW	Anne Wagstaff	KL	Katie Lawler
B	By courtesy of the Bromley Local Studies Library including images from the Rob Copeland Collection – copyright held by Mr Johns	KW	The late Keith Whittingham
		LP	Linda Peake
		LW	Lyn Williams
		M&AD	Monica and Alan Duncan
BE	Reproduced by permission of Bethlem Royal Hospital Archives and Museum	MC	Marjorie Coles
		MM	Marjorie Mather
BP	Bob Pack	MMc	Monica McCarthy
BM	By courtesy of the British Museum	MOTG	Townswomen's Guild, Monks Orchard
BR	*London Bridge to Addiscombe*, Middleton Press, for British Rail pictures	MRD	Mr Dellar
		NL	Nigel Lawford
CL	Chris Latham	NT	Nancy Tonkin Collection from Bill Tonkin
CR	By courtesy of the Croydon Local Studies Library	OH	Olive Hamer
		OV	Olive Varney
CW	Carol Walklin (née Jeffries)	PB	Pat Baxendale
DB	David Bebbington, photographer, for permission to use the David Bowie bandstand photo	PD	Peter Duncan
		PF	Paul Faires
		PG	Phyllis Greenslade
DE	Derek Eldridge	PT	Phyllis Tear
DH	Dave Hitchins	PW	Pam Warden (née Holland)
DS	David Stoneham of Masters	RB	Ray Burden
EH	Maps by courtesy of English Heritage a) 1991 Crown copyright NMR b) 1946 English Heritage NMR RAF Photography	RH	Ritchie Hepburn
		RP	Roddy Petley
		RW	Ray Whittingham
		SK	Stan Kelly
EN	Eden Park Nurseries and the Bartholomews	SM	Sheila Meakins
		SMI	Peter Smith
ES	Eric Smith	STM	The late Stanley Mitchell, with special thanks for the cover photo
FB	Felicity Boyden (née Edden)		
FF	The Faviell Family	STD	St David's College
FFC	Fulham FC	SW	Shirley Willis
HB	The late Hugh Bean	T&NP	Thelma and Norrie Pedgrift
HS	Howard Smith	TF	Tim Feltham
JB	Jean Bedford	TJ	Tony (Anthony Copeland) Johns
JAB	Janet Berlin	TW	Trevor Woodward
J&B	Joan and Bert Durling	VS	Valerie Sheldon (née Thornton)
JF	Jane Fabb (née Webber)	VW	Veronica Watkins
JH	John Hazelton	WG	Wendy Gowell

Introduction

The Monks Orchard estate comprised two adjacent farms, Park Farm and Eden Farm, which met at the county boundary between Addington, Surrey and Beckenham, Kent. Landowners called Munke who owned parts of Addington in 1552 are the most likely origin of the name Monks Orchard. There was once a Monks Orchard Wood of 44 acres running across the county boundary and on the 1820 map of the sale of the Langley estate were three fields belonging to Eden Farm, each called Monks Orchard. In 1854/5, when Lewis Loyd needed a name for his new mansion, he chose Monks Orchard and the name has been retained for the modern estate. Present-day descendants of the Loyd family have supplied a wealth of detail about their forebears – we are especially grateful for two volumes, one the family tree (more than 28 A3 pages) and the other a who's who of all those mentioned, as well as many family photographs.

The name Eden came from the lease of farmland by Langley estate owner, the great Peter Burrell, to William Eden, First Lord Auckland, in 1782. The information about the Edens comes mainly from journals and books written by Lord Auckland himself, his daughter Emily and other family members, including Sir Anthony Eden, Lord Avon.

This book, however, is dependent on all its contributors, who so patiently and willingly acceded to requests for photographs and for stories of their pasts. Without them there would be no book on Monks Orchard and Eden Park.

The aerial view on the title page shows Wickham Road in the foreground and encompasses the grounds of the Bethlem Royal Hospital (once the mansion of Monks Orchard) and, in the distance, the housing of Eden Way and Upper Elmers End Road. The rectangle of the walled garden, dating from 1850 if not earlier, with the Dower House on the site of Wickham Park, will be lost in the building of the hospital extension in the near future (2005).

Park Farm, seen on the middle left of the same photograph, taken in 1991, had by 1994 been demolished, unfortunately before it could be listed by English Heritage (EH).

Bill Tonkin takes a party through the stable arch at Park Farm, 1992. (J&B)

Some of the Contributors

Far left: *Jane Fabb.*

Left: *Janet and Margaret Lambert.*

Joan (née Freeman) & Bert Durling

Living for decades in Altyre Way, Joan and Bert's interest in local history has not only provided us with a reliable source of pictures and detail but a seemingly inexhaustible source of names of neighbours to contact for further anecdotes. They supplied the names of the party-goers at the Aylesford Avenue VE Day celebrations, reminding us that in those days adults were not generally known by their first names.

Phyllis Greenslade

Although she lives far away in Somerset, Phyllis was our first contributor as she has a friend, Marjorie Mather, who still lives in Cheston Avenue. She brings clearly into focus the hard life of a farm worker in the 1940s and her respect for the steward, Mr Ablewhite, shows through.

Jane Fabb

One of our main contributors, Jane has lived in the area her whole life and has a lively interest in photography. The shot of Stanhope Park taken from her bedroom window reminds us of the lost world of trust and fun that was enjoyed by the youth of the 1950s. Today one of her main interests is adopting animals such as orphan lambs. She also enjoys theatre and astrology.

Janet & Margaret Lambert

Since 2001 Janet and Margaret have moved from Beckenham to Longfield in the Darent valley, where they are ideally placed to research their family history. Their great-great-grandfather, a master carpenter, was responsible for much of the carpentry in St Margaret's, Horsmonden, including the pulpit, angel carvings and a handsome signed chair. Ex-policewoman and probation officer Janet, a keen county cricketer in her day, and her sister Margaret, a telephonist, have raised well over £15,000 for an arthritis charity by making 3D cards and selling them through their friends and their local coffee-evening group.

Eric Smith

Born the youngest of a family of three in Beckenham, Eric was educated at local schools and has an incredibly vivid recall of those times, probably because he took an active part in all that was going on. He worked for the same company in the City for 53 years as a shipping and forwarding agent, a job that he thoroughly enjoyed. He continues to be a dedicated member of the community in Tonbridge, where he lives today. Eric belongs to the Lion's Club International, members of which believe that it is the men and women in a community who are in the best position to know who needs help and why. Worldwide, there are 1.4 million members in more than 180 countries.

Howard Smith

We are indebted to Howard for all the details he supplied about local footballers. You can read his own story in Chapter 2.

Olive Varney (née Chilver)

Born at Eden Park Farm shortly before it disappeared under the housing of Stanhope Grove, Olive also spent her childhood on Kelsey Manor Farm and played in the Kelsey Park ice well. Her unique memories and photos have been very welcome.

Felicity Boyden (née Edden)

We have Felicity to thank for the many civic photos she supplied as the daughter of the late, much-respected Dr R.P.S. Edden, OBE, JP, of Eden Park Avenue. While taking care of her husband, son and twin grandsons, she still, in 2003, managed to win, with partner Margaret Milne, the Doxford foursomes trophy, the Invicta Horse of Kent, to which all lady golfers of the 'Wildernesse' club of Sevenoaks aspire.

Phyllis Tear

Niece of Alderman James Crease, the loyal Beckenham Council member for some 50 years after whom Crease Park is named, Phyllis now lives in

Charles Stevens (left) was eight years old when he led out the Beckenham Town football team in 1948 (see page 112). He followed the team from Balmoral to Stanhope and such was his interest in football that he went to Bromley Grammar School instead of the rugby-playing Beckenham and Penge Grammar School.

Eric Smith.

Howard Smith.

After working for 40 years as a buyer for Sainsbury's he retired to a life of squash and golf although he remains as keen on football as ever.

Ferring but has her roots in Beckenham. She married David Munro, a talented writer, 'father figure' of the Beckenham Salon and friend of Bob Monkhouse. She has supplied us with photographs from her uncle's day.

Cliff & Veronica Watkins
Cliff has lived for 40 years in the Eden Park area of Beckenham. He married in 1965 and he and his wife Veronica made their first home in Eden Road. Veronica taught for some years at Monks Orchard School and their son Crispin was a member of the

choir and the cubs at St James' Church, Elmers End. Cliff is well known for his active interest in and concern for local affairs. He probably knows more about celebrated Beckenham personalities such as Enid Blyton, her nephew Carey Blyton and David Bowie than anyone else in the town. His help and advice, along with the numerous photographs he provided, are greatly appreciated. Not to be outshone, Veronica has not only contributed to collections of short stories but her novel, *Searching for Martin Barrett*, was published in 2004 under the pen name Veronica Lloyd.

Class Upper 1, 1966, at Marian Vian. Left to right, back row: *Julia Coles, Stephen Dennis, Ann Strachan, Howard Sharman, Karen Dormer, Bill Harding, ?, ?, Christine Miles;* third row: *Aubrey Davey, Geraldine Crossley, Derick Clarke, Dilys Jones, Stephen Blake, Gillian Trueman, Dave Skindle, Loraine Rumph, Ian Muir;* second row: *Paul Thomas, Diana Bowden, Nicola Garratt, Hilary Brightman, Valerie Smeeton, Elaine ?, Sarah Snell, Alison Beddington, Linda Peake, Julia Burgess, Ian McPhillips;* front row: *Stuart Clarke, Stuart Knowles, Gary Goode, John Kirkman, Brian French, Barry ?, Robert Hume.* (LP)

The Authors

Pat Manning and her beloved dog Jenna.

Ian Muir.

Pat Manning

Patricia Ridler was born at Blackheath in 1929, daughter of Alfred Ridler (who for 18 years was verger of St Paul's, Brackley Road) and the youngest in a family of three. Educated at the Beckenham County School for Girls and Imperial College, London, she is a scientist rather than a historian but, as a lifelong Beckenham resident, the town's history has become an engrossing study. In 1951 she married Michael James Manning, a merchant navy engineer, and they had three sons, David, Philip and Peter, and a daughter, Gillian. Teaching fitted in with raising a family and she taught mathematics and science – specialising in biology – at her old school, which had moved to Park Langley.

Retirement gave Pat the chance to write and in order to publish three books she established Jenna Publishing in memory of her dog, Jenna. Research into the fascinating Cator family provided material for her fourth book, published by Authors Online Ltd. None, however, has been as much fun to put together as this book about Monks Orchard and Eden Park! Lucy the West Highland terrier and Troy the Bearded Collie are/were also Pat's dogs.

Also by Pat Manning and obtainable from the Beckenham Bookshop are: *Churchyard Memorials of St George's, Beckenham; Thoughts on Beckenham's Rivers; The Road Names of Beckenham Tell their Tales; The Cators of Beckenham and Woodbastwick.*

Ian Muir

There can be few residents better qualified to compile a book about Monks Orchard and Eden Park than Ian. Although born in Scotland, Ian grew up in Merlin Grove in the 1960s with his brother Robin and sister Sheila. He was educated locally at Marian Vian

and Hawes Down. Here is Ian's Beckenham as he knew it:

When I think of Marian Vian and Hawes Down the first thing that comes to mind is the school dinners. At Marian Vian the dinners were vile and we were made to eat all our greens. It was no wonder there was always somebody being ill in afternoon assembly. I could not believe it when I went to Hawes Down and saw chips being served – pupils even asked for seconds. During research for this book it was a great pleasure to meet Kit Bailey, who some may remember as a teacher at Marian Vian. Kit is sharp as a tack and remembered all our names.

In the winter nearly everyone wore a black duffel coat. If it got a bit too warm you would just put the hood on your head without putting your arms in the sleeves.

Our bikes had what we called drop handlebars, or cow horns, like a Harley Davidson motorbike. Some of us even shared a tandem. I can recall Ray Lotto and myself paying a boy we called Lurch £4 for his tandem. After using it for a while somebody offered us more money so we sold it.

It was a long ride uphill from Eden Park to West Wickham so we used to cut through Hawksbrook Lane (we called it 'the tranny', after the London Transport Sports Ground), then along the golf course road (Red Lodge Road) into Hawes Lane. Going home was different, downhill all the way. The noise we made going to school was very loud as we were all very excited – not about lessons but about seeing all our mates and getting into mischief. Going home it was even louder. I would say that there were nearly 200 bikes in the bike sheds at Hawes Down.

If we did not ride to school we got the school coach that ran from the Robin Hood in Penge, stopping at Elmers End, the Rising Sun and alongside the Esso

Garage at Eden Park. It took you all the way to the front gate at school, avoiding the long walk from the bus stop outside West Wickham swimming baths all the way down Hawes Lane. To this day I do not know who organised the coach. I do know it was run by Clark's Coaches and we paid the driver three old pence.

My friends and I roamed freely in the surrounding fields and parks, particularly in the hay meadows of the Bethlem Royal Hospital, where some residents of Eden Way, according to their house deeds, are still permitted to walk. We did have problems when we decided to enter one of the many private sports grounds – the Standard Bank of South Africa (now Amida) sports ground, for example, was next to Stanhope Grove and had some great tennis-courts about 100 yards from the pavilion. The groundkeeper lived in an apartment in the pavilion. We would enter the courts and usually play for about five minutes before he saw us. Instead of creeping up on us, he would come charging out of the pavilion every time and shout, 'Oi, you, get out of there!', and off we would pelt. We once nearly got caught, we were laughing so much.

In those days the council gave scholarships to promising swimmers and I swam, with the Manning boys (Pat's three sons), as a member of the Beckenham Swimming Club. Those boys were too fast for us. My good friend Phil Ibbs and myself both attended training

but it was so hard we even resorted to cheating by pulling ourselves along by the ropes used as lane markers. We didn't make the Olympic team – I wonder why not?

In 2002, when Eden Park School was being demolished, I went onto the site to take some photos and was shown around what was left of the school by the janitor. We went into a room with all the school cups and trophies and I noticed a cup with the words 'Philip Ibbs, Swimming Champion 1965'. After hearing that everything was to be thrown out, I took Phil's cup home and waited for a few weeks until I presented it to him. 'Where did you get that?' he declared. We returned the others to the school at Wickham Court.

One very hot day in 1965, Beckenham Town had a pre-season game against Fulham FC. The spectators were in for a treat because Johnny Haynes was playing. Since 1952 he had played for Fulham 658 times, captained England 22 times and received 56 caps. The Fulham team arrived in a coach and entered the ground by the top gate. They were all dressed in club blazers and walked across the pitch in pairs to the changing rooms, followed by two men carrying the kit in an enormous container. We were more used to teams arriving in old cars and vans. Although nearing the end of his career, Haynes played the game as though it was his first. I shall never forget the sight of him in gleaming white and black kit going to the centre of the pitch to meet Beckenham Town's captain. There was another pre-season match (1965/66) against a professional club, this time Millwall. Town lost both games but the score did not matter to the supporters. It was brilliant.

My memories include running errands for my mother with the added bonus of being able to keep the change as a reward. While planning my own purchases I would forget the order and then go into the fishmonger at the Rising Sun (which is what we called the area) for some fish. 'What kind?' he would ask. After a long silence he would phone my mother to ask her.

Did you ever do that?

Above: *The view from No. 109 Stanhope Grove across Stanhope Park in the 1950s.* (JF)

Right: *'The other side of the door' at Beckenham first-class baths on an important gala night.* (M&AD)

Going to the barbers was like going to the dentist. We were given strict instructions to ask for a short-back-and-sides. You have to remember that this was in the 1960s and the Beatles, the Rolling Stones and the Searchers were very popular with the kids, though not so popular with the grown-ups as they were loud and did not have short hair. We would go into the barber at the Rising Sun and ask for a haircut like the Searchers and the barber would say OK but still give us a short-back-and-sides.

I remember the echoing screams and shouts and the swimming-bath smells while waiting impatiently for a ticket at the kiosk, and the excitement when occasionally the door to the first-class baths would open and give a glimpse of what was going on. Why were we only allowed up the right-hand staircase to the café to get our sticky bun and hot Ribena? Even after getting a tanner (6d.) bag of yesterday's buns on the way home from Lampards, the bakers in Croydon Road, we still ate all our dinners!

We played football all year round at Stanhope Grove Park. In those days you had to get to the park early just to get on to the pitch, as there were up to 50 kids playing there. We only had one football. It belonged to David Ward and if he did not come down to the park somebody would be despatched to his house to borrow it. I remember when he was ill in bed we still decided the right thing to do was to go and get the ball. Bromley parks all had park-keepers whose job was not only to look after the park but to organise games, etc. One such 'parky' was the late Alf Killick, to whom we all owe a debt of thanks. Alf was a dedicated man who did much for visitors to the park. Stanhope Rovers and Beckenham Town Football Club played on Saturdays at Stanhope Grove and were our heroes. When I was doing research for this book I managed to track down Howard Smith, who was secretary of both Town and Rovers. When I went to see him he remembered me and said he had something belonging to one of my mates. He then produced Paul Faires' Beckenham Town scrapbook, which Paul had either lost or left with Howard years before.

In the summer months we played in the fields and woods in the Bethlem grounds. There was an unwritten law that nobody went past the bowling-green. Local residents had allotments in the grounds behind the houses in Eden Way and Altyre Way. Our entry to the grounds was by a path between two houses in Eden Way (the original path to the Monks Orchard mansion), where the gate was always open. Just past the gate was a Day Centre (formerly the Evening Standard Sports and Social Club), which even had a croquet lawn. We 'borrowed' this lawn on Sundays when nobody was there and used it as a cricket pitch – Paul Faires even arranged a game with another team.

The paths that ran inside the woods were great to ride bikes around at high speed. I can recall one of our gang saying that he had seen a map of the Bethlem grounds showing a large lake to the south. We spent

years trying to find it, making expeditions by day and night to no avail. I have discovered since that the lakes were drained and filled in just after the Second World War – the map was obviously an old one. Nevertheless, we had great fun trying to find the lake and in 2002 we did find a weir and lots of old gates and fences that I now know belonged to the mansion. At the end of summer we would play in the hay bales.

We all went to Inters and Junos at St John's in Eden Park Avenue – we saw it as a better version of the Scouts. In those days we rode or ran everywhere and once walked from Eden Park to Keston Ponds and back.

The Eden Park café was a favourite with us, not for the excellent food but for the pinball machine. The reward for being top scorer of the week was to have your name highlighted on a blackboard. This board often showed the names of Crystal Palace Football Club players, who used the café after training at the London Transport ground in Hawksbrook Lane. Palace also trained at the Beckenham rugby ground in Balmoral Avenue. In 2004, Palace continues that tradition – their training ground is in Copers Cope Road.

Another playground was the Eden Park Hotel car park, nicknamed the Black Patch. We would roller-skate and use a very early version of a skateboard. Robert Gibbs was best on the board, with Mick or Lawrence Turton coming a very close second. The Turtons moved to Devon in 1969, which was hard for us, having been a very close group of friends for many years. It was all part of growing up. Paul Whale, if I remember, had the best bike and could outride us all, so we let down his tyres.

We all still went down to Stanhope Grove to play football in the evenings, even when we had left school and started work. After the game we would sit on the fence by the alley outside the Rising Sun. We would go into the off-licence and buy tins of lemonade and packets of crisps and sit there talking for hours. We even had our own football team, Harvington FC, managed by Reg Swift, whose son Adrian played as a centre-forward. When we were old enough we went into the Eden Park Hotel. Then we all grew up and got married and although only a few of us kept in contact there was a bond between all of us, as with any group of friends. After all, these were the people who shared the good and bad times, who together moved from junior to senior school, who went on holiday together, who were even best man at each others' weddings.

What I will always remember is the laughter. We held a reunion in the Eden Park Hotel during Christmas 2003. It was a day to remember as some of us had not seen the others for 30 years. It was as if we started where we had left off – laughing.

I would like to pay tribute to our fantastic parents, many of whom are no longer with us.

The steady loss of open land to building has hit Ian particularly hard. He fears a time when the parkland of the Bethlem Royal Hospital will become over developed.

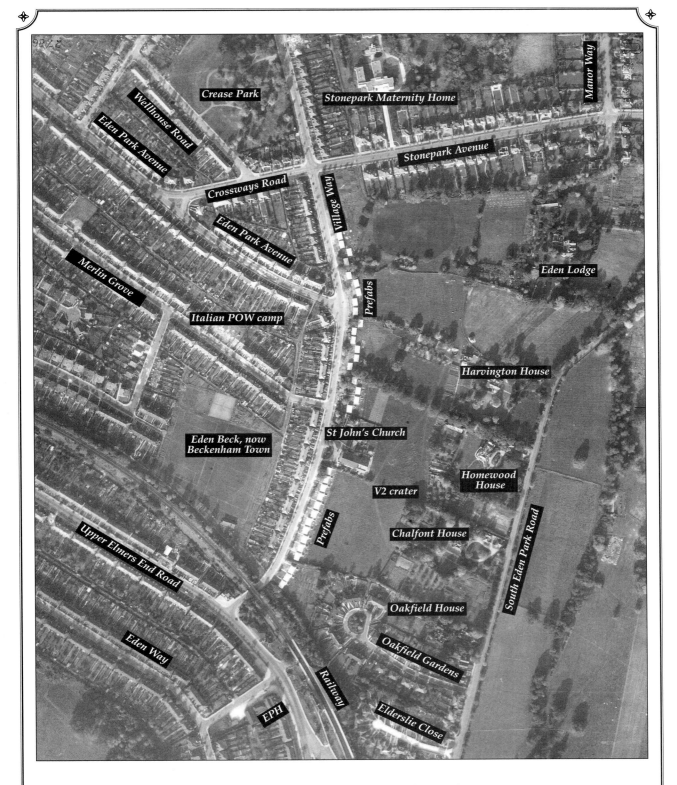

An aerial view of Eden Park showing many features long gone.
Note the circle (behind St John's Church) – this is the V2 crater. (EH)

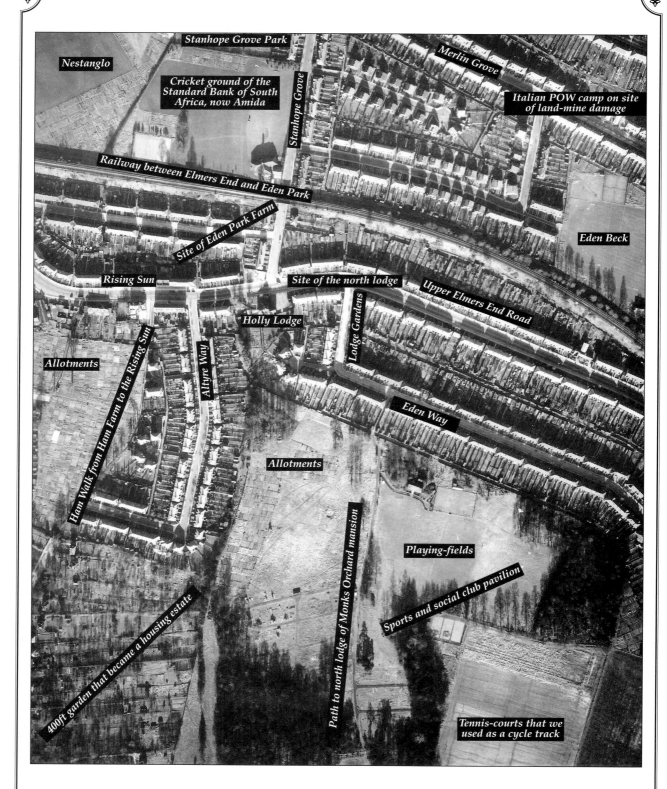

An aerial view of Upper Elmers End and the sports fields of Bethlem Royal Hospital grounds. (EH)

CHAPTER 1

History

The Lloyds' farmhouse in 1910, seen among the trees (above) *and, in 2004, as a holiday home* (left). (AL)

Where it all Began

The story of Monks Orchard begins far away in the farms of west Wales, close to the village of Cilycwm, Carmarthenshire. The land there is largely owned by the Queen and, for its population of about 390 adults, forestry is more important than farming.

Thomas Lloyd and his wife Gwenllian were staunch supporters of the church at Cilycwm and it is fortunate for us that its records run from 1701. The list of burials tells us that Thomas and Gwenllian lived into their eighties and we can calculate that Thomas was born in about 1653 and his wife some ten years later.

Of their children, son William died in 1701 when only a few days old, while Mary, Catherine and Lewis survived into adulthood. Lewis and his wife Jane had seven children, of whom William (1729–1800) provided the line leading to Beckenham and Monks Orchard. William inherited the farm at Cym-y-To-Fach, when his father died in 1758 and was still farming the same 56 acres in 1795. He married Anne Williams in 1765 and they also had seven children, all baptised at the church in Llanwrda. William made sure that his four sons were well educated and was rewarded by all four moving to England and changing the spelling of their name to Loyd! Lewis, especially, was highly successful and died in 1858 worth nearly

£2m. Between 1795 and 1798 William farmed the 24-acre Court Henry Farm at Cym-y-To-Fach, which stayed in the family until 1881.

The four boys who broke away from Wales were Lewis (1768–1858), William (1770–1828), Thomas (1775–1853) and Edward (1780–1863).

In September 1789 Lewis, on a lively white pony, rode to Manchester, where he entered the Manchester Unitarian Chapel and became a preacher. A member of the congregation, Samuel Taylor, recognised his

Lewis Loyd senr, from a portrait by E.U. Eddis. (AL)

gift for figures and accounts and Lewis, after his marriage in 1793 to Sarah Jones, daughter of the banker and tea dealer John Jones, entered the London & Manchester Bank. On 25 September 1796 their only son, Samuel Jones Loyd, was born at Lothbury, London, inheriting his father's wealth. On 10 April 1835 Lewis obtained a grant of arms registered at the College of Arms in his father's name to include his brothers and their descendants. This includes a double-headed eagle with a buck's head for the crest and the motto *non mihi sed patriae*. Lewis purchased the Overstone Park estate in Northants, where he died on 13 May 1858. He was buried there.

Samuel Jones Loyd became one of the great figures of British banking, his correspondence running to three volumes in the Cambridge University Press. He was created Baron Overstone on 5 March 1850 and it was he who came to live in Addington, his name being remembered locally in Overstone Gardens, off Orchard Way. The area is now part of Beckenham because of an exchange of land between the present boroughs of Croydon and Bromley.

Samuel Jones Loyd, Lord Overstone,
from a photograph taken in 1886. (AL)

Samuel was MP for Hythe from 1819–26 and in 1929 he married Harriet Wright. Their only son, Henry Jones Loyd, was born in December 1832 but died three months later, Samuel thus having no male heir to whom he could pass his title on his death in 1883. His daughter, Harriet Sarah (1837–1920), survived and went on to marry Lt Col Robert James Lindsay VC, KCB, in 1858, at which time Robert incorporated his wife's name with his own, becoming Loyd-Lindsay. He was made Baron Wantage of Lockinge in 1885. Robert's VC was awarded for defence of the colours at Alma in the Crimea in 1857.

Edward, the youngest of the four Loyd brothers,

also came to live in Addington but not until his retirement in 1848. He had joined the London & Manchester Bank as a clerk, working his way up to become a partner of the Manchester branch of the Jones Loyd bank in 1821. He married Sarah Taylor of Lancashire in 1809 and, unlike his brother Lewis, had a number of children. Of his three sons and five daughters it was Lewis who became Samuel's heir. Edward and Sarah leased Coombe House in Coombe Lane and both died in January 1863. They were buried beneath a large red-marble chest tomb on a tiered base of grey marble in St Mary's churchyard, Addington. Their son Lewis and his wife Frances Harriet were buried in the same tomb, Lewis in 1891 and Frances in 1902. Beneath a large yew tree, the tomb is hidden by ivy, which seems to have preserved the inscriptions – to Edward and his wife Sarah on the south side and to their son Lewis and his wife Frances Harriet on the north side.

South side inscription:
Edward Loyd of Green Hill Manchester
Born 30 Jan 1780
Died at Coombe house 30 Jan 1863
Sarah his wife born 5 July 1785
Died 10 Jan 1863

North side inscription:
Lewis Loyd of Monks Orchard banker
Born at Manchester 10 August 1811
Died at Monks Orchard Addington 19 July 1891
Also his wife Frances Harriet Loyd
Died 27 Jan 1902

With costly remedial work carried out under the auspices of English Heritage, Coombe House is a Grade II listed building, purchased by Croydon Health Authority for use as a day centre for the mentally handicapped and now called Geoffrey Harris House, after a Croydon MP.

With Victorian additions, the original inner shell of the building is eighteenth century. In the grounds there is an eighteenth-century red-brick ice house, also Grade II listed, consisting of a domed circular storage chamber half sunk into the ground.

Another of the four Loyd brothers, William, also moved to Manchester, where he married Martha Kirkman in what later became Manchester Cathedral. They then moved to London, where William worked as a warehouseman in Cheapside and Clapham. Success in business eluded him, however, and the family had to clear his considerable debts. He was the first of the four brothers to die and was buried in Bunhill Fields, East London, in 1828, leaving five sons and two daughters.

Thomas Loyd was the only unmarried brother and was a calico printer of Ardwick Terrace in Manchester. In 1823 he was head of the Cannon Street calico printers, Loyd & Price, later Loyd,

An early Welsh kitchen. (AL)

Buchan & Welsh. He remained a humorous conversationalist and good company to the end of his days. When he died in January 1853 he left £80,000 to his Welsh relatives. Incidentally Thomas, while acting as witness at his sister Jane's wedding, was the first of the four observed to use the name Loyd.

The London House of Jones Loyd & Co. at 43 Lothbury was sold in 1864 and absorbed by the London & Westminster at 41 Lothbury. It became the City office of the National Westminster Bank.

It is thanks to the work of two of the present members of the Loyd family – Peter Haig Loyd and his fourth cousin Alwyne Loyd – that we have

The Loyd family arms. (AL)

discovered the story of their ancestors. Together they formulated a family pedigree and 'who's who' with all family connections explained.

The Lloyds' house at Cwm-y-To-Fach, in the photograph taken in 1910 (page 15), appears much as it would have in the eighteenth century and seems little changed now it is a holiday home – although it is doubtful that the kitchen still has a cooking pot suspended over an open fire. The view of the house nestling in the valley has probably been the same for centuries. The church of St Michael, where the Lloyd forebears worshipped and were buried, is beautifully kept. A document dated 1535 gave the church's value then as £100.

Samuel Jones Loyd and Park Farm

Park Farm was shown on the 1762 Rocque's map of Surrey as West Shirley Farm, the home farm of Shirley House. In 1807 the Burrells acquired it from John Smith and in 1820 it was described as 'a most desirable estate for a sportsman' in the Lord Gwydir sale of the Langley estates. Paul James Le Cointe bought it in 1822 and his widow Sophia sold out in 1829 to Henry Alexander. In 1836 Park Farm went to Samuel Jones Loyd. It is uncertain whether it was James le Cointe or Samuel Jones Loyd who built the mansion Wickham Park, but the name first appears on maps and documents in 1836.

The farm buildings were situated at the south-east corner of a large lake and Samuel Jones Loyd's initials, with the date 1843, could be seen over the doorway of the farmhouse that he had rebuilt. Sadly the stables were deemed dangerous and demolished in August 1994 and the adjacent farm buildings were lost the same year in a fire on 10 November. English Heritage attempted to save the stables and the Department of Historical Manuscripts took photographs of the elegant ironwork of the stalls and the herringbone brick floors but the Grade II listing came too late.

The Addington charge list dated 4 August 1842 shows Samuel Jones Loyd as the self occupier of Wickham Park and 236 acres, for which he paid £36.18s.6d. annually. The mansion of Wickham Park stood where the Dower House is at the time of writing, the only original feature being the remains of the walled garden. The mansion was reached by three long drives, each with a lodge on a main road. There were two lodges similar in style – one being the White Lodge in Wickham Road with its twin in Upper Elmers End Road, where it remained until 1928 when housing was planned for both sides of Upper Elmers Road as well as Eden Way and Lodge Gardens. A deed in the Bethlem archives details the purchase of the land and dwelling-house called Eden Park Lodge by Edward George Miles and William Henry Gorham, builders, for £450. Mr Burchett, the head gardener was given a week's

Above: *The archway, Park Farm stables.*

Left: *Dated shield on Park Farm stables.*

Below: *The farmhouse, Park Farm.* (BE)

Gardener's cottage in the walled garden of Park Farm. (BE)

Top: *Haymaking in the south field, with the apple orchard in the background.*

Above: *Cutting the north-east field of Park Farm.* (BE)

notice to quit on 5 September 1928 with a recommendation that he be retained on the staff. He had occupied the lodge for two years at a rent of 7s.6d. out of his £2 per week wages.

Various papers held by the Bethlem Museum show how Samuel Jones Loyd extended the property, buying up Eden Park Farm from John Woolley in 1838 and further land at Upper Elmers End, including the Rising Sun in 1847. The Spring Park estate was also acquired in February 1847.

It was at about this time that Edward Lawford was leasing Eden Park, William Eden's mansion in what is now Crease Park. His son, Melville Lawford, kept a diary between 1842 and 1843, details of which are found in Chapter 2.

In 1850, Samuel Jones Loyd was Commissioner for the Great Exhibition and Senator of London University. He sold Wickham Park, Spring Park Farm, Eden Farm and the Rising Sun with its cottages to his cousin Lewis in 1853 and in 1861 had a new house, Overstone Park, built in Northants at the wish of his wife, Harriet. She died just over three years later, from which time he preferred to live with his daughter at Lockinge or in Carlton Gardens in London. In 1865 he was declared one of the wealthiest people in the world with a fortune of five million pounds.

His own son having died in infancy, Samuel Jones provided extensive financial support to the widow and eight children of his nephew, Thomas Kirkman Loyd, who was killed in the Indian Mutiny at Humeerpoor in 1857.

The Dower House remains something of a mystery. The 1851 census shows Wickham Park to be a house of considerable size, but the Dower House described in the 1920 Monks Orchard sale is much smaller, with only two bedrooms. Perhaps Lewis Loyd had the old house replaced by a house which, upon his death, would be more suitable for

The Tudor Lodge in Wickham Road. Note the design of the chimney-pots. (BE)

The north entrance to Park Farm and Monks Orchard in the snow, viewed from 415 Upper Elmers End Road before the even-numbered houses were built. (J&B)

The north lodge in Upper Elmers End Road, in a picture used on a postcard. Compare the fencing to that in the snow scene above. (CR)

The south lodge, now the White Lodge, in Wickham Road. (BE)

In these 1830 portraits by Maclise are, above, *Edward Lawford with his wife Maria and son Melville and* right, *four of the Lawford children,* left to right: *Charles (who later became a curate at the Shirley church), Henry, Maria and Baring. The lake in the background is possibly Kelsey Park Lake.* (NL)

his widow than the Monks Orchard mansion – hence the name 'Dower' House – although Lewis' widow was still living at the mansion according to the 1901 census. The present Dower House was built in about 1929 but is likely to disappear with the proposed extension of the hospital. Let us hope that the tulip tree (*Liriodendron tulipifera*) in the garden survives the upheaval.

Lewis Loyd

When Samuel Jones Loyd sold Park Farm and Wickham Park to his cousin Lewis Loyd in 1853, it was not long before Lewis was playing an important part in the community. In February 1854 a preliminary meeting was held at Wickham Park to form a committee to be responsible for the building of the new church of St John the Evangelist at Shirley. Lewis contributed £1,000 of the tender for £3,960 and the foundation-stone was laid on 9 September 1854. For nearly 30 years there were no choir stalls or pipe organ and the main source of income was from pew rents, not abolished until 1919. In 1881, Lewis Loyd had an organ chamber built on the south side of the chancel into which he installed a manually pumped Lewis organ. He also had choir stalls incorporated. Thereafter, music became an important part of worship at St John's. Lewis founded another St John the Evangelist in Waterloo Road, Cheetham,

Manchester, at a cost of £20,000 and endowed its benefice with an income of £200 per annum.

Lewis was born in Manchester on 10 August 1811, eldest son of Edward Loyd and Sarah Taylor. Edward had retired in 1848 to live at Coombe House in Coombe Lane, which is possibly how Lewis came to live in the area and to buy Wickham Park from his cousin, Lord Overstone. Educated at Eton and Trinity College, Cambridge, he was a banker in the London House of Jones Loyd & Co., a JP, Surrey High Sheriff in 1863 and Commissioner of Lieutenancy for the City of London.

Although according to its occupants in the 1851 census Wickham Park was a large mansion, Lewis wanted to build his own house nearby, which is how the mansion of Monks Orchard came into being. It had eight principal bedrooms, seven secondary rooms, and a top floor of four double and two single rooms, as well as separate domestic accommodation. Inside high walls there were three vineries and separate glasshouses to grow peaches, melons, cucumbers, tomatoes, ferns and carnations. There was an orchard, a rose garden, an Italian garden and three fish-ponds for boating and coarse fishing. On 19 June 1845 at St George's, Hanover Square, Lewis had married Frances Harriet, eldest daughter of Rear Admiral the Hon. Frederick Paul Irby of Boyland Hall, Norfolk, but sadly they had no children to fill their mansion.

Lewis Loyd of Monks Orchard and, above right, *his father, Edward Loyd (1780–1863).* (AL)

Monks Orchard mansion with a view of the lake. (B)

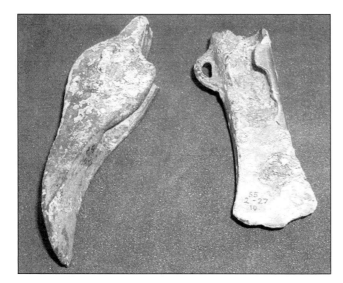

Winged axe heads (top) *and a gouge and ferrule* (above) *from the Wickham Hoard, kept at the British Museum.* (BM)

During the building in 1855, late Bronze-Age relics were unearthed that were dated to 700BC. They included winged axe heads, socketed axes and moulds, parts of spears, a portion of a hilt broken from a sword and gouges, all of bronze, and a quantity of imported copper cake. Known as the Wickham Hoard (grid reference TQ 371625), it can be seen at the British Museum in the Department of Prehistory and Early Europe. A similar Addington Hoard was found in 1914, when a bunker was being dug out on the golf course (grid reference TQ 365640). The same types of Bronze-Age relics are found right across France and the Netherlands and in south-east England they are centred on Carshalton.

The water-supply for the house came from a seemingly inexhaustible well some distance away in the 47-acre Kennel Wood, opposite the Addington Golf Course, although the St James' stream surfaces north of the mansion and other springs rise in the arable land.

The tall alders in marshy ground to the west suggest that there may have been a river flowing from the region of Miller's Pond off Bridle Road. This may have been the river that was used to supply the three ornamental fishponds.

Lewis became a respected member of the commu-

nity. His role as a financial advisor was valued by Emily Hall when he recommended that she buy the 12-acre Lodge field adjoining Ravenswood, extending her property down Beckenham Road.

Lewis was always looking for opportunities to extend his estate. William Little, a tailor from Vauxhall, was the owner of Pond House at the west end of West Wickham High Street. When William died in 1863, Lewis bought the property, which was next to Monks Orchard, for £1,130 when it was sold by auction at Garroway's.

Pond House was the old coaching inn, known as the King's Arms when listed in the *Licensed Victuallers' Registers*, 1753–1816. When William Little bought the property in 1821 its licence went next door to the White Hart. The present White Hart was built on the same site in about 1908. Pond House had many different tenants but eventually the flying bomb that hit this end of the High Street damaged it beyond repair. It was demolished in 1946 and replaced by Crittenden Lodge.

Lewis was also generous and quick to see local need. He donated land at the same end of West Wickham, almost opposite the Wheatsheaf, for an infants' school. The foundation-stone was laid on 5 October 1861 by little Ellen Cator, who put a dab of mortar on the stone with a silver trowel before it was lowered into place. The school was later converted into a church, St Augustine's, at a cost of £1,000, borne by Lewis Loyd.

In 1881, the census provides us with details of the lifestyle of Lewis and Frances, who was five years younger than her husband, at Monks Orchard. Lewis's cousin, Lt Col William Kirkman Loyd of the National Royal Artillery, aged 61 and unmarried, was living at the mansion. Major James Rodd of the National Militia, aged 59, was visiting with his wife

A horse enjoys his nosebag as he waits by the pond at Pond House. (BE)

Monks Orchard mansion. (SMI)

Geoffrey Harris House.

The Château Napoléon.

Elizabeth Ann, aged 60.

There were ten servants, none of them local, to care for the household. William Laynes was the butler, with Herbert Dennett as under-butler, Charles Fricke as footman and Mary Roberts as housekeeper.

The housemaids and kitchen staff were Martha Spooner, Rhoda Lorick, Mary Davenport, Jane Ellis and Margaret Brummett. There were two lady's maids, Ann Witts and Maria Benckendoff. The coachman, George Dartnell, his wife Alice and the groom James Watson lived over the stables, while bailiff Thomas Marchant, his wife Mary Ann and daughter Rebeca *(sic)* occupied the farmhouse.

Lewis also had a house in town at 20 Hyde Park Gardens, SW7.

Although only a few garden balustrades remain of the Monks Orchard mansion, his father Edward's residence, Coombe House, is still in existence. Another historic building close by is Coombe Wood House, now the restaurant Château Napoléon, built by Arthur Lloyd in 1898. There were three Lloyd brothers although they are not related to the Loyds. At St John's Church Arthur has a memorial striking in a graveyard full of impressive gravestones. Off Oaks Road there is also Coombe Farm, now a hostel, consisting of a Tudor building with nineteenth-

century additions by Herbert Lloyd. To complete the trio there was Frank Lloyd, a newspaper magnate who bought Coombe House in 1892 and discovered the Pilgrims' Well in the grounds. Lloyds Park owes its name to these Lloyd brothers.

Since Lewis and Frances had no children of their own, his heir was his brother Edward's eldest son, Frederic Edward Loyd of Amwell Grove, Ware, Hertfordshire. The true extent of the Loyd wealth is indicated by the 1920 sale of the Monks Orchard estate by Frederic. There were 46 lots making up 1,538 acres stretching from Long Lane in the west to Spring Park Woods in the south and down past Oak Lodge along Upper Elmers End Road to Elmers End.

The Monks Orchard mansion and grounds did not sell immediately and it was 1924 before a sale was made to the governors of the Bethlem Royal Hospital. Complications over the Southwark lease led to the property being conveyed to the Corporation of London. It was then leased back to Bethlem for the remainder of the 999-year term, which began in 1674.

When the Bethlem Royal Hospital governors first acquired the property in 1924, farmer Philip Edward Headington was the sitting tenant of Park Farm, which he had leased since 1921. He continued to hold the lease until 1927, while the governors advertised their acquisition. Mr Headington leased two of the lakes to the West Wickham fly-fishing club in 1925 and the remaining lake to a Mr G. Youngman. As a young man Philip had played table-tennis for the Windsor Constitutional Club in a six-a-side team. In 1901, the homely game of ping-pong, until then played on the dining-room or kitchen table, became a national sport and was played everywhere. This was only a passing phase, however, and by 1904 enthusiasm had waned and did not resume until the 1930s. Cippenham in Slough, home of Philip and Louise Headington before they came to Park Farm, restarted its table-tennis club in 1973 and is now in the top British League. It is interesting that some of the cards of 'cat' artist Louis Wain, who spent much of his later life at Bethlem, showed cats playing ping-pong.

Louis William Wain was born on 5 August 1860, his father a traveller in textiles and his French mother a designer of church embroidery and carpets. He studied at the West London School of Art and became an art journalist famed for his cat drawings. H.G. Wells said of him that he invented a cat style, a cat society, a whole cat world. His cats inhabit a comfortable domain which closely resembles the ease, flamboyance and lifestyle of Edwardian society. They wear top hats and monocles, play tennis, give tea parties, make after-dinner speeches and divert themselves at the seaside.

An eccentric, mild-mannered man, Louis became violent towards his sisters and was certified insane in June 1924. He went from Springfield at Tooting to Bethlem but never came to Beckenham, being transferred in 1930 to Napsbury, where he died on 4 July 1939. In *Louis Wain's Cats* by Michael Parkin, the following poem describes the kittens playing ping-pong:

Soon cats demure and kittens small
Were learning how to place the ball
And with what strength to deftly smack it
All pusstown then was on the racket
The craze spread to the nursery room
The children there each afternoon
Discarding corals, bibs and rattles
Gave bottles up for ping-pong battles.

There are many examples of Louis Wain's cats in the Bethlem Museum archives, although not the one of the ping-pong kittens. In addition to some 30 pictures there are annuals for 1907, 1908, 1910/11, 1914 and 1915. We are indeed fortunate to have our very own museum so conveniently at hand but perhaps we fail to make enough use of it!

The land towards the north of the hospital was turned into playing-fields leased to sports clubs such as the London Scottish and the Evening Standard for football and cricket from 1928. The AB Sports Club from Eden Park Hall in Croydon Road had a 14-year

Louis Wain cats, 1930s.

lease from 1927–41 and in 1928 the Ruskin (Croydon) FC paid a pitch rent of £20 p.a. The Parkhouse Rugby FC moved from their ground on Baston Farm in 1931 with Sir Henry McAuliffe supporting their application. The Kenilworth Association FC had a lease from 1938. The land became an unofficial playground for the children from Eden Way and the developing housing estates. Peter Rees remembers his twin breaking his nose when jumping onto a loose plank that was lying around and being unable to report the accident as they had no right to be there.

Efforts were made to preserve the Monks Orchard mansion but it was considered that the dry rot was too advanced. As the Bethlem Royal Hospital building was erected in the middle of fields and woodland with no access roads other than the three approaches to the Monks Orchard mansion, it was decided to use a branch line from Eden Park station to transport the materials required. There were two and a quarter miles of 4ft 8.5in. track for a steam locomotive and three miles of 2ft temporary track for five petrol locomotives and many tip wagons. As the building progressed the temporary track was moved to suit. A 20h.p. petrol tractor was used for excavations at the 'quiet unit'.

From 31 December 1928, with the clerk of works laid up with sciatica and severe weather for the following three months, 16,598 hours were lost by all trades. There were three complete weeks when it was impossible to lay stone or bricks. By June, systematic overtime was started and good progress was being made with the superstructure of the nurses' home and the 'excited patients'. The severe winter was followed by a hot, dry summer. By the end of September 1929 the demolition of the old Dower House was virtually complete with the new one in its place retaining some of the high wall that was probably originally around the 1822 manorhouse, Wickham Park.

Queen Mary officially opened the hospital on 9 July 1930. It was based on a villa system and had four houses, Tyson, Gresham, Fitzmary and Witley. The joint architects were John Cheston (hence the renaming of Cheston Avenue) and Charles Elcock.

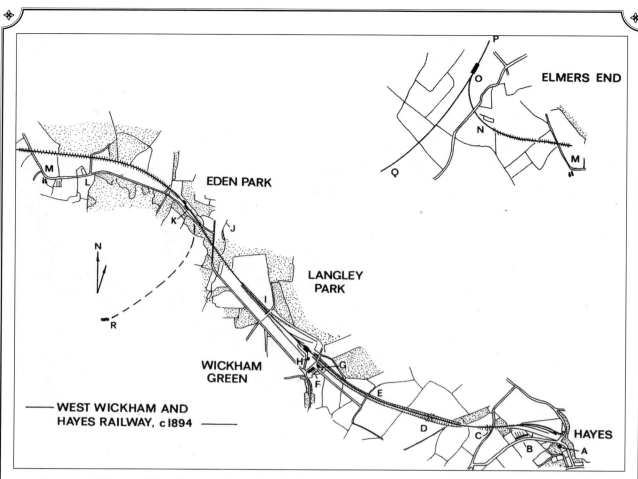

A Brewery; *B* Bourne Way Cottage; *C* cattle arch; *D, E and I* footbridges; *F* Leather Bottle; *G* Railway Hotel;
H Stationmaster's house; *J* Beck; *K* Eden Park Station; *L* Eden Park Farm; *M* West Kent Brewery;
N Brickworks; *O* Elmers End Station; *P and Q* Addiscombe railway. *The dotted line to* **R** *shows
the temporary spur to Bethlem Royal Hospital, which operated between 1928 and 1930.* (TW)

*The construction of the
chapel* (left) *and the Gate
Lodge.* (BE)

The stone store for the buildings, later the site of the bowling-green. The fencing marks the path to the north lodge in Upper Elmers End Road. (BE)

By 1995 the villas had increased in number and included Alexandra House, Longfield House, Wickham Park House, Larkbarrow, the Wakefield unit and Winchilsea (one-time home of Mr Ablewhite, steward of Bethlem Royal Hospital).

In 2003 an action brought by Bromley Council failed to stop further development spreading westwards through the grounds with the loss of historic structures associated with the Loyd habitation and the potential progressive loss of the metropolitan open land to the north-west.

The Hayes & West Wickham Railway Company

The Mid Kent line between Elmers End and Hayes was opened on 29 May 1882 – only a month later than planned, in spite of difficulties from local landowners. Alexander Beattie and Col Sir John Farnaby Lennard were directors and Charles Emmanuel Goodhart a shareholder, 8,000 shares being issued.

William Rudd Mace owned much of the land required by the railway company. It was recorded in the company's minutes that there was a long discussion as to how much would be needed for Eden Park Station. The house, Elderslie, stood in five acres of grounds with stabling, greenhouses and ornamental gardens. Both the occupier, a Mr Mace, and his tenant, Mr Wallace, were unwilling to let the railway company buy just the land they needed (one rood 38 poles at the extreme corner). In the end, during 1881, the company gave Mr Wallace £3,250 for the lease of the house and Mr Mace £7,500 for the freehold of all the land.

The company's troubles were not over. The next tenant, Mr Baker, who leased Elderslie from the company for seven years at £325 per year, asked for the signal-box to be moved to the end of the down platform and for a fence to be constructed at the bottom of the embankment. Mr Baker paid a lease of two guineas a year to use the strip of land beside the railway, where, it is said, he would flag down trains to pick him up.

Eden Park Station and the stationmaster's house were built on the upside and the downside was reached by a tunnel. The original buildings remain today, although the tunnel, in particular, is marred by graffiti and the accumulation of litter.

A railway journey from Elmers End to Hayes in 1902 was remembered by Brigadier John Faviell in his book *The Railway Journeys of my Childhood*. Born in 1898 in Blackheath, he had a distinguished military career over two world wars. During the Arab Rebellion in Palestine in 1936 he won the Military Cross and was awarded the OBE in 1943 and the CBE when he retired in 1950. He retired to Great Maytham Hall in Kent, where he eventually decided to pass on his memories of childhood railway journeys to his grandchildren and great-grandchildren. He writes:

When our mother thought a day in the country would be a change for us from walks on the heath or Greenwich Park, she took us to Hayes Common. We were quite a party. There was Mother, Nanny, a seven-year-old boy, a girl of five and a boy not quite four (me) with our spaniel puppy Jim. We had with us all the impedimenta of a picnic: a hamper, a rug, my sister's Teddy and my mother would have had her parasol. First we took a horse tram to Lewisham, then by train to Elmers End. There we changed and waited for the branch line to Hayes. It is clear to me now that this small branch line was run by completely antiquated engines and rolling stock. The engine was probably built in the 1860s and had been put out to grass on the small branch line. Vaguely I see this engine as a 2-4-0 with a topless windscreen type of cab.

In June 1928, when Bethlem Royal Hospital was being constructed at the Monks Orchard site, a temporary spur ran from the West Wickham side of Eden Park Station to the hospital, a distance of three-quarters of a mile. The contractors were Harold Arnold & Sons Ltd, of Doncaster. The firm had been erecting Crane Houses at Wollaton Park – steel-framed houses infilled with concrete panels – but only half the 1,000 houses commissioned were finished. The firm's next assignment was to construct the Bethlem Royal Hospital. HRH Prince Arthur, Duke of Connaught KG,

'Changing at Elmers End, ready for the train to Hayes'. The Faviell family at Elmers End Station in 1902. (FF)

laid the foundation-stone in July 1928. Messrs Arnold & Sons presented the Prince with a golden trowel and the architects gave him a golden cigarette case.

A Clergyman Investigates Monks Orchard

The following are extracts from an account written by the Revd O'Donoghue for the monthly magazine *Under the Dome*, December 1924/25.

It was on a solitary day of sunshine in the midst of a week of rain that I ventured forth to catch a glimpse of the park in Kent upon which the fourth Bethlehem Hospital is to rise into a clearer, bluer sky. Away from grinding tramcars and lumbering buses, out of sight of revolving wheels and trucks of excavated earth, towards a Canaan, which later on will be fragrant with the scent of azaleas and gay with variegated blooms from myriad rhododendrons.

Just a journey of half an hour carried us from London Bridge and its sordid streets by way of Lewisham, Catford and Lower Sydenham to Eden Park, a station almost lost in the woods. Mrs O'Donoghue and I were bound for Monks Orchard, a large park on the other side of the line, which strides from the parish of Beckenham into the parish of Addington. Whether once upon a time contemplative monks paced up and down this estate in their hours of recreation or whether a less saintly and more prosaic Mr Monk once farmed these pastures and gathered crops of apples, I do not know.

As we passed out of the asphalted road through the Beckenham gate into our new domain, some migrant birds from Norway were feasting upon the luscious fruit of the ubiquitous holly and the airmail from Croydon to the Continent was purring contentedly overhead.

It would be easy to copy from the auctioneer's ample catalogue and the tattered bills still hanging on the palings. The figures tell us, in cold black and white,

that we have purchased an estate of 337 acres, or more than thirty times our present site. But there is nothing in the particulars of the sale that will give the reader a just idea of the varied charms of the garden of Eden, destined hereafter to seclude our Adams and Eves from a noisy inquisitive world. I do not think there are any pheasants still lingering in the coverts but you may hear the trilling of the nightingale and the hooting of the friendly owl.

There are however numbers of burnished copper beeches and plantations of all sorts of graceful trees. But on the Shirley edge of the estate, red brick houses are springing up about the golf course and the thirty-nine red-tiled blocks of the Bermondsey Schools are to the left of the water tower of the Croydon Corporation. Not so far off gleamed the Crystal Palace like a sheet of water under the December sun. As we made our way towards the balustraded mansion, the woodland was bare and gaunt but there were rabbit pies and blackberry puddings under those thorns and briars of the dense undergrowth.

The mansion bore a rather anaemic look in contrast to the ruddy complexion of the new houses towards Addiscombe. Its handsome rooms are spacious and lofty and bear traces of having always kept the best of company in the country. From the windows of the nursery with its delightful frieze of horses and dogs we looked down on gardens and conservatories. No doubt three or four years ago, the gardens had been the glory of the manor with a promenade of happy dancers on a summer night. Moorhens were still swimming on the lake and over yonder towards West Wickham were the green pastures, the Dower House, a real farm, real haystacks and real cows.

Maybe in the years to come, a red brick palace reproducing the stateliness of the second hospital may look down on the same landscape. Or it may be that as in American institutions, detached pavilions and single storey wards may peep out among the firs and oaks.

The Revd O'Donoghue looks round West Wickham

Through another lodge and we are in the long straggling street of West Wickham where its occasional fine brick Georgian mansion makes the humbler weatherboarded neighbours sink into themselves. Beyond the tea gardens, a war memorial and a garage appears a truncated elm of girth and years. We are committed to a walk of a mile to the Tudor house of the Lennards and the ancient parish church. The court with its red brick walls and turrets is the same, which Anne Boleyn so often visited. A step or two from the house is the church looking down from a grassy hill upon a widening valley. In its dimly lighted aisles there is some very old stained Flemish glass with some beautiful modern glass.

Many memories of the eighteenth century statesmen, sailors, poets and archbishops haunt West Wickham, Addington, Hayes and Keston. Lord Chatham who drove out the French from our American colony lived at Hayes. William Wilberforce planned the abolition of slavery at Keston and the poet Richard Glover loved Wickham Court.

If it is ever dull at Monks Orchard, there are delightful shops in Croydon! But in the summer and autumn,
our new park will be at its best and life will be one long ecstasy with picnics, rambles and drives in the garden of England.

The Revd O'Donoghue visits during the construction of the hospital

It was a glorious Spring day when I visited the 'Orchard' on the Wednesday in Whitsun week. Outside the White Hart callow ducklings were enjoying all sorts of adventures on a small muddy pond. In front of the inn our workmen were sitting on the benches or sprawling on the sun-baked ground with their nose-bags and their glasses of beer or stout. Within the park also men were lying about the grass or in the shade of a tree dozing away the dinner hour. It was a very hot day and yet some of them were blithely carolling snatches of song from the wireless or the gramophone.

Misty fields of bluebells, the fearless song of birds and the tender leaves of waving trees invited me to take a seat on a silver birch, which had been felled by an axe. I could not see in this paradise the grim girders of the rising buildings and the dazzling stone of foundations was mercifully hidden from my tired eyes. But I could hear the children as they raced over the tussocky, lumpy grass with their butterfly nets and now and again I could see a family with their picnic. Velvety bumblebees were buzzing about and overhead was the drone of an aeroplane. It was a drowsy afternoon and I longed for a nap.

And so I came reluctantly back to spitfire engines, twisted skeins of railway lines and the obstacles of trenches and embankments. Here sunburnt navvies were laying down a bridge of sleepers to enable the excavator to cross the rails. There stonemasons were sawing through blocks of French 'Portland

Construction of the boiler-room (left) and rolling stock used to carry materials to the Bethlem site, 1929. (BE)

Stone' and at intervals in the noisy music I could hear the ring of the bricklayers' trowels on the bricks. On that day there were four hundred men, mainly Londoners, at work. In some of the buildings they were ready to put on the roofs but in others they were still busy with the foundations. I marked out where the gardens were to be and admired the proportions of the Nurses' Home. Finally I discovered the pegs that indicated the length and breadth of the chapel. The rich red bricks satisfied my Tudor taste and I was glad to see that monotonous straight lines were to be broken up by louvres and bow windows and wings of masonry.

The house of the Physician Superintendent will be built on the site of the Dower House and the Steward's house near the junction of the new road with Wickham Road. Now I wanted no more than a pot of tea at Croydon and the large trucks from three railways and a real locomotive belching black smoke in the woods, hurried my departure.

Returning in the autumn, a week before Founder's Day, the Revd O'Donoghue was met by the sight of broken, twisted fences and bonfires of wood blazing high.

Mutilated and dismembered trunks of trees lay here and there in the fields where a hefty man with the swinging axe had felled to the ground every tree that obstructed the advance of the new highway to Wickham Road. A few minutes later we were watching the woodman's wife picking her way cautiously over the treacherous grass with a can of steaming tea. But whistles were sounding and something was exploding under the monstrous stump of a tree so we hurried away to safety and the Croydon bus.

The visit of Her Majesty Queen Mary, 1934

The Queen was wearing a chiffon dress, flowered in shades of rose and blue, and was carrying a pink parasol when she entered the grounds of the new hospital. She passed between a Guard of Honour recruited from nurses and attendants both on entering and on leaving two hours later. They gave the Queen three hearty cheers and sang the hymn 'Thou to whom the sick and dying'. Then the Queen had tea with the President and Governors and was presented with a bouquet. Queen Mary was given a valuable antique Chinese vase, possibly an opium jar, from the associated architects that was five or six hundred years old. It was six inches high and covered on all sides with carved ivory figures and foliage painted in bright colours.

The man who probably most enjoyed the Queen's visit was a workman who sat down in her fine gilt and brocaded chair. He said as he rose, 'I've never sat in a Queen's chair before and it's beautiful.' The papers mixed up the reporting of the visit. The Daily Mail printed that its object was to open a Railway Hospital and jumbled up the list of roads that purported to show where she would go. There was one tragic event the next day when a child of a fireman crossed the street to see the bunting put out for the Queen. She was knocked down and killed by a lorry.

Queen Mary on her visit to the Bethlem Royal Hospital in 1934. Left to right: Miss Sarah Hearder (matron), Mrs Kathleen Porter Phillips, Walter Ablewhite (Steward), Dr John Porter Phillips (physician superintendent), ?, ?, Her Majesty Queen Mary, assistant matron, Sir Lionel Faudel-Philips (treasurer), Sister Chinnery, ?, Albert Coston (chief male nurse). (BE)

John Allford Cheston MC 1889–1930

It was only eight days after Her Majesty Queen Mary's visit to open the new hospital that its permanent architect collapsed with pneumonia, from which he died on 24 July 1930. John Cheston had worked day in and day out to finalise the details of the nurses' home in time for the great day of inauguration but it was too much for his weakened lungs.

During the war he had served in the 24th Royal Fusiliers, winning the Military Cross for gallantry and leadership and attaining the rank of captain. His citation read as follows:

During the attack on the strongly held enemy system about the Canal du Nord on 11 and 12 September 1918 he led his company deep into the hostile trenches, overcoming a fierce resistance and accounting for numbers of the enemy, besides taking many prisoners. In the heavy bombardment of a counter-attack, he moved his men from the main trench to the forward shell holes, thereby saving many lives as the trench was then obliterated.

However, his sense of duty did not save him from the deadly effects of gas in the trenches, which impaired his health for the rest of his life.

He was born in Chelsea on 8 January 1889, the son of Horace Cheston, surveyor to the hospitals – an office that John took over on his father's death in June 1919. During his attendance at Haileybury School he was captain of the rugger, won three cups in hurdle races and was exceedingly musical, playing anything by ear without being able to read a note of music. He continued at the AA schools, served his articles with T.E. Collcutt and became a Fellow of the Royal Institute of British Architects in 1919. He enlisted in August 1914 in the HAC when only 15 years old but his gentle, cheery personality led him to say little about the war to anybody. He married in June 1927.

John Cheston was associated with C. Ernest Elcock as joint architects for the new Bethlem Royal Hospital although, as the permanent surveyor, John was always regarded as the senior man. Ernest appreciated him with the following words:

His untimely death cuts short an association, which to both of us was exceptionally pleasant. From the very start of the work we never had a moment's unpleasantness and although we frequently had divergent ideas the eventual finding was always perfectly amicable.

Many of the roads round the hospital take their names from historical figures of the locality and it is not surprising that Cheston Avenue is included among them.

The Coronation Pavilion

The Bethlem Royal Hospital Sports Club was formed in July 1932 to provide cricket, football, tennis and bowls. Lord Charles Wakefield of Hythe was the president and the steward, Mr Ablewhite, was hon. secretary and treasurer.

In their first cricket season the club won 17 of their 27 matches, with Mr Ablewhite as captain. There were 16 other clubs in their cricket league, each playing twice during the months of May to September. They played Beckenham Art School, Old Bendonians, St Paul's, King Edward's School, Hayes cricket club, West Wickham cricket club, Blackheath Wanderers, Southend village police, Wickham Park, North & Associated Social Club, Old Croydonians, SNB Fitters, Croydon mental hospital, Addiscombe Nomads, Croydon Phoenix and Old Addeyans.

The football fixture list was just as crowded, with Bethlem winning 16 of their 25 matches against Park Langley, Croydon Highways, Old Krocks, Bermondsey Borough Council, King Edward's School, Beckenham Bedouins, Kenilworth, Croydon Casuals, South Norwood, West Wickham Wednesday and Beckenham Art School. Tennis matches were arranged against Wickham Park, the Inland Revenue and the George Street Institute.

A new pavilion was presented in 1937 by the president of the sports club, Lord Charles Wakefield, to commemorate the coronation of King George VI and Queen Elizabeth. It was completely up to date, with showers and buffet, but sadly the war brought most of the activities to an end.

Why Monks Orchard?

Mavis Cocks (née Webster) tells an interesting story about Monks Orchard. Her godmother, Ethel Wells, believed that everyone had a guardian angel – hers being a Native American. She lived at 37 Bridle Road and was the housekeeper of widower Walter Westacott.

Walter was subject to nightmares involving monks being hanged from the trees in his garden. When his front wall needed repair, he was amazed to see when it was finished that it was set with a Native American symbol. Had the guardian angel come to save Walter from the fate of the monks of Monks Orchard?

Mavis told me this story on a Sunday in May 2003, when the old church of St Mary's Addington was open in the afternoon to those interested in its history. There has been a church on the site since 1080, with the first tower built about 100 years later. The initials WC over the porch are not intended to offer relief to the weary traveller but stand for William Cantuar, the title of William, Archbishop of Canterbury, who was buried in the chancel in 1848.

The Revd O'Donoghue, who was cleric of the Bethlem hospital during the time of the acquisition of the Beckenham estate, felt that it could possibly have

The Native American symbol on the wall in Bridle Road.

The badge of Monks Orchard Townswomen's Guild.

been in the possession of monks before the Reformation. It appears that towards the close of his reign, Henry VIII exchanged lands in Addington for the farms and woods owned by Nicholas Leigh at Ashstead, Headley, Walton and Leatherhead. Part of the Addington estate had belonged to the priory of St Mary Overy, Southwark, but when Henry VIII suppressed them in 1534, he put what belonged to the monks into his own pocket. Perhaps Prior Ballard's Wood was an earlier name for Monks Orchard. Nicholas Leigh became Lord of the Manor of Addington and died in 1582 during the reign of Elizabeth I.

It is generally believed that the area has something to do with monks. Jane Fabb's son Ben says he used to hear monks chanting when he was in bed at night. Was this just the radio or a party along the road? Another friend thought she had a monk's spirit living in her house!

Certainly the ladies of the Monks Orchard TG used their imagination when designing the badge for their tablecloth – it consists of a monk walking through colourful orchards.

However, as the introduction suggests, Monks Orchard may just have come from the names of the fields owned by Munke in 1552.

Properties in the 1920 Monks Orchard Estate Sale

1. Monks Orchard
2. Ham Farm
3. Eden Park Farm and Holly Lodge
4. An acre of pasture land
5. Small building site
6. Small building site
7. Home Farm and Holmhurst
8. The Rising Sun
9. Eight cottages and gardens
10. Six cottages and gardens
11. Ham Lodge Cottages
12. Five acres of pasture land
13. 17 acres of allotments
14. Long Lane Wood
15. Beckenham Golf Course
16. Cottage and garden
17. Cottages and gardens
18. Cottages and gardens
19. Cottages and gardens
20. Cottages and gardens
21. The Cricketers public house
22. An acre and a half of building land
23. Shirley Farm
24. Spring Park
25. Spring Park Farm
26. 69 acres of accommodation land
27. Sandpit lodge
28. 22 acre smallholding
29. Thatched cottage and gardens
30. Three cottages on 10 acres of land
31. Kennel Wood
32. Spring Park Wood
33. The dairy
34. Oak Lodge Farm
35. The Laurels
36. The White Hart
37. Pond House and cottage on 2 acres
38. 16 acres of accommodation land
39. Two cottages and plantation of one acre
40. Row of four cottages and gardens
41. Pair of cottages, allotments and plantation of 3 acres
42. Pair of cottages with gardens
43. The Alders
44. The Nest
45. Nos 1–7 Victoria Terrace
46. Plantation Cottage with shop

Victoria Cottages, West Wickham. (B)

Right: *An early-twentieth-century postcard showing Ham Farm Walk, now the alley next to the Rising Sun. The old wooden fence was replaced by metal fencing after the mansion was built in 1855.* (RW)

Orchard Way in 1932, showing Orchard Rise. (CR)

Left and top: *Ham farmhouse in winter.* (SMI)

Above: *Horseshoe pond, used by the elephants of the Carmo circus.* (SMI)

Ham Farm

Climb steadily up The Glade from Long Lane or along Orchard Way from Upper Elmers End and you come to the source of the most easterly branch of the Chaffinch, the ancient Ham Farm. There exist many postcards from the first decade of the twentieth century that show the Ham Farm footpath into Elmers End by the Rising Sun and the path is still there. In the fifteenth century the land here was part of the Monks Orchard estate, owned by the Squery family, the estate remaining intact until Baron Gwydir died in 1820. It was then divided up into lots and Ham Farm was sold separately from the rest to John Maberly for £10,000. Eventually it was purchased by the Loyds to increase their land holding until the great sale in 1920.

Ham, meaning farm, homestead or estate, is a common name for old English settlements. In earlier references, 'hamm' means meadowland by a river. The ancient manor of Ham was described as an open-hall timber-framed medieval house. It was rebuilt in the 1850s and survived until 1935, by which time it had lost most of its land to the second suburb-building boom of 1920–35. By 1920 estate agents Percy Harvey were advertising plots for sale with no attempt at planning – houses were built by small firms and individuals with little experience. There was no mains sewerage or reliable water-supply and such roads as existed were impassable in winter.

Until it was pulled down in 1935 the 1850s farmhouse could still be seen on the left behind Nos 1 and 3 The Glade. When sold in 1921 it was listed as a property with buildings, orchard, lawn, arable land, two ponds, a stream and a spinney. The horseshoe duck pond lay to the east of the farmhouse and the

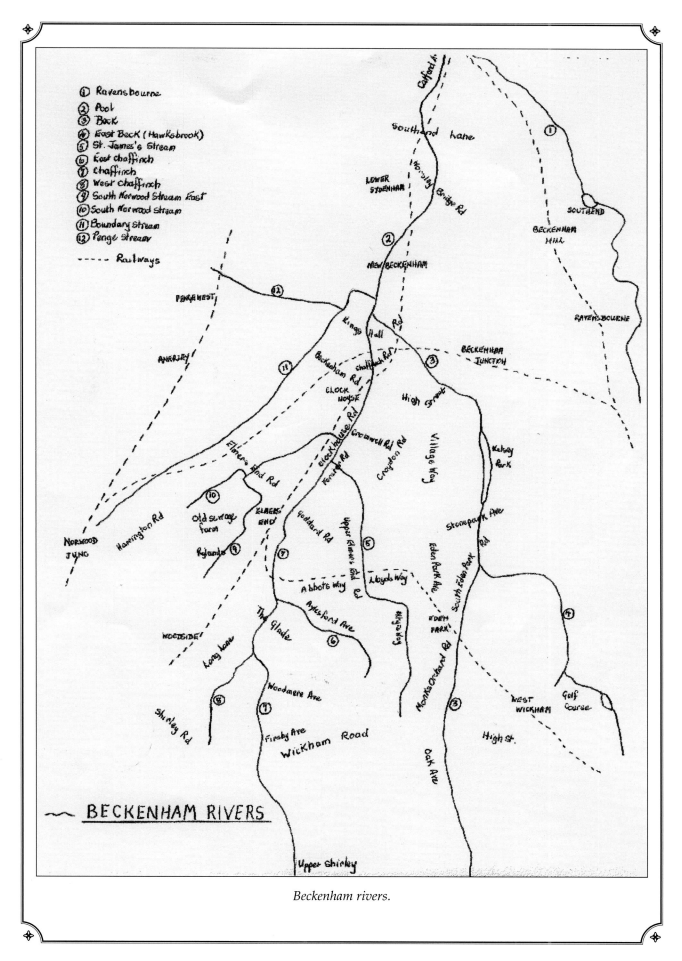

Beckenham rivers.

stream was the East Chaffinch, which ran between Gatton Garden Mead and Park Field along a line of trees to Elmers End. By 1937 there was a population of 4,000 in some 1,500 houses, but few shops and only one school and one church. This lack of foresight can be seen in the irrational road patterns of today, with Orchard Avenue and The Glade now rush-hour private 'motorways'.

With the development of the housing estate, the river was diverted underground, partly because it was felt to be a health threat in the days before immunisation against diphtheria and antibiotics to control scarlet fever. It can be seen at the foot of the allotments near Abbots Way and Aylesford Avenue, where it runs along an open culvert and meets the branch that flows near Stroud Green in Shirley. What can we see to remind us of Ham Farm? Traces of the Ham Shaw (wood) remain in patches of woodland at Long Lane, the bird sanctuary, between Lorne Gardens and The Glade and along Woodland Way.

Aldersmead Avenue is the only reminder of The Alders, the old woodland by which the Chaffinch flowed. There is also a road called Ham View off Orchard Way.

Spring Park Farm

Spring Park Farm faced Park Farm across the road from West Wickham to Croydon. Previously called Cold Harbour, it was then a miserable, worthless farm with cold, poorly drained soil. It was owned by Col John Maberley, who went bankrupt in 1832, at about which time Hewitt Davis took over the tenancy. He was variously described as a surveyor, a farmer and a land agent. By building roads across the farm and installing drainage he was able to convert Cold Harbour into a model 500-acre farm renamed Spring Park. Between 1836 and 1847, when Hewitt was farming both Spring Park and Oaks Farms, Hewitt and his wife Maria had two sons and six daughters. Three of their children died, however, and are commemorated in St Mary's Church. The Davis family lived at the eighteenth-century Spring Park House, which survived until 1963.

When Hewitt's tenancy came to an end in 1849/50, Samuel Jones Loyd bought Spring Park Farm and it remained part of the Loyd estate until the 1920 sale.

Miller's pond owes its name to Edward Henry Miller, who occupied part of the farm with Bayne in

Spring Park House at the time of the 1920 sale.

Holly Lodge (later Eden Park School) at the time of the Monks Orchard sale in 1920.

1916. The purpose of the ponds on the farm, of which there appear to have been five, was to soak the wooden wheels of the carts to swell them. Miller paid a rent of £54p.a. for an old cottage, cowstalls and stabling, the north barn and two new cottages, sharing the cart-shed with Bayne. The south side of the farm was rented for £168p.a. by Bayne and included the farmhouse, blacksmiths' and wheelwrights' shops, pigsties and fowl houses. Although the lease did not expire until September 1930, Lewis Loyd's heir, Frederic Edward Loyd, sold the farm to Samuel Amos Worskett of Chislehurst for £7,000 in 1924.

The land agent for the Loyds at this time was William King Brown, their agent for about 30 years. He lived at Holly Lodge in Upper Elmers End Road from about 1915 until he retired to Westbourne Villas, Hove, in 1931. His son of the same name lived at Holmhurst.

In 1929 Samuel Amos Worskett sold the farm for £15,000 to Herbert Ferris Worskett from Shirley, Alfred Temple Bennett of Winchmore Hill and James Oswald (whose share was taken over by Alfred's son, Stuart Morris Bennett, when Oswald died in 1932). They formed the company

Gower Builders (London) Ltd and built the western side of the estate.

By 1936 Spring Park Farm was no more and a housing estate had replaced it. Leslie Seymour, a commercial traveller from Norfolk Road in London, bought 75 Bennetts Way for £760 – another road was Temple Avenue.

The Development of the Land Round Bethlem as Seen by the Bartletts

I [Doreen Bartlett] *celebrated my fifth birthday at 31 Monks Orchard Road in March 1932, just two or three weeks after we moved in. It was still an unmade road with no street lighting, although telegraph poles were in place carrying phone lines to the very few. The new nurses' homes were opposite. We were on the odd-numbered side up to about 101 and beyond that it was open fields to Wickham Road. In our back garden our father took months digging out the roots of a huge tree on which meanwhile my sister Brenda and I played see-saw on a plank. The woodland beyond was unspoilt, with little paths leading to a stream where grew marsh marigolds in profusion, big*

Doreen Bartlett racing at St David's sports day, late 1930s/1940. (STD)

37

Monks Orchard Road in 1931 when the houses were first built, with a solitary silver birch at the roadside. (AB)

daisies, aconites, violets, primroses and bluebells that were a sea of blue in the spring. Householders were able to extend their gardens by 30ft but then our beautiful secret garden became a landfill site with lorries dumping rubbish by the ton.

The avenue of horse chestnut trees now in Monks Orchard Road did not exist then and the silver birch in our neighbour's front garden was quite a landmark. Light woodland stretched all the way down to Eden Park Station and a well-trodden path wound its way up and down through the bushes, brambles and trees. Links Way did not exist and to this day anyone would understand that 'to go across the footpath' meant walking our way to the shops or station. Never mind that it is now a bus route with houses on either side!

In the early days there were just a few shops opposite the station. Miss Herbison MPRS ran the chemist shop dealing with prescriptions and making up her own hand creams, etc. Mrs Kidd's newsagent's was a joy because besides stationery and sweets it was an adult lending library and she sold books for children. I saved my 2d. per week pocket money for weeks for a copy of Children of the New Forest, which cost one shilling. On the station side there was the clean, butter-smelling shop of the United Dairies, where there was always a flat basket of brown eggs in the window. There were two milkmen delivering milk twice a day, the orange United Dairies and green and cream Bowyers, which we had. Many other tradesmen came: the butcher's boy on his delivery bicycle, the baker three times a week with horse and cart like the milkmen, the paper boy on foot, the rag-and-bone man pulling a cart and occasionally the oilman. In the summer the men came on tricycles with refrigerated boxes containing

ice-creams and water-ice lollies at 1d. each. Walls were best, with their 'Stop me and buy one', but Eldorado were cheaper.

St David's College was round the corner with no roads to cross and I was able to come home for dinner when I went to this friendly kindergarten. My mother could see and hear me from the kitchen when we went to play out the back in the field. The principal, Mrs Davies was much loved and respected and she cooked dinner for those who lived too far away to go home.

There was a grand parade to celebrate the inauguration of Beckenham's first mayor in 1935. Floats assembled at the Wickham end of Monks Orchard Road early in the morning. Brenda and I spent all the morning watching about 50 floats being made ready with every local shop, trade and organisation taking part. Such costume and colour rivalled the Lord Mayor's Show!

This account, by Doreen Wilson (née Bartlett), is taken up by her youngest sister, Ann, ten years her junior.

I was born at 31 Monks Orchard Road in 1937 and lived there until 1968. My most striking memory is of the rhododendrons of many colours planted opposite. Queen Mary would come every year to see them in bloom in May and I remember waving to her as she swept past, always sitting bolt upright in her big, shiny car. Sadly the bushes have deteriorated over the years and reverted to mauve.

Like my sisters, I remember particular shops but I was frightened of Mrs Kidd at the newsagent's. The sweetshop on the corner of Monks Way was popular and nearby was Mrs May's haberdasher's, stuffed with

Mature pink and white horse chestnut trees, 70 years old, in Monks Orchard Road in 2003.

pins, needles, sewing cotton, ribbons, trimmings, wool, knitting needles, patterns, materials and goodness knows what else!

My earliest memories are of the war years. Dad was a Home Guard officer. One day a platoon of soldiers ran through our garden with their rifles and disappeared through the back gate into the woods. We went to McAndrew's to see the King but I did not believe it was him as he was not wearing his crown. As we grew our own vegetables, Dad would rush out to collect steaming hot horse manure from the horses of the delivery men, and we kept chickens too. The eggs were lovely but we were not so keen on eating the birds when their useful life was over. Mum was a fire-watcher on the roofs opposite. Cycling home with her one day, some German aircraft flew over very low and we could see the pilots quite clearly. We were evacuated from our house one night when a bomb fell in the hospital grounds but no one was hurt. The rubble from bombed houses was dumped in the woods and we used to play on the stack of old doors and windowframes, trying to get from one end to the other without touching the ground – about 50ft below. Quite dangerous but good fun!

I attended Mrs Mallick's school, which gave a very good grounding in all subjects, including algebra and geometry and a little French. The lovely garden had a pond with a willow tree and in fine weather we had our lessons outside. The school supported the Red Cross fête held in the grounds of a big house in South Eden Park Road, probably Harvington.

When the war ended, my idyllic childhood living in Monks Orchard Road became much the same as

anywhere else and in 1954 I started at the Beckenham County Grammar School, travelling from Eden Park to New Beckenham.

Why Eden Park?

Eden Park was part of Langley. There were three farms close together which are easily confused. Eden Farm was the name given to the land leased by the Eden family where Crease Park is today. Eden Park Farm was the area where Stanhope Grove joins Upper Elmers End Road. Formerly called Elmers End Farm, it was part of Eden Farm, all owned in 1838 by John Woolley. Close by, opposite No. 415 Upper Elmers Road, was the north lodge of Park Farm, built in the 1840s and the property of Samuel Jones Loyd. This was later called Monks Orchard Lodge when Samuel's cousin, Lewis Loyd, built his mansion where the Bethlem site is today. Finally, to confuse still further, the mansion built on Eden Farm became Eden Park, the eventual name for the whole area.

The bailiff's house across the road from Eden Park Farm was known from 1881 as Holly Lodge. In the 1881 census, the occupant of Holly Lodge was an Australian agent, Paddy Pascoe and his wife Elizabeth and baby son Kenneth. All occupants from this time could be considered middle class, for example Ernest Esdaile, a lecturer with the War Office, was there in 1901 and, as already mentioned, the estate agents for the Loyds, William King Brown & Son, from about 1915–25. At about this time the frontage of Holly Lodge was built out to form the building seen in the 1920 sale brochure for the Monks Orchard estate. It became Eden Park School, formerly Holly Lodge School, and was demolished in 2002, despite its history, to make way for Asprey Mews.

The south lodge of Park Farm can still be seen on the approach to West Wickham from Shirley on the left-hand side of the road – a small white building with columns. The north lodge was taken down in 1933 when Lodge Gardens, Holly Crescent and Eden Way were built.

The name Eden comes from Sir Robert Eden, created baronet in 1672. He was the ancestor of the much-respected politician Sir Anthony Eden (1897–1977), foreign secretary and Prime Minister 1955/57 who became Lord Avon. Thus we have Eden Park Avenue, South Eden Park Road, Eden Way, Eden Road and Stanhope Grove from a family who married into the Edens. There were also Eden Cottage and Eden Lodge off South Eden Park Road but neither survives today. It was William Eden (1744–1814) who leased land in Beckenham from Peter Burrell in about 1782. William's brother, Robert, Governor of Maryland, was the great-great-grandfather of Sir Anthony Eden. Letters written by William to Robert showed that the brothers did not

The demolition of Eden Park School in 2002, showing the old part of the house as distinct from the newer extension.

agree politically and that Robert's sympathies lay with the colonists. When Robert died in 1784 he was buried in Annapolis, Maryland.

Of the 14 children of our William and his wife Eleanor Elliott, whom he married in 1776, only George and Frances appear in the local baptisms. George was baptised at St George's Church in 1786 and Frances in 1800. Several of the other children were born abroad, as Eleanor accompanied her husband in his travels overseas. There were six boys and eight girls, but of the boys only George and Robert John lived to a reasonably old age. The burial records of St George's register the early deaths of Henry (aged seven) and Charles (aged nine). In the churchyard beneath a yew tree is the box-shaped pink marble vault of Mary Dulcibella, sixth daughter of William, First Lord Auckland, which bears the following inscription:

South face:

CHARLES DRUMMOND Esq.
of Stratton St London died 23 August 1858 aged 67

'Thou wilt keep him in perfect peace whose mind is

stayed on Thee because he trusted in Thee'
Isaiah XXVI.
Also the Hon. MARY DULCIBELLA his widow
6th daughter of WILLIAM 1st Lord AUCKLAND
died 20 March 1862 aged 68

Another grave is that of her sister, the Hon. Emily, who died in Eden Lodge, Kensington, in 1869, at one time mistaken for Eden Lodge in Beckenham, which the family left in 1818.

When William died, George, his second son, became the Second Lord Auckland. A marble memorial in St George's Church shows how enormously successful and well liked George was.

It is not known when the elegant mansion, later called Eden Park, was built but in 1820 it was surrounded by parkland with many large trees. Looking at Crease Park today, the mansion stood on the flat ground at the top, the rest sweeping down to Wellhouse Road (named after the housing of the well) below. Crease Park was named in memory of Alderman James Crease, freeman of Beckenham.

Groveland Road (Greater and Little Groveland Mead) and Broomfield Road were named after Eden

Eden Farm, the home of William Eden, Lord Auckland (inset). (NL)

Farm fields when the area was developed in 1932. The firm of developers, Clout & Tysoe, also named Derrick Road, Gordon Road, Ronald Close and Ernest Grove after their sons, and the names Birchwood Avenue and Cherry Tree Walk echoed the trees planted in the vicinity. To see the pink cherry blossom against a blue sky in the spring is unforgettable. Glanfield Road was named after Messrs Riley & Glanfield of the Eden Park Estate Co.

Before the Edens came to Beckenham in about 1782, the area was called Bure Gates. Old maps show a cluster of buildings just below Beckenham's highest point of 175ft, now the Crossways and Village Way traffic lights.

What leads us to believe that the date was 1782? When Peter Burrell died in 1820 there were 34 years of the lease remaining. It is likely that the lease had been taken out for some 72 years from 1782. William Eden and Eleanor Elliott had married in 1776 and by 1782 they had four daughters and a baby son born earlier in the year. Their fourth daughter, Caroline, had been born in Ireland in 1781 when William was Chief Secretary, a position he resigned in 1782. Time was ripe for the growing family to have a home of their own and letters written by William in the

summer of 1782 show that this was to be in Beckenham. Then, in August 1784, their second son, George, was born at Eden Farm and baptised at the parish church of St George's in Beckenham.

William was spending his time haymaking and working in the fields with his hired day labourers. It was a particularly bad season and William wrote from Beckenham on 8 August 1782 in a letter to Lord Loughborough:

My pastures are wet and poked full of holes by the horses, our Guinea chickens are dying of ague, pears and apples are dropping in cartloads, and the melons are rotten instead of ripe. I am wet up to the knees six times a day and cannot get the 6th part of the day's work out of my day labourers.

Exactly where they lived at this time is not clear. It is generally thought to be at the farm buildings shown in the 1838 tithe map close to the mansion site. Certainly by 1790 William was paying window tax for 74 windows. The mansion shown in subsequent pictures of Eden Farm must have been in existence by 1790. William was also paying 'hair powder' duty at Eden Farm in 1795 on behalf of the American nurse

Hannah De Grave and the housekeeper Mrs Gibson.

The name Eden Farm was regularly used from 18 September 1794 because 'we were obliged to give a name to our place to avoid a new penny post, which goes to the Beckenham village.'

William continued to accept appointments in Europe and his wife and family always accompanied him. Henry was born in Paris in 1786 when his father was envoy to the court at Versailles. Mary Louisa was their 'nice little señorita' born in 1788 when William was Ambassador to Spain. Charles was born in The Hague in 1791 when William, now Lord Auckland, was appointed Ambassador to Holland. William Eden, as First Lord Auckland, had no overseas appointments from 1793 but was for seven years the confidential adviser of Mr William Pitt the Younger. He was appointed Postmaster-General in 1798, the year in which he lost a second son, Charles, buried at St George's aged seven, Henry having died of a fever in 1794. By 1800 William and Eleanor had produced 14 children, six sons and eight daughters although only four of their sons survived – and there was worse to follow. After a year as President of the Board of Trade, William retired in 1807.

His letters show that he enjoyed living at Eden Farm. He writes in August 1794:

I visit the small works going forward on my farm and in the neighbourhood. I pursue a disjointed sort of reading in the library.

I ride, walk and swing with my daughters and I play at skittles, pick fruit and take wasp nests with my sons. I act as coachman when Lady Auckland goes out in the phaeton. Our four girls are growing into tall young women and are pleasant companions to us.

On 26 June 1799, William and Eleanor Eden gave a ball to celebrate the marriage on 1 June of their eldest daughter Eleanor with the widower Lord Hobart. Previously Eleanor had been the love of William Pitt's life but, as he was in debt at the time and nearly 20 years older, marriage was deemed unsuitable. Less than a year later Charlotte married Lord Godolphin. Three of the girls married in 1806, Caroline to Arthur Vansittart, Catherine to Nicholas Vansittart and Mary Louisa to Andrew Wedderburn Colvile (who became Colvile by Royal Licence on 22 June 1814). Mary Dulcibella waited until 1819 to marry Charles Drummond and the remaining two girls, Emily and Frances (Fanny), set up house with their unmarried brother George.

The year 1810 was a sad one for the Edens. Their eldest son, William Frederick Elliot, drowned in the Thames and Catherine Vansittart died in August.

Only one of William and Eleanor's boys (Robert John) had children to carry on the name of Eden but Charlotte, Caroline, Mary Dulcibella and Mary Louisa each had numerous children – the latter had 17. Morton had died at the age of 27 in 1821 but

Robert John became Bishop of Bath and Wells and had at least seven children with Mary Hurt. He became the third Lord Auckland on the death of his brother George.

William, First Lord Auckland, died in 1814 followed by his wife in 1818. The family left Eden Farm and never returned. George arranged to lease the farm to a widow, Mrs Wildman, for seven years at £600 per year but the death of Peter Burrell in 1820 led to the auction of most of his land. Eden Farm was Lot 21 and covered over 300 acres. If we think of the farm in terms of the modern road layout, the mansion was in Crease Park with access by a woodland ride along the ridge where Village Way runs. One of its lodges was somewhere near the top of Kelsey Way with meadows stretching away on either side. Fields belonging to the farm ran down to the Chinese roundabout and a short way along South Eden Park Road, although they did not include Harvington playing-fields. The farm occupied all of today's housing estate down to Croydon Road, where there was a second lodge at Elmers End. Fields extended on the south side of Upper Elmers End Road to Monks Orchard.

In the 1920 Monks Orchard sale, the farm called Eden Park Farm was situated at the end of Stanhope Grove with a frontage of 700ft on Upper Elmers End Road. This was the farmhouse, garden and homestead listed in the 1820 Burrell sale of Eden Farm as No. 102 on the sale map. The mansion was not called Eden Park until about 1838, when it was shown thus in the 1838 tithe map, although the 1820 sales map shows the farm's parkland as Eden Park.

The education of the 14 children of William and Eleanor was the responsibility of their mother, who left a detailed diary of their upbringing. In it she writes that during their wanderings 11 of the children had smallpox, along with outbreaks of whooping cough, measles and scarlet fever. Mrs Eden became known as Haughty Nell and her nursery was variously described as the Brattery, the Light Infantry and the Little Parisians. Of the children, we know most about George and Emily. George became the Second Lord Auckland on the death of his father in 1814. By 1840, the name Auckland was used for the New Zealand city, George having been a friend and mentor of the Governor.

Emily's correspondence with her sister Eleanor started when she was 17 and later included her friends Theresa Villiers and especially Pamela Fitzgerald Campbell, leaving a priceless record of the social life of the time. Her great niece, Violet Dickenson, granddaughter of Emily's brother Robert, edited her letters. Emily was a keen Whig politician and was clever, amusing, critical and a loyal friend to her brothers and sisters.

Letters to a variety of people, including family as well as Theresa Villiers and Pamela Fitzgerald Campbell, were written from Eden Farm until she left

A painting by Rosemary Hatt of Eden Park Farm in 1929.   (J&B)

in 1818 to set up house with George and Fanny in Grosvenor Street. Later she wrote from Park Lodge, Greenwich, from their home outside London and then from the Admiralty when George was promoted. She wrote from Langley Farm when visiting her sister Mary Louisa Colvile and from Eastcombe, Greenwich, the home of her eldest sister Eleanor, known as Lady Bucks.

George and his two sisters had to give up their own homes at Grosvenor Street and Greenwich when he was promoted to the Admiralty but they rented a small villa at Ham Common to give the sisters some privacy. Then, upon their return from India in 1842, they re-settled at Eden Lodge in Kensington Gore. Emily also had a cottage at Broadstairs where she spent most of her time after George's death.

Visits further afield were made to her youngest brother Bob at Eyam and Hertingfordbury, to Lord and Lady Bath at Longleat, to The Grange in Hampshire, belonging to Alexander Baring, and also to Bowood, Stackpole, Woburn and Chatsworth. Her sister Charlotte with her husband Lord Godolphin lived at Bigods, Essex. Emily's astute observation of social class is shown in her two novels, *The Semi-Detached Couple* and *The Semi-Detached House*, in which she shows herself to be on a par with Jane Austen.

In November 1828 Emily wrote from Grosvenor Street as follows:

We came to London last Monday having passed a whole summer at Eastcombe. It is very odd that the Duke of Wellington [Prime Minister 1828–30] will not say a word as to the intentions of the Government. I begin to believe what some people say, that he has no plan and doesn't know what to do.

Two years later, she wrote:

Have you seen the second volume of Lord Byron? It is a wicked book and it is unlucky that I feel myself obliged to own that it is much the most interesting book I ever read in my life!

There are many references in Emily's letters from India to her childhood at Eden Farm. In September 1838 she wrote:

Such nice clear air and altogether it feels English and exhilarating. I think of you and Eden Farm and the Temple Walk, Crouch Oak Lane and the blue butterflies. I should like to go back to childhood and youth again. There was great enjoyment in them.

Crouch Oak Lane today would be a walk along the top of Eden Park Avenue towards Eden Park Station and the Eden Park Hotel. Crouch Oak Wood was part of the woodland still remaining in the Bethlem parkland. A clue to the whereabouts of the Temple can be found in the diaries of the son of a subsequent resident at Eden Farm, Edward Lawford. Melville Lawford writes in 1844, 'When we came home, Baring and I went on in the cart to the bamboo temple and took my tool box there. We then went on and pulled the boat a little.' (Their boat was on the lake in Kelsey Park and the temple seems to have been beside the River Beck as it entered the lake.)

In January 1839 Emily wrote:

We are more mad than ever; at least, we have got ourselves into one of those scrapes that mad people do. There is a wretched little rivulet, a thing not so big as that ditch by old Holledge's at Elmers End. This little creek which is dry for 10 months of the year suddenly chose to rise in the night and there is now 7ft of water.

Two days later she added:

That little ditch is quite pompous with 20ft of water. The only way of passing the camels was by tying six of them in a string to the tail of an elephant who then swam across dragging them all after him.

Her letters contain details of her family which would otherwise have been lost. She loved her King Charles' spaniels – Chance, who accompanied her to India, and the less lively Zoë.

Emily herself had the chance to marry widowed Prime Minister Lord Melbourne, but elected to stay with her beloved brother George. As for children, her sisters had plenty! When visiting Langley Farm in 1827, two of her sisters had 18 small children between them. She cared for two of her brother Robert's sons when her sister-in-law was lying-in after the birth of her sixth child, the eldest just five years old!

She was a godmother several times over. Her friend Pamela, ultimately the mother of 11, wrote to ask on the birth of a 'big monster of a seventh girl' if she could give her new daughter the name Eden as it sounded 'Eve-ish'. Pamela had thought of 'Rhinocera' but the baby was baptised Caroline Frances Eden! A letter written in 1834 commented on Louisa Colvile having her 17th child, Mary

Drummond her ninth and Mrs Eden (Robert John's wife) about to have her seventh. Remarkably for the period, few of the children died. Emily sadly recalls the death of her brother Morton in 1821 and her niece Eleanor Colvile died at the age of 16 at Langley Farm. The 1881 census indicated that at least four of Mary Louisa's daughters remained unmarried – Emily, Jane, Charlotte and Isalen Colvile were living on private means at Berry Pomeroy in Devon.

Her brother Robert's daughter, Lena, was not expected to live at birth but survived to be Emily's companion in her declining years. George died of a stroke on New Year's Day, 1849, during a visit to Lord Ashburton at The Grange, Alresford, and his sister Fanny died only three months later. Thereafter Emily lived the life of a semi-invalid, dividing her time between Broadstairs and Kensington, but she outlived all the family except her brother Robert.

She left two novels and also wrote two books about her stay in India from 1836 to 1842 – *Up the Country* and *People and Princes of India*. She was a gifted water-colour artist, with three volumes of her paintings sold at Christies in 1907 and now in the Victoria Memorial Hall in Calcutta. Emily's sister, Fanny, also wrote, producing a book called *Golden Interlude*.

In September 2003 an album containing 27 of Emily's hand-coloured lithographs entitled *Portraits of the Princes and Peoples of India* was sold at Christies for £28,000 at the Arts of India auction in London. The collection belonged to Mildred Archer, who used to run the prints and drawings department of the India Office Library.

Sources
The preface to Emily Eden's novels is by Lord Avon.
Extracts by Geoffrey Tookey from Lord Auckland's journal, held by Beckenham library.
Minutes of Beckenham Council meetings, c.1928.
Emily Eden's letters edited by her grand-niece, Violet Dickenson, Robert's granddaughter.
Up the Country by Emily Eden.
Nigel Lawford, whose ancestors lived at Eden Farm c.1826–54, provided the picture of Eden Park mansion.

CHAPTER 2

Memories

Phyllis Greenslade at Park Farm and Cheston Avenue

Phyllis Greenslade was educated at Croydon High School and the commercial college at Purley. She lived with her parents at 33 Cheston Avenue, a large detached house built in 1935 on land belonging to her uncle, Percy Greenslade. He also owned the land, bought in June 1930 for £1,000, that became the Parkfields Recreation-Ground. The deeds for these transactions are held in the Bethlem Museum archives. After working on a Welsh farm for the first year of the war Phyllis, then of conscription age, returned to London to join the other workers (two cowmen, a pigman, a poultryman and a carter with just one horse in the stables) at Park Farm, where the baillif was known by her uncle.

Every morning at 6a.m. Phyllis started work by milking the shorthorns. She had just one Sunday off a month and another 'three parts of the day' when she could go home after milking the cows. Her day ran from 6a.m. until 5p.m. but she was allowed home for breakfast with an hour off for lunch. She used a heavy bicycle with a milk carrier at the front to deliver quart bottles of milk to nearby properties and remembers the double-fronted red-brick house,

Phyllis Greenslade with her cow. (PG)

'Winchilsea', on the corner of Monks Orchard and Wickham Road, where Walter Murray Ablewhite lived. He was the steward in overall charge of the farm, the hospital catering and the gardens, greenhouses and walled garden. After serving in the First World War, Walter Ablewhite had been appointed in June 1919 to Southwark before transferring to the Monks Orchard site, retiring from there in March 1948. The farmer – first Mr Balchin and then Dick Russell – lived in the house at the corner of the farm.

Phyllis earned a wage of £3 per week but after working all through the war the long hours and hard daily routine took their toll. From the council she rented a smallholding at the back of the houses in Cheston Avenue and ran her own business. She had goats, a cow, chickens, cats and a collie dog and also raised heifers and pigs. On one occasion the piglets all escaped when the electric fence around their enclosure failed – fortunately all they managed do was consume large numbers of acorns from the many oak trees in the area. At another time a hand-reared piglet was befriended by the collie and they would sit together by the fire with the cats.

Eventually the running of the smallholding became too much and for a while Phyllis took in young bank clerks as paying guests. Her neighbour in Cheston Avenue, by the name of Brown, ran a bakery business with some ten shops and Phyllis ended up working for the branch in Shirley. At the time of writing she lives happily in Somerset, still with the company of a border collie.

Other local people who remember the farm are Bill Tonkin, who would cycle from Herne Hill for a day out visiting the local hostelries in Biggin Hill with Dick Russell. Bill's wife, Nancy, was co-author with Eric Inman of the book *Beckenham* and Bill has catalogued the Nancy Tonkin collection of postcards and other memorabilia used in this book.

Janet Berlin (née Couchman)

Janet Berlin, whose husband Marc is related to Irving Berlin, remembers keeping her horse, Pepe, in a field close to Bethlem.

She had been riding for some years at the Selsdon Park Stables when her parents agreed that she could have a pony of her own. Although she had saved £90 to buy a pony she had nowhere to keep it and had no luck when the Bethlem Royal Hospital refused her offer of giving riding lessons to patients in exchange for part of a field! On her way home to Addison's

Above left: *Pepe giving rides to children in his paddock. Behind the railings is Bethlem parkland, 1962.* (JAB)
Above right: *Janet puts Pepe through his paces, 1962.* (JAB)

Top: *Janet Berlin* (centre), *between her parents* (on the left) *and her brother, who is talking to Vic Woolgar, 1962.*

Above: *Ken Couchman in conference with Vic Woolgar, 1962.* (JAB)

Monica McCarthy on Pepe, 1962. (MMc)

Close she passed the Nissen hut used by the Girl Guides, close to an overgrown orchard where there was a caravan belonging to Fred and Victor Woolgar. To Janet's delight they had been to Stanley School with her father, Ken Couchman, and let her use the field free of charge.

Pepe, a bay pony of 15 hands, was bought from his owner at Chipstead. Her parents gave Janet a saddle and her father built Pepe's stable in the corner of the field next to the boundary railings of Bethlem.

When her parents insisted that she paid for the upkeep of her horse Janet spent Saturdays giving riding lessons at 2s.6d. for half an hour. One of her pupils was Monica McCarthy (née Scholey), who also remembers buying eggs from Phyllis at 33 Cheston Avenue.

Janet outgrew Pepe and her next horse, Buccaneer, was stabled at Hayes Farm from where Janet sometimes rode him to Buller's Wood School, where she worked. Does anyone remember the riding group organised by Janet when she was a PE teacher there?

In 2004 living in Downshill Road, Beckenham, Janet and her husband have a beautiful garden and won first prize for Bromley in Bloom in 2001 and 2002, withdrawing in 2003 to enter the London competition instead. They came second in that! In June they hold a visitors' Open Day.

Marjorie Mather

In the 1920s John Mather bought an acre of land when the Monks Orchard estate was split up. At that time the stony, unmade road was called Park View. John married Avice Cooper, the only daughter of Thomas Cooper of Mill Cottage by the Shirley windmill. He was the carpenter who made the gates to Ham Farm, diagonally opposite where Shirley library now stands. The gates survived for years – there remains a similar pair of gateposts, also made by Thomas Cooper, at the entrance to John Mather's house at 21 Cheston Avenue (Park View having been renamed after the architect at Bethlem). In the garden are two old hawthorn trees dating from around the 1920s, when cows rubbed against the bark and the huge oak tree beside them was a mere sapling.

This information is supplied by John's daughter-in-law, Marjorie Mather, who twice married into the Mather family – her first husband was John's son Harry Thomas Mather, an electrical design engineer who died after suffering for some 18 years from MS, and her second husband was Harry's cousin, John Martin Mather, a furrier, son of William Mather and his wife Harriet Martin.

When Thomas Cooper died in 1933, his wife, Elizabeth Cooper, went to live with her son-in-law John at 21 Cheston Avenue. She survived into her 90s at the attractive four-bedroomed house, the garden was large even with one-third of an acre used for building No. 23 next door. Marjorie has many family treasures and photographs, including the original of Mill Cottage which appears in Ray Wheeler's collection of postcards of Shirley and Addington credited to George Edwards rather than Thomas Cooper.

Harry and Marjorie Mather came to live at No. 21 in 1948, having previously lived in Bridle Road. Marjorie started work in the Midland Bank, although she had always wanted to be a nurse. With her husband's health deteriorating she left the bank and

Marjorie Mather (centre) *and Renée Asherton meet the Queen Mother at the 1978 Ideal Home Exhibition.* (MM)

trained as a Red Cross nurse at the Mayday Hospital. Returning one day in 1944, she had just reached home in Bridle Road when a V1 dropped by the White Hart, killing a woman doctor in her car. Marjorie picked herself up to help the bus drivers who had been taking their tea-break in the café opposite. On other occasions she was on duty when a shelter received a direct hit and when a bomb, landing on a canteen, caused grave injuries from scalding.

After the war less onerous duties came her way both at the Festival Hall and at St James' Palace, where she was on duty while the public filed past the wedding presents on the occasion of the wedding of Prince Charles and Lady Diana in 1981 (the weather was very hot and many people fainted in the heat), though she never worked at Buckingham Palace.

Marjorie did not miss meeting the Queen Mother altogether. In the 1960s, at the Ideal Home Exhibition, Marjorie was waiting with friend Renée Asherton, hoping to catch a glimpse of the Royal Personage, when they were spotted and to their everlasting delight were included, like honoured guests, in a press

The gates to Ham Farm, the work of Thomas Cooper. The last remaining gatepost was erected with a plaque in the churchyard of St George the Martyr and is now at Edenham School. (MM)

Barry Chapple, Mick Bates and Jeff Runacre (above) posing behind Witley Ward, and (below) with their 'mobile wheelbarrow' taking a breather from gardening in 1969. Sadly, the original mansion gardens and walkways have since been allowed to become overgrown. (DH)

photograph, the Queen Mother asking them how long their hours were and if they had had many patients.

Marjorie was made Commandant and became well known locally for organising Red Cross collections. She has always had a soft spot for dogs and black labrador Josie is her treasured companion. A friend of Marjorie is that other lady from Cheston Avenue, Phyllis Greenslade.

Eve Morin

Eve has lived in Cheston Avenue for 40 years, her children – two boys and a girl – attending local schools. She remembers Phyllis Greenslade walking her dog to the park and Janet Berlin riding her horse, Pepe.

During the Second World War Eve worked to rehouse bomb victims but had a hankering for the Land Army and, through *Country Life*, found a job helping with the poultry at a manor-house in Devon in the severe winter of 1946. During the following long summer evenings, with double summertime, Eve found it tedious waiting for the chickens to go in at night so, in 1947, decided to take a trip round the world, leaving Southampton with very little money on a Polish liner bound for New York. A family with six children helped her out on the train to Canada by doubling up in their sleepers so that Eve could have one.

Within three weeks she had met the man she was to marry and that was the end of her world tour! Her husband was an architect working about 100 miles from Ottawa. Their children came in quick succession but sadly her husband died when the children were aged four, six and eight years. Eve returned to England and to Shirley where she was near her brother, who lived in West Wickham.

At the time of writing one of Eve's main interests is following the top tennis players in the Grand Slam tournaments. With Janet Berlin's mother, Jean, Eve was one of the founder members of the Shirley tennis club. They started playing in a private garden and went on to form the Midweekers' group on the courts near St John's Church.

Park Farm in the 1960s

Douglas Croker's first job when leaving school in 1960 at the age of 15 was as a gardener at Home Farm, part of the Bethlem Royal Hospital. He remembers many employees at the farm – Reg Herbert was the head gardener living in the house in the corner of the walled garden and responsible for the beech, douglas fir and larch plantation, which was named in his honour when he retired; Les Burroughs was a gardener first class and the union rep for COHSE (Confederation Of Health Service Employees); Fred Truncheon worked in the greenhouses but had previously worked at Castle's, opposite Dick's, the nurseryman in Elmers End

Road near Beckenham cemetery. The foreman, Horstmayer, was a German airman prisoner of war who never returned to Germany.

Peter Bristow was a tractor driver living in tied accommodation in the old farm buildings and was one of the first owners of a Messerschmitt bubblecar. A local dealer took a photograph of Peter driving it past the old farm archway. The Messerschmitt KR200 was developed by former Luftwaffe aeronautical engineer Fritz Fend as an invalid carriage on three wheels. It was intended for injured pilots and was powered by pushing the handlebars to and fro in a rowing action. Fritz joined forces with aircraft manufacturer Willie Messerschmitt, who was no longer allowed to build aircraft. By 1952 they had produced a two-seater car powered by a 200cc engine. This was called the KR200, or Kabinenroller 200cc. Produced in 1960, the final model was the TG500, the Tiger with a 500cc engine. Only 450 were built and Douglas Croker is not certain which of the models Peter Bristow drove. Peter also won the *News of the World* Amateur Golf Championship in about 1959 while working as an artisan at the Addington Golf Course. Another tractor driver was Jim Marchant who drove a Humber Hawk and was the caller at the Beckenham Folk Dance Club at St Barnabas' Church in Beckenham.

One of the jobs that Douglas had was sitting on the tractor and operating a seed drill which had originally been horse drawn. He disconnected the ten drills feeding barley at the end of each row while the tractor turned to make its next run. The barley field remains as a pasture beside the Wickham Road.

Throughout the hard winter of 1962/63, with deep snow on the ground, Douglas grew cabbages in the field on the other side of Monks Orchard Road beside High Broom Wood, where the land has since been developed for housing.

Steve Isted was another youngster who worked with Douglas. Steve started at Wisley and moved to Bethlem in 1964, staying for 37 years. He became an expert in the kitchen garden, providing vegetables such as parsnips and January King cabbages. Douglas also remembers Taffy Amae, a former miner who became a gardener for health reasons, and Les Beckway, who did the propagating in the greenhouses. When the stable block was demolished he used some of the pinky-yellow bricks from the herringbone floors to build a well in his garden at Selsdon.

The patients in the wards of King's College Hospital, Cane Hill and Maudsley, as well as in Bethlem, always had fresh flowers grown by the gardeners. Daffodils and tulips were grown in old tomato compost, forced outside the walled garden on cinder beds. Everything was recycled – a lorry-load of extremely smelly fish boxes would be scrubbed out before use; old turf would be chopped and put though the sterilising machine to make compost which would be mixed with sand, loam and peat

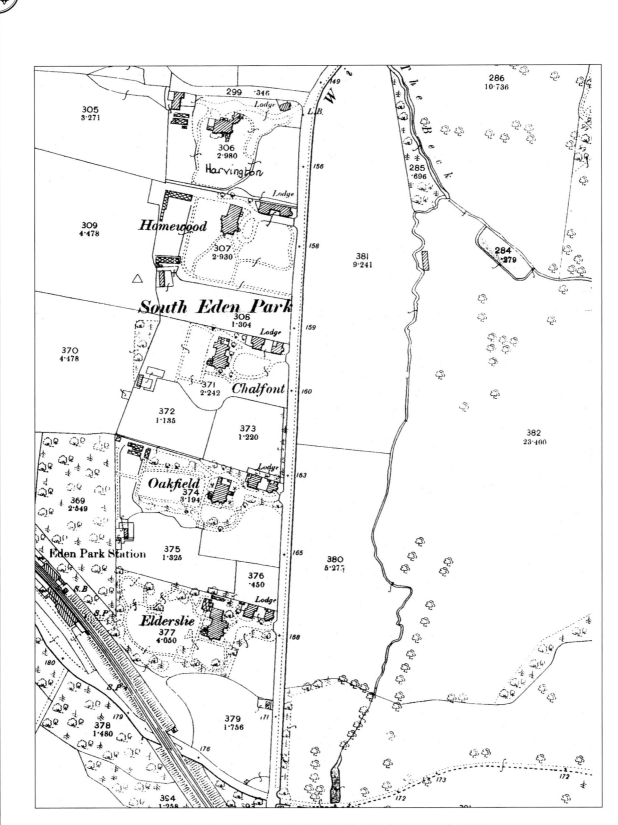

A map showing the five houses in South Eden Park Road in the 1870s. (B)

Elderslie, replaced in 1939 by Elderslie Close. (NT)

Above: *Bertrand Theodore Petley and Florence Ada Petley (née Chappell).*
Below: *The Petley family with* (from left to right) *Dorothy, Hugh, Philip and Florence.* (RP)

according to its purpose. All the pots were re-used, being stacked according to size and scrubbed out with cold water on the floor by the drain.

Notable trees that Douglas remembers were the tulip tree, *Liriodendron tulipifera*, in the Dower House garden, and the lily of the valley tree, Forest Flame, which was 20ft tall.

Douglas worked at Park Farm for five years earning £3 a week and then became part of the 'heavy gang' for L.B. Bromley Parks Dept from 1966 to 1968. He was part of the gang landscaping the old peoples' home off Goddard Road and working on school tarmac and fencing projects, earning a more respectable £8 a week.

For the years 1954–56 some of the names of the cows on Park Farm were Betty, Mistletoe, Rosebud, Aurelia, Aurora, Geyser, Tansy, Blackie and Prunella. The Bethlem Museum holds their milking records.

The Harvington Estate

In the early 1870s, five houses were built along what is now known as South Eden Park Road. At least some of the land, if not all, belonged to William Rudd Mace, whose daughter Emily had married George Stanley Lutwyche. The houses most closely associated with them were Elderslie and Oakfield but there were also Chalfont, Homewood and Harvington. How did the whole area become known as the Harvington estate?

It is all to do with the Petley family, Bertrand Theodore and Florence Ada, who lived here from 1919, bringing the name Harvington with them – it being the name of the village near Kidderminster where they became engaged to be married. They took the name to Burma for their house in the hill-station at Maymyo and then back again for their house in Beckenham at the bend in South Eden Park Road. Harvington was described as an imposing red-brick house with a slated roof, roughly square in shape with a frontage of 60ft. A 20-ft billiard room had been added to the original building but had suffered some damage when a V2 fell near St John's

Ordnance Survey maps from 1914 (above) *and 1933.*

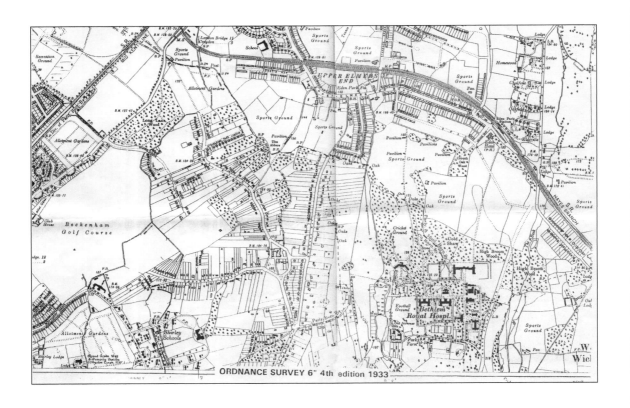

The waterfall at Harvington in the 1960s. (AC)

Above: *Mark Williams in his pram in Eden Park Avenue, 1964. Note the prefabs (see also page 13).* (LW)

Below: *Looking across the fields from the kitchen garden at Harvington to Eden Park Avenue. The oak trees are 100 years old at the time of writing.* (RP)

Bottom: *Marguerite Oliffe's dancing class shows off its skills at Harvington.* (WG)

Church on the other side of the fields. The other two houses, Homewood and Chalfont, were of white brick and perhaps the lodges still existing – Harvington constructed of red brick and the other two of grey materials – reflect the different construction of the houses. Oakfield was described in 1904 as a picturesque building in the style of an Italian villa. It was built using Staffordshire brick with ornamental stone dressings and mouldings.

Harvington was thought to be the oldest, built in 1871 according to the date carved by the builders above one of the first-floor windows.

As a young man Bertrand Theodore Petley became a forest manager for Messrs J.W. Darwood & Co., Burma, living far from civilisation. He was known in Upper Burma for the force of his personality and his intimate understanding of the country and its people. In November 1898, at Rangoon Cathedral, Bertrand married Florence Ada Chappell, daughter of iron founder Henry Pegg Chappell, from Staffordshire.

Left: *Elmville football team, 1949/50. Left to right, back row: Bob Miles, Bert Durling (secretary), Roy 'Birdie' Nightingale, Bob Francis (chairman), Lennie Ralph, Alan Morgan, Joe Norris (treasurer), ? Holloway, Ken Francis; middle row: Ken Garret, Derek Heritage, Harry Holloway, Bob Pearce (son of the fishmonger next to the Rising Sun), Ken Everett, Len Davis; front row: Derek 'Turbie' Parson, Don Gasson.* (J&B)

Their eldest son, James Bertrand, died in Burma from dysentery at the age of two years, four months, 20 days and they had two other sons, Hugh Henry and Philip Theodore. Their daughter, Dorothy Florence, was born in Katha on 20 September 1899 and baptised in May 1900 in Mandalay. The following description of life in Katha comes from a history of Messrs J.W. Darwood & Co.:

The Katha forest manager lived in a ramshackle bunga-low adjoining the native quarter. It poured heavily and relentlessly in the summer. Age-old newspapers and paperbacks were ravaged by silverfish and white ants. Heavy mosquito netting thwarted the whisper of a breeze. Overhead, a steady stream of bats flashed along the veranda and the occasional lizard would fall with a plop.

Did the magnificent bougainvillea compensate for the tough life into which Bertrand and Florence brought their daughter Dorothy?

In 1904 Bertrand joined the forest staff of Messrs Steel Brothers and became responsible for much of the firm's success. Following a serious shooting accident while hunting tigers in 1910, when he lost an eye, his career in Burma came to an end and he returned to England. In 1914 he joined the London Board of the company and the Petleys came to live in Beckenham at No. 31 The Avenue. By 1919 they were living in the house at the bend of South Eden Park Road, which they renamed Harvington. Here they ran a dairy farm next to another small dairy farm, Kelsey Manor, which stretched across to Kelsey Park. Locals remember hearing the cattle in the fields – Mrs Petley prided herself on this being the longest surviving working farm in the district.

In 1926 Bertrand Petley became chairman of the board – the only forester to become chairman of Steel's, work in the jungle not normally leading to the boardroom! He held many other posts and was known as a staunch churchman of great dignity. He retired from business after a debilitating stroke in May 1929 and died on Boxing Day 1930, sorely missed by his wife and children. He had attended

Mr Hills, complete with suspenders, offering a tray to Mr Bird at the VE Day party in Aylesford Avenue. See them also in the photograph on the opposite page.

Christchurch for nearly 20 years but was buried at Downe cemetery near to the local church.

How the family came to be in Burma is a fascinating story. By the middle of the nineteenth century, three families – the Peggs, the Chappells and the Petleys – had associated as iron founders and ship owners trading with outposts of the British Empire.

Bertrand's father James was a sea captain. After an incident in the Bay of Bengal in which he was washed off the bridge and miraculously returned on deck unconscious and clutching a rope, James decided to stay on in Rangoon negotiating hardwood conces-sions. At Nan Cho in the Karen Hills, close to Toungoo, he established a tea and coffee plantation which he cultivated until the coffee leaf disease struck Burma in 1898 and the estate had to be abandoned. James was buried in Toungoo in 1903 and if it were not for his granddaughter, Elizabeth Marion Heptonstall, leaving notes for her nephews and niece, the exciting story of

VE party in Aylesford Avenue in 1945. The names were supplied by Joan Durling (née Freeman), who can just be seen (No. 62). 1 Audrey Wright, 2 Mrs Jamieson, 3 Mr Southeren, 4 Mr Darby, 5 Mrs England, 6 Mrs Sheffield, 7 Joan Knott, 8 Mr Gaved, 9 Mrs Hope (Rene Peacock's mother), 10 Mrs Pickering, 11 Mrs Edwards, 12 Mr Collis, 13 Mrs Collis, 14 Mrs Gaved, 15 Audrey Edwards, 16 Mrs Ratcliffe, 17 Mrs Aynesworth, 18 Mrs Southeren, 19 Mr Gascoigne, 20 Mr Bird, 21 Mrs Pratt, 22 Tony Hansley, 23 ?, 24 Mrs Drinkwater, 25 Rene Peacock, 26 Mrs Turner, 27 Wally Burgess, 28 Mrs Gladstone, 29 Geoff Taylor, 30 Mrs Darby, 31 Eileen Kelly (née Minter), 32 Mr Wetheral, 33 Mrs Wetheral, 34 ?, 35 Clifford Darby, 36 Les Darby, 37 Vera Wetheral, 38 Yvonne Sandecombe, 39 ?, 40 ?, 41 ?, 42 Jean Simmonds, 43 David Skipp, 44 Peter Simmonds, 45 Pam Shepherd, 46 Ronald Pratt, 47 Yvonne Sandecombe's fiancé, 48 Jean Sheffield, 49 ?, 50 ?, 51 Jimmy Atwood, 52 ?, 53 David Hill, 54 Pat Gaved, 55 Barry McGrath, 56 Margaret Longley, 57 ?, 58 Yvonne Biddle, 59 Jean Edwards, 60 Brenda Muncey, 61 Shirley Biddle, 62 Joan Freeman, 63 Peter Gladstone, 64 Michael Luckman, 65 John Gaved, 66 ?, 67 ?, 68 Anne Perran, 69 ?, 70 ?, 70a Mrs de Solar (?) and youngest child, 71 Joyce Pickering, 72 Dorothy Pickering, 73 ?, 74 Margaret Ridgewell, 75 Joan Ridgewell, 76 Mr Hill, 77 Betty Percival, 78 Barbara Sheffield, 79 Anne Shepherd, 80 Diane Morgan, 81 Brenda Greenslade, 82 ?, 83 ?, 84 ?, 85 ?, 86 Pam Kettle, 87 ?, 88 Hazel Kettle, 89 ?, 90 Vicky Bird, 91 Anne England, 92 Mr Pickering, 93 John England, 94 Jill Southeren, 95 Rita Ratcliffe, 96 Joan Knott's sister (?), 97 Clive Turner, 98 Pat Venables, 99 Ann Greenacre, 100 Eileen Greenacre, 101, ?, 102 ?, 103 ?, 104 ?.

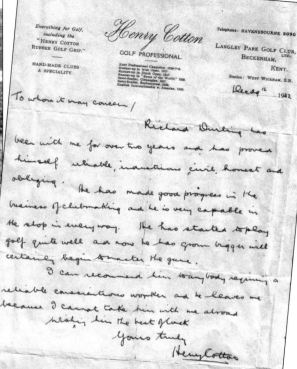

Above: The cottages at The Alders where Bert Durling was born. The River Beck flows from left to right in the foreground, towards the White Hart, early 1930s.

Right: The reference written for Richard Durling by Henry Cotton. (J&B)

Elmville FC party, New Year's Eve, 1949. Percy Jones is eighth from the left in the third row from the front. (J&B)

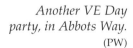

Another VE Day party, in Abbots Way. (PW)

the Petleys in Burma would largely have been lost.

Soon after Bertrand's death, his widow Florence gave the land for St John's Church to be built in Eden Park Avenue. Its foundation-stone was laid in 1932. She gave the new church her full support and donated the organ in her husband's memory. This did not mean that she forgot Christchurch. The annual outing to Harvington was by horse-drawn coal-cart for a tea in the house followed by a visit to see the farm animals – geese, chickens, dogs, pigs and cows. Florence played the church organ and had a grand piano in the house that eventually she willed to her son Philip. She was playing the organ at the church when a V2 dropped in the field in February 1945 killing two Jersey cows and a hen but thankfully not even waking the vicar's baby, asleep in the vicarage garden.

The Harvington estate as owned by the Petleys included the houses called Homewood and Chalfont, together with their lodges and stables. During the war Florence Petley leased out Homewood and Chalfont to the Metropolitan Electric Light & Power Co. for their offices.

When Florence died in 1946 at the age of 73, Beckenham Council bought the 37 acres of land for £36,000, including the land used for allotments between Chalfont and the adjoining house, Oakfield. In her will, Florence had hoped that her unmarried daughter, Dorothy, who had assisted in the running of the farm, would take over the Harvington house. In 1935 Dorothy wrote a reference for William Chilver, of neighbouring Kelsey Manor Farm, who was applying to work at Wellcome's, his farmland having been taken over for the construction of Stone Park Avenue.

All three houses were leased to the LEB (London Electricity Board) for ten years from 1948. When the leases expired, the lodges continued as rented accommodation for the Park's staff but the houses were demolished in 1960 by the firm of Sid Bishop. The stone bearing the family crest with the motto *Toujours Prêt* (meaning Always Ready) was sent to Hugh Henry Petley at his house in Old Heathfield, Sussex, where it remains.

As for the family, Dorothy lived at 70 Manor Way and continued as a Sunday-school teacher at the church. Hugh Henry was a stockbroker with offices in Great Winchester Street, while Philip Theodore was a company director at 56 Warwick Square. Both the boys were keen members of the Beckenham Cricket and Tennis Club.

They dedicated the St John the Baptist stained-glass window in the church in Eden Park Avenue to their parents, Bertrand Theodore and Florence Ada Petley.

Both boys married and had children but only Hugh's family had children in their turn, these being two daughters and a son, Roddy, who took over his father's house at Heathfield.

Sadly, not long before she died, Florence had to submit to the compulsory purchase of 20 acres of her land along Village Way and Eden Park Avenue. To help solve an acute housing shortage at the end of the war, Beckenham had 165 prefabricated houses to place in the borough. At first it was requested that the land should be available on lease but Mrs Petley contested this because it was agricultural land. She offered to sell the land to the council on condition that on her death it would be held as open space for the benefit of the people of Beckenham for all time but the council would not agree to this and acquired the land by compulsory purchase. By September 1946, the site was drained and the bungalows were in place. Florence died shortly afterwards. The prefabs were vacated between October 1967 and July 1968, having doubled their projected lifespan of ten years. In their place were built old people's flats and two- and three-bedroomed houses.

Roddy Petley, Florence's grandson, says all the Petleys he meets own signet rings bearing the family crest. There were Petleys in the Kent village of Downe over 600 years ago and there is still an early eighteenth-century house called Petleys, built of flint and red brick with white doorway and cornice.

The Durlings

Now residing on land that was once part of the Monks Orchard estate, Bert Durling is descended from an old West Wickham family, certainly as far back as his great-grandfather William. Before then the Durlings were Kentish Men from Downe,

Lance Corporal William Chilver with his first-born son, Bill, and his wife Nell. (OV)

Left: Nell Chilver holding Bill at the door of Ham Farm cottage, with her mother and an unknown child. (OV)

Below: The Chilvers at Eden Park Farm with Ken, Bill, Cyril, Lesley and Eric. The Rising Sun would be to the left and Loyd's Way to the right. (OV)

Coloured GREEN and numbered 322 and 323 on Plan

"EDEN PARK FARM"

An Area of

Valuable Accommodation Pasture Land

together with

Two Cottages and Extensive Farm Buildings

situated in the Parish of Beckenham, to the North of and with a Frontage of about 700 ft. to Upper Elmers End Road, and covering an Area of about

6 a. 1 r. 28 p.

THE FARM BUILDINGS

for the most part built of brick and tile, with some corrugated iron and timber, are substantial and consist of: Two Loose Boxes, Cooling House, Cow House for 20, Cake and Meal House, Loose Box and Root House, Bull Box Closed Cattle Shed and another Loose Box, Three-bay Open Implement Shed, Cart Shed and Loose Box.

THE TWO COTTAGES

formerly a Farmhouse, are well built of brick, with tiled roof, and contain the following total accommodation: Seven Rooms and Two Sculleries, all on one Floor. Outside: W.C., Wood House, Good Garden and Orchard. Company's Water and Gas are laid on, and the Drainage is on the Cesspool System.

This Lot is let with Lot 15, and Possession may be resumed in the same way. Apportioned Rent, £10.

OUTGOINGS:—Tithe Rent Charge, Beckenham Parish (Rectorial), 18s. 6d.

NOTE.– The Purchaser of this Lot will be granted such right of way over the roadway, Ord. No. 321 on the Plan, as the Vendor is entitled to.

Details of the 1920 sale of Eden Park Farm. (OV)

Right: *Bill Chilver holds his brother Brian at Kelsey Manor Farm.* (OV)

Left: *The Chilvers at 10 Fairfield Road in 1938.* Left to right, back row: *Ken, Cyril, Bill;* middle row: *Olive, Eric, Lesley;* front row: *Alan, father William, mother Ellen, Brian, Freda.* (OV)

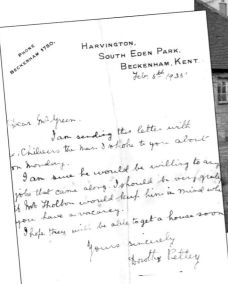

Above: *The old coach-house of Charles Hoare at Park Langley.* (B)

Left: *The letter written in 1936 by Dorothy Petley recommending William Chilver for employment at Wellcome's.* (OV)

Cudham and Eynsford. William and his brother Thomas lived in adjoining cottages built for them in The Alders by Sir John Farnaby of Wickham Court and there were at least 12 little Durlings born to William and his wife Caroline. Their son, Albert, moved a few yards along the road to No. 6 The Alders, where both Bert's father Ernest and Bert himself were born. He was the youngest of five children – Nellie, Albert, Fred, Doris and Herbert (Bert). Their home was one of four wooden cottages numbered five to eight with The Alders and the River Beck running across their front gardens, often causing the cottages to flood.

Ernest was a gamekeeper and gardener on the Loyd estate but the sale in 1920 eventually led to the loss of his job. The cottages were condemned and the Durlings were given notice to quit on 11 August 1937. The family moved to Goddard Road in Elmers End, where the children attended Marian Vian School. Bert helped his sister Doris do the family shopping at the Co-op (dividend number 61607) and they played in Stanhope Grove Park. Their mother was thrilled to see Winston Churchill on his way to Chartwell taking a short cut through Goddard Road and the boys cheered the endless convoys carrying planes along Upper Elmers End Road – the fuselages were carried on separate vehicles to the wings.

Bert decided that his future lay in being a despatch rider but started work as an office boy for an export business in the City, where he remained all his working life. His brothers worked locally, Fred as a porter at Elmers End and Eden Park Stations in the days when they were kept spotless and adorned with flower gardens, while Albert ran the Smith's bookstall on Eden Park Station, where he served Julie Andrews' father. This was when Julie attended Woodbrook School and was described by Miss Mead, the headmistress, as having the voice of an angel. Their second cousin, Elsie, well into her eighties at the time of writing, worked at Harvington for the Petleys, as did her father Joseph, while her brother, Richard Durling, a promising golfer given a reference by Henry Cotton, was killed at Monte Casino in the Second World War.

Despite having no proper football pitch at Stanhope Grove Park, Bert and some other boys put together a football team to play friendlies on the pitches of other teams, including those of patients and staff at the Bethlem Royal Hospital. At first they called themselves Elmers End Rovers, and played in the West Wickham District Youth League. Their strip had to be simple black and white because the white shirts that they played football in on Saturday had to be washed ready for work on Monday! They moved, as Elmville, to the more influential Beckenham League in 1948, with Percy Jones, owner of Twinlocks in St Margaret's Road, as their president. Their new strip was black and amber.

Conscription caught up with Bert in February 1950 and, after the initial shock of leaving home, he quite enjoyed it – especially in Kenya. Before that there were a few months at Devizes where he remembers having to scatter fresh snow over the parade ground to cover the flattened snow when a visit from Emanuel Shinwell was expected.

Demobbed in February 1952, it was back to Elmville for Bert. The fun and games extended to outings to the coast and parties, especially at New Year. He left after the 1959/60 season, the demands of married life with Joan Freeman taking their toll, with too much to do on the house in Altyre Way. Joan is another local. In the mid-1960s Elmville disbanded for good, although Joan and Bert remained strong supporters of local football and have for many years followed the fortunes of the historic Bromley Town FC in Hayes Lane.

Years later, when he retired, Bert and Joan turned to family and local history. We are grateful for several of their photographs and many reminders of the not so distant past included in this book.

Kelsey Manor Farm and the Chilvers

Beckenham's farms were fast disappearing as their land was turned into housing estates. William Chilver had previously worked on Ham Farm, where he lived in one of the farm cottages now in Elstan Way. By 1927 he was the last tenant farmer of Eden Park Farm, owned by Harry Joseph Chilver, his uncle, who lived opposite at 204 Upper Elmers End Road, then called Holly Lodge (now Asprey Mews) and which was at one time Eden Park School. By 1931 Stanhope Grove had been driven through Eden Park Farm and its cottages, where Olive Chilver was born in 1927. Olive's memories include the Kempton pie factory and the tiny confectioner's shop by the Rising Sun. She also can remember the muffin man, a tray of muffins on his flat hat, ringing his bell to come and collect all the naughty children!

The Chilvers then moved to Kelsey Manor Farm, off South Eden Park Road, which was the property of the Barnard family from at least 1885. Olive Lucy Ellen Varney (née Chilver) was the sixth of nine children of William and his wife, Ellen Eliza Hales. She has memories of playing in the brick-built ice well with her brothers and only sister, Freda Margery. There was no problem getting in as the door had disappeared! They also had a horse, Dolly, which she remembers pulling the cart on a Sunday outing to the Green Man at Peter Pan's Pool, where they ate large 'Brighton biscuits'.

The farm was next door to Eden Cottage, which dated from before 1838. From about 1924 it was the Sir Frederick Milner home for ex-servicemen, known as Eden Manor, which formally closed at the beginning of the Second World War. The building stood until 1953, when Beckenham Council bought it and pulled it down. All that remains of Eden

Cottage/Manor is the coach-house of Charles Hoare (a previous resident at Eden Cottage) on the site now occupied by the local rangers who police the parks.

Kelsey Manor Farm had been demolished by 1936 to make way for Stonepark Avenue while earlier, in 1929, the Park Langley garage was built and Stone farmhouse gave way to the Park Langley shopping parade, with grocers Messrs W.H. Cullen occupying the actual site of the farmhouse. The manager at the garage was Mr Molyneux who had three sons, all older than Olive and who lived in a house beside the garage. One day, when Olive was about six, Mr Molyneux came to her aid. Sent to bring her brothers in to dinner, Olive swung on the farm's five-bar gate which collapsed on her and broke her leg. Mr Molyneux brought his car in through the farm's entrance in South Eden Park Road and took her to Beckenham Hospital, where her leg was put into splints – no plaster casts in those days!

The Chilvers moved to 10 Fairfield Road, where two of Olive's unmarried brothers live at the time of writing, and William Chilver worked as the cowman at Wellcome's on the recommendation of Dorothy Petley of Harvington. Olive will never forget when, at only 17, she came home on leave from the Wrens to find a policeman barring the way to Fairfield Road. A V1 had fallen on the air-raid shelter at the top of the road which now (2004) divides the car park in two. Most of the bombed-out people had gone to Marian Vian School but poor Olive could not find her family there – they had gone to her brother's house in Durban Road, where Olive found them playing cards! Their black and white dog, Joe, had been rescued but

Eden Manor.

Langley Farm. (NL)

Olive's father had a blood-chilling tale to tell. He had seen the doodlebug heading straight for their house when it had tipped the church spire and was diverted onto the shelter. The blast had blown him – together with the front door – through to the back garden!

Nigel Lawford's Ancestors

The great-grandparents of Nigel Lawford, from Farnham, Surrey, came from two notable Beckenham families, the Lawfords and the Hollands.

Henry Holland, born in 1745, was the first son of a leading London builder who worked with Lancelot Capability Brown. Among the many projects completed by Henry was Althorpe, home of Earl Spencer, and the Brighton Pavilion, whose oriental exterior was not added until 1815, nine years after Henry's death.

It is possible that Langley Farm was built to Henry's design. Henry and Bridget had seven children with only two sons, the second born in 1781 and named Lancelot. At age 18 Lancelot was in the 1st Regiment of Foot Guards, rapidly rising to Lt Col. He married the beautiful 19-year-old Charlotte Peters, who had reddish-gold hair, a brilliant complexion and pretty teeth. They had ten daughters and five sons and lived at Langley Farm from about 1828 until Lancelot's death in 1859.

Edward Lawford was solicitor to the East India Company and clerk to the Drapers' Livery Company and as such had a well-appointed townhouse in London. Beckenham was accessible from the City, especially as the railways developed, and so Edward leased the late William Eden's mansion at Eden Park – possibly from 1826, when a previous sub-lease to a Mrs Wildman expired. By 1842, Edward and his wife, Maria Bowring, had nine children. The eldest, Henry Smith Lawford, born in 1815, was Nigel's grandfather. The others were Maria (1817), Charles (1818), Emily (1823), twins Frances and Jane (1825), Edward Melville (1826), Augusta Smith (1828) and Henry Baring (1829).

Edward Lawford's four sons were educated at Eton and while there Edward Melville kept a journal of events at school and in the holidays. Melville was a great sportsman and became a cadet in the Indian Army when he left Eton. His diaries, written between 1838 and 1843, show that he had free access to the lake at Kelsey through Kelsey Field from Eden Farm. He refers to rowing, punting, bathing, fishing and ice-skating on the lake and mentions meeting Mr Hoare while rowing, so the Lawfords must have owned a boat. There was an ice house in the wood, about 200 yards away from Wickham Lodge, that was filled on 16 January 1843. He mentions days out where they took the donkey cart down to Eden Park Farm and then went on foot to Mr Loyd's pond to catch perch. His companion was often his younger brother, Baring.

This was when Samuel Jones Loyd was first in occupation of Park Farm. On other occasions they would go on horseback to Coombe and return by Mr Loyd's wood – the woodland beside Long Lane, between Bywood Avenue and The Glade.

Their social life brought the Lawfords and Hollands in contact with others in the district, such as the Cators and the Loyds, as well as with the various clerics from St George's Church. They had tableaux evenings to which, among others, the Peter Cators and Jones Loyds, the Hollands and the Whitmores would come. There were balls in Croydon and Bromley and dinner parties that were attended by Sir Charles and Lady Farnaby. By 1843, Lewis Loyd was also visiting.

Nigel's grandmother was Emily Frances Holland one of the ten daughters of Lancelot Holland and Charlotte Peters of Langley Farm. Emily married Henry Smith Lawford on 30 September 1852 and they lived for a time at the Cator mansion, Beckenham Place.

The occasion of their wedding day has been preserved forever in a letter written by Elizabeth Cator, who had married Emily's brother Revd Edward Holland. He conducted the ceremony that Elizabeth described for her sisters-in-law, Emma Holland and Julia Travers (née Holland):

October 2 1852
Saturday
Camerton Rectory
My dearest Emma and Julia,
I know you will like to hear the particulars of Emily's wedding and I have promised Mama to write them for you although she is herself writing and will I dare say tell you everything else. She is looking much better than she did when she arrived and I will try to persuade her to stay till the middle of the week as it suits her so well. I am sure Edward will try to keep her so I hope she will consent to the arrangement but you know how impossible she thinks it. Anything can go on at home without her and she is full of objections and difficulties but I think we shall prevail.

I must now enter upon the subject of my letter, which I need not tell you has engrossed my heart and thoughts the last few days. Emily and Eleanor have kept me constantly supplied with the account of everything going on and the latter sent me a beautiful account of it all written yesterday but I must put everything together and give you as concise an account as I can of my own.

On the wedding morning dear Emily was not only free from nervousness but beaming with cheerfulness and happiness. She had never waked all the night before and looked lovely in her wedding dress and her figure they say exquisite. It was all so beautifully made.

The party assembled at the church at eleven, the Lawfords of course from their own house and Edward and Charles went early in the brougham to wait in the communion rails. From Langley came the Rusts, Peters and their own open carriages containing

Henry, F.B. Wilmot and Fred, three bridesmaids in white silk and muslin over blue with net bonnets and blue sashes, Charles' wife nicely dressed, four more bridesmaids and then the closed carriage containing Papa and Mama Holland, the bride and Henrietta the principal bridesmaid.

The churchyard and church were so thronged with people that it was a squeeze to get in but they made way when the bride came. The organ which is a beautiful one and given by Mr Lawford struck up as she entered the church, the organist having come from London as a compliment to the Lawfords to play it. He played rather too long as of course the service was delayed till he finished. Emily looked a little pale and began to tremble a little, however after everyone making frantic signs to the organist he stopped and the service began.

Edward said the service almost entirely without a book, which had a very touching effect as he turned and addressed them in his touching tender voice calling them as he was accustomed to do Henry and Emily not Henry Smith and Emily Frances. Then the bells, the signing in the vestry and then all the party now fifty in number returned to Langley. Henry and Emily were in a chariot of their own drawn by four white horses.

Breakfast was at twelve o'clock and fifty sat down to one long table. Edward proposed the health of the Bride and Bridegroom. H.L. very nicely returned thanks. Peter Cator proposed Mr and Mrs Holland and he returned thanks. Bourdillon proposed Mr and Mrs Lawford and Mr Edward Lawford made the most beautiful and touching speech ever heard. Then the bridesmaids were toasted and Mr Maule the best man was very absurd, witty and ridiculous.

Then when Emily came down dressed for driving off in a dark plain silk dress for travelling she looked quite lovely. Their own chariot with four greys and H.L.'s man and her maid behind and Mr Wrench produced a shoe from his pocket and flung it after them. Edward went down to Ashford with Mr Peters and everybody dispersed even Fred back to Scotland.
I am ever Your most truly affec sister, Lizzie.

Lancelot and Charlotte's youngest daughter, Eleanor Mary (1831–1920), grew up on Langley Farm. She never married and many years later wrote down her childhood memories for the benefit of her great-nephews and nieces.

She remembered all their games – Tom Titler, battledore, shuttlecock, coronella, bagatelle, charades and play-acting. Coronella was a game of tossing shuttlecocks between long-handled cups.

Her sister Henrietta was a favourite with Mr John Cator, Aunt Elizabeth's uncle. He was a big, stout man who was always suggesting that the children had a half day's holiday from the schoolroom. Eleanor had loved her nurserymaid, who had spoiled her, and was miserable when at age seven she had to join her sisters in the schoolroom and learn her tables and spelling and all the rest. Henrietta was pretty, quick-witted

Bomb damage in November 1940 at Nos 93–103 Merlin Grove (above left and right) with Nos 101 and 103 (left) completely destroyed by parachute mines. The photographs were taken from No. 98 by the late Bernard Tyson. (AH)

and full of imagination so was always chosen as the Princess or Beauty in *Beauty and the Beast*. The schoolroom was shut off from the rest of the house and Eleanor had to attend lessons with Henrietta and Emily in that dull place until she was 11. They had Monsieur Colinet for French, Miss Holmes for music and there was also a dancing mistress. Gardening was a delight, each sister with her own bed.

Eleanor wore her nursery pinafore at early dinner or luncheon held in the big dining-room which was a big, formal room with a long, broad table, mahogany sideboard and handsome chairs. The only picture was a Gainsborough but there were bronzes on the chimneypiece and Japanese vases on the floor.

The children delighted in seeing the planets and their moons through the telescope on the lawn and Eleanor also loved her father's microscope. Her brother Wilmot married Margaret Wells and lived at Langley Lodge so with Henry and Emily at Beckenham Place there were always men dropping in and coming to dinner. They were such a large party in those days, with eight Misses Holland (until Sophia married), and they often had archery parties (Melville mentions in his diary that Sophia won the ladies' match).

Where is all this today now that the land has been turned into an estate of 500 houses? Little do the children of the Unicorn School realise that they are not the first children to play there!

The Merlin Grove Mob

Dave Baker and Jack Nightingale were the best of friends from the age of three, when they would race their tricycles along the pavements on opposite sides of Merlin Grove. They were forbidden to cross the road and since Dave's father was a policeman he knew he must do as he was told!

It was the second year of the war when a pair of parachute mines, designed to explode above ground and cause maximum blast damage, were dropped on the moonlit night of 15 November 1940. From Anderson shelters could be heard, catching against trees, the lines which trailed from the bombs. One fell over Greenways and the other at the back of 103 Merlin Grove, damaging 300 houses. Two women, Mary Anne Frances Drew and Jessica Redington, both widows, died at 103 Merlin Grove, but the whole Sargent family, Leonard and Cecilia with their sons John and Brian, died at 58 Greenways. Dave lived further down at 52 Merlin Grove and Jack lived opposite. Bernard Tyson, who lived opposite the bombsite at No. 98, took photographs of the devastation, passing them to the current owner of No. 97 in 1982. The pre-war builder, Edward Barrs, rebuilt the houses in their original style after the war.

Later in the war, when a rocket fell behind the church in Harvington, Jack, rushing from the house with plaster on his head, was delighted to think that

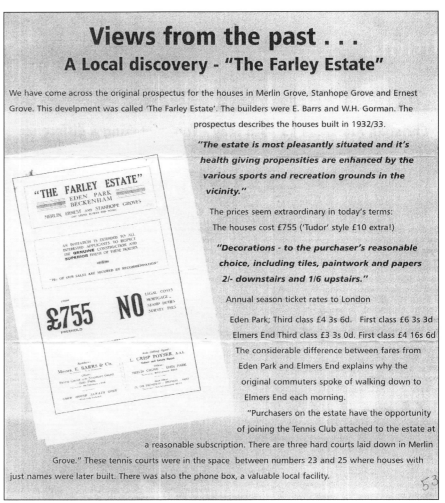

Above: *Dave Baker and Jack Nightingale of the Merlin Grove Mob.*

Right: *Farley estate brochure from the 1930s.*

Views from the past . . .
A Local discovery - "The Farley Estate"

We have come across the original prospectus for the houses in Merlin Grove, Stanhope Grove and Ernest Grove. This develpment was called 'The Farley Estate'. The builders were E. Barrs and W.H. Gorman. The prospectus describes the houses built in 1932/33.

"THE FARLEY ESTATE"
EDEN PARK
BECKENHAM
MERLIN, ERNEST AND STANHOPE GROVES

£755 NO

"The estate is most pleasantly situated and it's health giving propensies are enhanced by the various sports and recreation grounds in the vicinity."

The prices seem extraordinary in today's terms:
The houses cost £755 ('Tudor' style £10 extra!)

"Decorations - to the purchaser's reasonable choice, including tiles, paintwork and papers 2/- downstairs and 1/6 upstairs."

Annual season ticket rates to London

Eden Park; Third class £4 3s 6d. First class £6 3s 3d

Elmers End Third class £3 3s 0d. First class £4 16s 6d

The considerable difference between fares from Eden Park and Elmers End explains why the original commuters spoke of walking down to Elmers End each morning.

"Purchasers on the estate have the opportunity of joining the Tennis Club attached to the estate at a reasonable subscription. There are three hard courts laid down in Merlin Grove." These tennis courts were in the space between numbers 23 and 25 where houses with just names were later built. There was also the phone box, a valuable local facility.

he might miss school. He went to the school at Holly Lodge for a while but was pleased to transfer to Marian Vian and then to Hawes Down with his best pal, Dave.

The whole block of six houses, from Nos 93–103, was demolished where the mine fell. The land was later used as a camp for Italian prisoners of war. The group of children known as the Merlin Grove Mob, thinking the prisoners were Germans, would goose-step after them, giving the Nazi salute. German prisoners of war moved in later and their building of Balmoral Road to connect with Upper Elmers End Road gave it the nickname 'the German road'. An aerial map of 1946 shows the long huts where the prisoners were housed. The children remember playing in the white house (Eden Lodge) and the red house (Eden Manor), both derelict in the 1940s and '50s. They also imagined that the men working for the electricity board at Chalfont, Homewood and Harvington were spies!

Others in the gang were Alan Cooper and Eric Sullivan, Gillian Rogers, twins Rosemary and Patricia Gower, Marcia Burns, Janice Trimmer, Jill Rogers and Ann Selby. When Pat went on to Sydenham High she announced she was having 'elocution', whereupon one of the younger ones assured her that it didn't hurt if you shut your eyes (inoculation!). Another Merlin Grove family who remember Dave are the Grants. John Grant and his younger twin sisters lived at the top of the road.

Alan Cooper was always in trouble. One day when they were playing bows and arrows he wrapped a piece of lead round his arrow to see if it would go faster. It did – unfortunately through the rear door of Mr Ross' car. With so few cars on the road in those days this was really bad luck, made worse by the fact that Mr Ross, of builders Ross &

Hansley, just happened to be passing. Marcia Burns remembers Dave's poster at the time of the general election in 1945. The windows were full of posters so Dave made one of his own advertising free ice-cream and lemonade. Ann Selby ran a nature-study club based at the empty lodge of Homewood. The boys were interested in joining because of the girls, not the flowers, but found themselves in aprons clearing up and looking for lesser-spotted this and that in the woods, which was not what they had intended!

When Dave and Jack were working together as glass-blowers at New Addington, Jack's family emigrated to Australia. Dave and Jack corresponded until the 1960s, when Dave married Margaret Cloke and moved to Tonbridge. Jack changed his address in Sydney and seemed lost forever.

Then a few years ago Dave's daughter, Elaine, went backpacking in Australia and worked as an office temp in a government office. She mentioned that her father had a long-lost friend in Sydney and a colleague looked him up in the records on the sixth floor. Out of six Jack Nightingales, the first that Elaine found was her dad's old pal from Merlin Grove, who confessed that he had always felt homesick. Since then, Jack and Dave have revisited old haunts and their story appeared in the *Daily Mail* of 21 June 2003.

Children and teachers from Eden Park School, 1945. Left to right, back row: *Isabel Doughty, Betty Knopp, Pat ?,* *Gillian Buckle, Sheila Sweeney, Hilary Bird, Greta Stirling, Miss Rootham;* fourth row: *Mrs Boyden, Brian Cooper,* *Keith Adams, Colin Curtis, Anne Hollingsworth, William Ross, Roy James, Barry Jackson, Ian Law, John Ames,* *Mrs Mallick (principal);* third row: *Sheila Vallance, Janet Webber (now Jane Fabb), Gillian Burgess, ?,* *Shirley Moran;* second row: *John James, ?, Roderick Simmonds, Roger Cookham, Peter Ball, Ralph Lampard,* *John Lowry;* front row: *Christine Stenning, Hilary Whybrow, Anne Hutton, Doreen Howard, Mary Saunders.* (JF)

Margaret Cloke, Dave's wife, also has tales to tell. She went to the Beckenham Grammar School in Lennard Road from 1951–57, when Gillian Brown was head girl.

In October 2003 came the sad news of Dave's sudden, unexpected death and he is sadly missed by his wife, his brothers and all his old friends.

The Farley Estate

A 1930s sales brochure discovered locally advertised the sale of houses in Merlin Grove, Stanhope Grove and Ernest Grove through the sole selling agent L. Crisp Poyser of The Broadway, Bromley. This 1932/33 development was called the Farley estate and the builders were Edward Barrs of 1 Eden Way and William Henry Gorman. Houses were priced from £755 – Tudor style costing £10 extra – with decorations of the purchaser's choice, including tiles, paintwork and wallpaper, quoted at an incredible 2s. downstairs and 1s.6d. upstairs.

The estate was described as 'most pleasantly situated with its health-giving properties enhanced by the various sports and recreation-grounds in the vicinity.' Commuters could become healthier still by taking a brisk walk down to Elmers End Station rather than travelling from Eden Park, saving £1.0s.6d. on an annual season ticket to London!

There were no legal costs, survey fees or stamp duty and purchasers could join the tennis club for a reduced subscription. The three hard courts were in Merlin Grove, the houses since built on the site being distinguishable by their differing design.

Jane Fabb Tells Her Story

I was born Janet Webber at 80 Croydon Road, Beckenham, the local maternity home, and returned to 109 Stanhope Grove, which had been newly built following my parents' marriage in 1931.

I remember the day that the Second World War was declared although I had no idea then exactly what was happening. In September 1940 I started school at Albemarle College, a private school in Beckenham Road run by the Revd and Mrs Riley. This coincided with the start of the Blitz and was quite a long way from home, although sometimes Miss Petley, a teacher at the school,

65

Janet Webber (now Jane Fabb) with Felicity Edden. (JF)

Stanhope Grove playing-field, immediately behind our house. During the war, much of it was given over to growing vegetables and two old coal carts were kept there to block the field in case of enemy invasion from the air. To us they became chariots, ships and aircraft for our games. After the war, two tennis-courts were constructed and one of the workmen was an enchanting young Frenchman, one of the first foreigners I had ever met. My father was a founder member of the Eden Park Bowling Club with my uncle, George Webber, Dr Edden and other local gentlemen. The Ladies' Club was formed much later.

The landlord of the Rising Sun and his wife, Frank and Marjorie Tarbard, were friends of the family. New Year's Eve was special when Frank would walk along the bar ringing in the New Year with a bell. Another great occasion was to celebrate Princess Margaret's wedding in 1960.

Our 'crowd' used to play tennis on Sunday mornings and I would call from my bedroom window to the park keeper to book the courts. The games warden, Harry, also organised netball and rounders after school. During our first year at work in the West End, my school friend Annie Hornidge and I went to every first night, sitting in the gallery for two shillings or half a crown. I had loved the theatre from the days of pantomime and repertory at the end of Hastings pier, but this was an education. I had a passion for Evita, which I saw 82 times!

At one time there was a dance at the Eden Park Hotel every Saturday. [Many contributors recall this, with Billy Sumner as MC.] We also went to the jazz club at the Liberal Club in Fairfield Road. A passion for coffee bars followed, when we commuted between the Fiesta at Clockhouse and the Anne Boleyn at Hayes. Tony Jermy, who lived along the road from me in Stanhope Grove, bought a Bond mini-car, which we nicknamed 'Hairylegs'.

In due course I married a childhood friend, Rodney Fabb. He and his brother Alan were Beckenham and

would give me a lift home in her car. When Eden Park School was moved in 1941 from a house in Upper Elmers End Road to Holly Lodge, I was transferred there. Here I spent the war years under the strict discipline of Mrs Mallick.

When there was an air raid we used to go across the road into the public brick-built air-raid shelter where we would sing to drown out the noise of the bombs. The V2 that fell by St John's Church in Eden Park Avenue threw us all across the classroom so that we ended up on the far wall. At home there was no gas, water or electricity so my father took us to lunch in Verney's restaurant in the High Street. On the way home we passed the spot where the rocket had fallen and butchers were carving up the cows killed in the raid!

On VE Day in 1945, my friend Felicity Edden and I joined many others in the Beckenham Rec. for an afternoon of entertainment and celebration. Felicity was the daughter of Dr and Mrs Edden, who lived at the corner of Eden Park Avenue and Cherry Tree Walk. She married Alan Boyden, the grandson of Mrs Boyden, who was our maths teacher at Eden Park School.

In 1946 I started at the Beckenham County Grammar School for Girls in Lennard Road, travelling by train from Elmers End Station with my cousins from Birchwood Avenue. My sixth year was spent at the Bromley Tech, now Bullers Wood, where I learned shorthand and typing.

While growing up, I spent a lot of time in the

Jane Fabb by the Upper Elmers End Road shops in the 1980s. (JF)

Above: *Bowls at Stanhope Grove, 1938.* (FB)

Right: *Women bowling at Stanhope before the war. At the time of writing they play bowls as part of the combined Beckenham and Stanhope Club at Croydon Road Recreation-Ground.* (FB)

Stanhope Grove Bowling Club with two mayors: Dr Edden and Councillor Atkins are fourth and fifth from the left in the middle row. (JF)

Souvenir programme (left) and members of the All-Stars celebrity team which played at Stanhope Grove in 1963: Bernie Winters (right), Pete Murray (below right) and Jess Conrad with fans (below left). (JF)

Penge Grammar School boys. There were rugger matches in the Balmoral Avenue ground, although I must say I preferred the rugger dances. Beckenham FC played at Stanhope Grove and one notable occasion was in 1963 when they played an All-Star celebrity side, including Bernie Winters and Pete Murray among others. The singer Jess Conrad's car was parked outside our house and young fans invaded our front gardens.

Centuries-old names were used for the flats in Upper Elmers End Road where I live: the name Huntingfield is first heard at the manor of West Wickham in 1278, when Sir Peter de Huntingfield, Sheriff of Kent, was lord of the manor.

Another of the houses is called Cade, which comes from an Eden Park schoolmaster of the eighteenth century. His pupils erected a gravestone to his memory in St George's churchyard. The engravings of pencils, a globe, compasses and other scholarly articles readily identify this, although the inscription is no longer legible.

The Lambert Family

Another good friend of Jane's was Janet Lambert, who was born in 1938 at No. 6 Cherry Tree Walk but moved to No. 71 Aviemore Way. She recalls:

None of my father's jobs was well paid so that buying a house was not an option. My sister Margaret Ann was born in 1935 in a rented flat in Langley Road but we stayed for 14 years at Aviemore Way.

In 1946, when new beds were unveiled at Beckenham Hospital, Janet was an in-patient suffering from TB. She spent six months there, her parents able to visit on Wednesdays and at weekends with Margaret, but in 1947 she was transferred to Holt in Norfolk where, because of tight family finances and her father's limit of two weeks' holiday, the family were only able to visit once in a whole year. Happily it was all worth it. Janet was given a clean bill of health and passed the 11-plus, then attended Beckenham Grammar School with Margaret.

In 1954 the Lamberts moved to accommodation over Herbert's Dairy in Thesiger Road. Janet's father, Edwin (Sonny), who had started there as a young milk roundsman, now returned as manager. In between he worked in a series of provision shops, including Tommy Lines in Upper Elmers End Road.

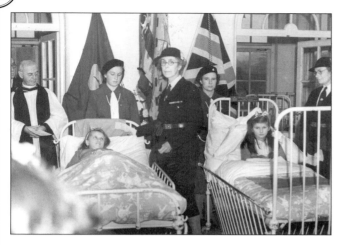

Right: *A 1930s advertisement for W.J. Herbert.*

Left: *New beds for Beckenham Cottage Hospital, 1946. Janet Lambert is the child on the right.* (JL)

VE Day street party in Aviemore Way. (JL)

VE Day fancy dress in Aviemore Way. Janet is the central shepherdess with the crook and Valerie Barrett is on her right. The shepherdess on her left with the bouquet is actually a boy, Tony Booth! Behind Peter Barrows (in the top hat) is Sheila Hewson as a doll in a box. (JL)

The Elmer Swifts, 1926/7 (top), with Sonny Lambert in the centre as captain.
Sonny Lambert also played in the Herbert Dairy football team (above). (JL)

In his twenties he had suffered from pneumonia and pleurisy and was judged medically unfit for the forces in the Second World War but played an active part in the Home Guard – he arrived home one night to find an incendiary bomb in the roof!

As a child at Marian Vian he was one of the favourite pupils of Miss Alice Maud Hayes, who kept up a correspondence with him until his death at Beare Green, Surrey, in 1987. Alice then continued to write to Janet and Margaret until she died in 1995, aged 104. Sonny Lambert played football locally for the Elmer Swifts and for Herbert Dairy, where he worked. At one time Cardiff City offered him a trial but his mother objected! After retiring to Bexhill in

1962, Sonny kept up his sporting interests at Sidley cricket and football clubs and was vice-president of the cricket club. Janet owes her cricketing skills largely to her father's encouragement.

Memories of Eric Smith (aka Smuts!)

Eric Smith lived at 360 Upper Elmers End Road from 1936–57. He was the youngest of three children. He went to Marian Vian School with his friends, Jim Hurley from No. 121 Merlin Grove and his wife-to-be Jeanne Levett from Cherry Tree Walk. As a youngster he worked for grocers Will and Nellie Whittingham,

Right: *'Unto Him Through and Through'* – the Campaigners' badge. (ES)

Left: *The badge of Balgowan School in the 1930s.* (ES)

The Rayner brothers outside their hardware shop in 1936. (RW)

their younger son Keith being his best friend. He also remembers Rayners the ironmongers, Finlays the tobacconist and Bill Smith at the stationmaster's house. He belonged to the Junos and Campaigners at St John's and was also confirmed there. The friends once tunnelled among a heap of bottles dumped by the brewers Whitbread at Langley, Eric unfortunately cutting the tendons in his hand on a broken bottle!

When building their dug-out air-raid shelter during the war the Smiths wrote 'Dug-inn' in the rendering of the inside walls – they shared the shelter with the O'Shea family next door at No. 362. Eric and the other boys collected shrapnel – sometimes too hot to handle – from dogfights and visited the ack-ack anti-aircraft guns on the Elgood playing-field, being scared out of their wits by the noise the guns made moving along the railway. Family games of cards, dominoes, draughts, chess and halma (a form of draughts) kept them busy in the shelters and the wireless was popular, with 'Dick Barton' (Snowy lived in Hampden Avenue), 'Children's Hour', 'The Ovalteenies', 'ITMA', 'The Billy Cotton Band Show', the music of Geraldo and Henry Hall, 'The Goon Show' and 'Friday Night is Music Night'. To supplement their rations the Smiths kept chickens and reared rabbits from three given to

the children for Christmas (Eric will never forget the smell of potato peelings being boiled up to mix with bran for the chickens!) and, of course, they had an allotment, behind the council-houses in Adams Road. When the doodlebugs started Eric was evacuated to Barnsley for eight months. He returned in time to experience the V2s and was sent home from school when one fell behind St John's. Eric's final wartime memory is of the British Restaurant at Elmers End near the cinema. His friend Jim Hurley escaped the bombs twice, first when the land-mine fell on Nos 93–103 Merlin Grove and then in 1944, when a doodlebug fell on the same site at about 8a.m. Fortunately the Italian POWs had just moved out!

Eric was disappointed not to go from Marian Vian to the Boys' Grammar School – his father could not manage the £4.4s. fee for non-scholarship pupils – and has some painful memories of the staff at Balgowan. The maths teacher, Mr Armitage, was a dapper gentleman who sat them all separately and made it understood that they were to call him 'sir'. He invited them to look at the cherry tree outside and to admire the cherries. 'All the boys I don't like get buried beneath that tree, which is why it has so much fruit.' Mr Armitage specialised in face slapping from

The Eden Beck football team. Left to right, back row: George Baxter, *Norman Snell, Cyril Cooke, D. Cockerhill, Alan York, Stan Bellinger, Pete Holder, Jeff Purkiss, Steve Ryder, Bill Ames;* front row: *Denis Powell, Eddie Lewis, Cyril Bedford, Ernie Allen, Basil Trueman.* (JB)

The Eden Beck cricket XI, 1946. Left to right, back row: *B. Townsend (umpire), L. Squelch, D. Wiseman, G. Harding, S. Wilkinson, B. Hart, S. Miles;* middle row: *B. Trueman, J. Plackford, ?, ?, ? Longhurst;* front row: *Basil Grove.* (JHU)

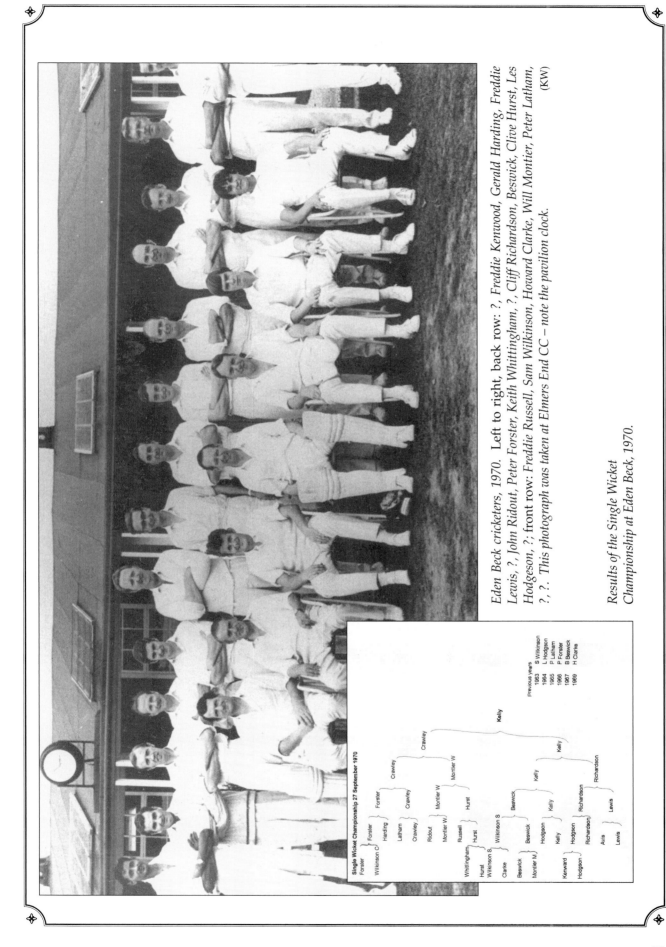

Eden Beck cricketers, 1970. Left to right, back row: ?, Freddie Kenwood, Gerald Harding, Freddie Lewis, ?, John Ridout, Peter Forster, Keith Whittingham, ?, Cliff Richardson, Beswick, Clive Hurst, Les Hodgeson, ?; front row: Freddie Russell, Sam Wilkinson, Howard Clarke, Will Montier, Peter Latham, ?, ?. This photograph was taken at Elmers End CC – note the pavilion clock. (KW)

Results of the Single Wicket Championship at Eden Beck, 1970.

Single Wicket Championship 27 September 1970

Forster
Wilkinson C
Harding
Forster
Latham
Crawley
Crawley
Ridout
Montier W
Montier W
Russell
Hurst
Whittingham
Hurst
Wilkinson S
Clarke
Beswick
Beswick
Montier M
Hodgson
Kenward
Kelly
Hodgson
Richardson
Avis
Lewis

Forster
Crawley
Montier W
Hurst
Wilkinson S
Beswick
Hodgson
Kelly
Hodgson
Richardson
Lewis

Crawley
Montier W
Beswick
Kelly
Richardson

Crawley
Kelly

Kelly

Previous years

1963	S Wilkinson
1964	L Hodgson
1965	P Latham
1966	P Forster
1967	B Beswick
1969	H Clarke

73

A newly built house in Upper Elmers End Road, 1928. (RW)

the back to the front of the classroom for answering back or failing to concentrate. Eric once had six of the best from the headmaster, Mr Goodspeed, and his name in the black book for chewing in class. He thought longingly of Mr Bailey at Marian Vian, who would let them eat some of their meagre sweet ration in class provided each child gave him two pastilles for his wife, Kit Bailey. Even he, though, kept a large rubber in his waistcoat pocket to hurl with deadly aim at any boy who was not paying attention!

Eric worked in the City as a shipping and forwarding agent, travelling from Eden Park Station on the same train as Bob Monkhouse when Bob was living at 17 Crossways Road. Eric remembers Bob as always scribbling on a writing pad with remarks like, 'Can't use that one, too rude'. Bob was not very complimentary either about his brother, John, calling him 'shorthouse'!

Eric played cricket at Eden Beck CC when the London Rifle Brigade owned the ground and would also take his turn working behind the bar. Cyril Bedford was captain of the football team and his wife Jean Bedford found the team photo. The Bedfords lived at No. 318 Upper Elmers End Road and Jean remembers John Monkhouse, Bob's brother, playing in the cricket team in about 1955 when living with his wife Kathleen at 350 Upper Elmers End Road.

Eric's sister, Joy, went to Marian Vian. Other friends were the Hardings – Sheila, John and Jerry – from Eden Park Avenue and the Coles. Doug Cole opened the Criterion restaurant near the Co-op and Arthur Cole was a photographer at ice hockey and tennis events.

Eric and Jeanne Smith (née Levett) announced their engagement on 9 March 1955 during a dance at the Eden Park Hotel and were married at Christchurch on 7 September 1957 by the curate from St John's, the Revd David Bubbers. Joy Smith met her husband, John Cecil Chapman, at an Eden Park Hotel dance and they were married at St John's on 17 June 1950. An invoice for eight copies of her wedding photos showed the price of £1.16s. Although living in Hereford by the time their son, Simon John, was born, they returned to St John's for his baptism on 11 March 1956. Eric's elder brother, Ken, was also married at St John's on 15 August 1953 to a South Norwood girl, Barbara Robinson.

Both Eric and Joy are able to recall the names of their friends. They are listed here; perhaps you remember them too: John Ames, John Lord, Florrie and George Down, Michael and Jerry O'Shea, the two brothers Bishop, Dennis and Margaret Cowley, Peter Latham, Rupert Groves (injured at Arnhem), Pauline and Georgina Larkman, Dennis Gardener, Eric Spooner, Tony Woods, Sheila Reed, Martin Garnett, Pip Manser, Iris Stockton, June and Julia McPherson, Dot Smith, Eric Stoneham, Jean Vardil, Kenneth Cox, Evelyn and Brian Luff, Pamela and Hazel Green, Brenda Curry, Glenis Creighton, Diana Clements (née Scott), Bill Aylett, Jackie Lane, John Stone, Gloria Sunderland, Marie and Cliff Redman, Ken and Margaret Symes, Norman and Leslie Snell, Ken Thomas, Joan Freeman, Jean Sheffield, Colin Watts, Doris Belbin, Pat and Winnie Williams, June Ridout, Yvonne Dunnett, Ken Sykes, Irene Bedell, Ken Thomas, Don Shorter, Sheila Ingram, Betty Jones, Gwen Evans, Sheila Chamberlain, Cynthia Emberry, Sheila Purchase, Kath Lewis, Barbara and Pauline Levett (Jeanne's sisters), twins Joyce and Pauline Yallop.

Pam Wardell

Pam Wardell can add memories from a slightly later date. Crossways Road to her was where you could sled at high speed in the ice and snow of the late 1940s and '50s or catch a glimpse of Bob Monkhouse waiting for the bus. Marian Vian was where Mrs Bailey taught needlework in the 'advanced' class and Harvington was where you could play in an old house and get into trouble for getting your shoes wet in the stream. When the steam train went through Eden Park Station early in the morning there was always a friendly hoot from the driver. A falling horse-chestnut tree crushed one of the prefabs next to St John's, where the Warners lived, but there were no casualties. Carole Warner became a well known ice skater and appeared on TV! Other families in the prefabs were the Cosams and the Camerons.

After racking her brains about Eden Park shops, Pam came up with some remarkable memories. She would go in to Whittingham's the grocer's for broken

Triple Green Shield stamps were available at the Eden Park Service Station.

KEEP UP
the value of
your car

with the

ESSO

A B C

LUBRICATION SERVICE

The simple-as-ABC way to regular lubrication.
The 'A' service operates every 1,000 miles, the 'B' every 2,000,
and 'C' every 5,000. Gives your car the right attention at
the right time. Ask us for details.

EDEN PARK SERVICE STATION

(A. S. MATHIESON)

LINKS WAY, BECKENHAM, KENT.

ESSO DEALER

The marriage of Pam Holland and Bob Wardell at St John's. The bridesmaid is Pam's sister Christine. (PW)

biscuits and sugar sold in blue bags bought by weight over the counter. She remembers Mr Whittingham as a tall, thin, kindly man (see page 96). Across the road was the sweet shop, Eden Court, run by two sisters, one large and one small. At the Eden Park Hotel, beer by the barrel was delivered by large dray horses that were kept waiting for ages after the beer was unloaded! Then came the off-licence, the paper shop, the greengrocer's, the secondhand shop, the electrical shop, the chemist's and the fish-and-chip shop. Somewhere in there was an antique shop and May's, the wool shop. There was also a haberdasher's called Catherine Parkins, run by the mother of Pam's friend, Ross. In those days the antique shop displayed its wares outside and Pam still has some plates bought there by her mother. There were more shops past the sweet shop: a café, a bakery that specialised in miniature Hovis loaves, another greengrocer's, an oil shop and Sage's the cobbler's. One of these shops was taken over by a hairdresser, Georgina's, that was very popular. Delivery of milk was in quart bottles, bread came by horse and cart and cockles and winkles were sold round the houses.

Pam's grandfather was George Henry Holland, who married Rose Annie Taylor – their son, Frederick Charles, born in 1911, being Pam's father. George and Rose lived at No. 26 Chancery Lane and then moved around the corner to 5 Limes Road, now in a conservation area. All their children were baptised at St Barnabas' Church, three sons before the First World War and two daughters and three more sons

after the war. Pam's father, Frederick, settled in Eden Park Avenue, where Pam spent the first 20 years of her life. There was no connection between Pam's family and the other Hollands in this book, as her family came to Beckenham from Derbyshire.

Bob Pack of Eden Park

Do you remember the Bobby Pack Trio jazz band, with Bob the drummer, Dave Crickenden on sax and Micky Harman? It started with a talent contest, won by Bob on drums, at Saturday morning pictures at the Elmers End Odeon. He played at the Studio with one of Mayor Curtis' sons and the trio regularly played in the bandstand at Croydon Road Recreation-Ground, known to everyone as Croydon Rec.

Until 1962, Bob lived with his parents, four brothers and three sisters in one of the two flats over the United Dairies shop at the corner of Eden Park Avenue and Upper Elmers End Road. Brother Billie was in the Campaigners at St John's and brother Roy, at the time of writing, still lives in Beckenham in Merlin Grove. Bob's father was in the ARP during the war and Bob's worst memory is of hearing his baby brother crying in the garden and finding that a piece of hot shrapnel had passed through the pram between the baby's legs, scorching them. Bob was evacuated for two years with his brother Jimmy and sister Marjorie to Huddersfield, but when an unexpected visit by his father found them running around barefoot they returned to Beckenham.

Bob's mother worked for Bob and Elizabeth Monkhouse in Crossways Road for a time between

Above: *Jimmy Pack (in his slippers!) shows off his motorbike.* (BP)

Left: *Bob Pack outside United Dairies, 1955.* (BP)

Below: *Admiring a car in the High Street in the days when you could park anywhere. Left to right, standing: Olly Oldfield, Dave Crittenden, Bob Pack and Ken Kitchener.* (BP)

1952 and 1955 and made baby Gary a doll. When she worked as a helper at Beckenham Hospital the family had to share out the chores and Bob Pack would push the pram to Kennedy's in the High Street to join the queue for pies and then collect coal from the greengrocer at the old fire station. An unexploded oil bomb once dropped onto the steps at the Regal, leaving an oil stain there for months. A sad memory was of a boy who was killed when he kicked an Army mortar bomb in a field at West Wickham.

When Bob went from Marian Vian to Hawes Down, his friends were Paul Bartholomew, from the Eden Park Nurseries, and John Crittenden, from West Wickham. John lost an eye when a thorn pierced it while he was collecting wood in the woodland. Bob's best friend was Peter Latham, from Holmhurst. They would all roller-skate to school to save the bus fare but would then spend the money on a slice of bread and jam at the café where the West Wickham baths are in 2004. Dinner money sometimes went the same way and they would often use 6d. of the 2s.1d. to buy one French loaf filled with chips between two of them. Underweight pupils at the school would be sent to the clinic next door to be given cod-liver oil and malt.

While Bob was doing National Service in Korea in the 1950s (after the Korean War), Peter Latham sent him a 10s. note in every letter. Peter married Betty Curtis and their daughter Angela used to run the bistro opposite the café where the boys bought their bread and jam. In 2003 the family had a grand reunion at the Eden Park Hotel and Bob noticed the telephone box outside Holmhurst, still in the same place. At the time of writing he is trying to trace Mike Harman, last seen at the rails of a ship at Aden when Bob was en route for Korea.

Derek Coles: Bevin Boy

Beckenham boy Derek Coles of Lloyds Way, educated at Marian Vian and the Beckenham Grammar School, was called up in March 1944 to be a miner in the Durham mines. He recalls:

The selection of men for mining was allegedly worked out on the basis of the last number on your identity card, i.e. 1–10. My number was 5! When I boarded the train at King's Cross to go to Durham via Newcastle General there were blokes on the train with every number from 0 to 9. No surprise really! After four weeks' 'training' in a place called Annfield Plain – can it possibly still exist? – and lodgings in Consett, I was deemed sufficiently experienced to work underground. This comprised getting empty half-ton

The corner shop opposite United Dairies at the end of Eden Park Avenue – one of the many photos Bob took from his top-floor flat. (BP)

Pharmacist Stanley Hamer (left) *and* (above) *in his dispensary before it was extended.* (OH)

BECKENHAM
AUXILIARY FIRE SERVICE
1938-1945

FIRST ANNUAL

Reunion Dinner

AT

The Public Hall, Beckenham

FRIDAY, 18th APRIL, 1947.

Chairman · · · · · *R. F. Leeks, M.B.E.*

Committee
Messrs. Badger, Brett, Burnham, Burt, Curtifield,
Drew, Houltham, Mackenzie, Marshall, Nash,
Preston and Weeks.

Joint Hon. Secretaries:
Messrs. Evans and Pamment

Joint Hon. Treasurer:
Messrs. Mogge and Lavington

The unveiling in December 1941 in Beckenham Cemetery and Crematorium of the monument to the auxiliary firemen killed in April 1941 at Old Palace School, Poplar. Mayor William Joseph Sampson is here addressing the mourners. (SK)

Notice of the 1947 reunion dinner of the auxiliary fire service. (OH)

Left: *Queen of the Fair at the West Wickham Flitch, 1938. The Mayoress is crowning Pamela Peacock, while Mayor Dr Edden looks on. The attendants include Pamela North, Sybil Freemantle, Vaughan Hyde, Geoffrey Walford, Alexander Ward and Eric Harding.* (FB)

Below: *Olive Hamer, President of the Inner Wheel.* (OH)

trucks called tubs to a landing from where they were moved further in to the coal face by men called putters, using a donkey or gallower as motive power. The men we worked with made us welcome, although at first I couldn't make out what they were saying. I was fortunate to be living at a bungalow with a nice old lady called Mrs Richardson, who cried when I left to go home. This hasn't happened very often since! As if to prove nothing changes, I understand that there was a shortage of miners during the First World War due to call-up; the same thing happening again in the Second World War.

When he returned to Upper Elmers End Derek started as a builder with Eason & Sutton, finding that it suited him very well. He knew builder Ted Barrs and worked for William Gorham, both men responsible for building local houses. Interestingly, half of the Lloyds Way houses were built by Miles & Gorham and a fence put across the the road while Wates of Norbury completed the rest.

Derek remembers all the shops at the Upper Elmers End Parade from the late 1940s into the 1950s (confirmed by Jane Fabb). They are listed here; see how many are familiar to you.

Starting on the side opposite the Rising Sun: Morgan's the cleaner's (John Hood) next to Randall Slade's, a bakery selling delicious food. Then Eley the greengrocer, camera shop Century Photos (run by Stan Quilter), the Post Office and sweet shop (Bill Smith) and the fish shop (Ben and Alice Pearce, who lived in the flat above). There was J. Bowron (the hairdresser) and then the Cole family's café (formerly a clock and watch repair shop) where you could buy Eldorado ice-cream. Pop Cole played the double bass at the Brixton Empire, where Derek would take the most expensive seats at 2s. a time. Doug Cole

eventually went abroad as a guide in Madeira and his brother Arthur worked for *Tennis* magazine, taking photographs at Wimbledon (Doug and Arthur were friends with Eric Smith).

Continuing along, there was the Co-op and then the builder's where Derek worked. Millicent Hadland's dress shop came next – her daughter ran the Baron dance school. Milly had a bad accident when she was knocked down while running across the road to get a paper. The shoe repair shop of Bill Lilleystone and his wife was followed by Rutter's the ironmonger (later Lennox), the off licence and finally the greengrocer – formerly Greenwoods, this was Eley's second shop.

There were fewer shops on the other side because the Rising Sun took up much of the road. Electrician Cyril Taylor was on the corner next to Bill Gent's newsagent's. Stanley and Olive Hamer's chemist shop was next to Tommy Lines the grocer, then Mr and Mrs Green the haberdasher's (straight out of 'Are You Being Served?') and later Sainsbury's. Whitby butcher's shop was beside the tavern. The manager Mr Tarbard lived at the Rising Sun with his wife Marjorie and their two sons and daughter.

On the other side, just under the railway bridge was a sweet shop run by two ladies called Mills – a favourite place to spend the sweet ration!

So there you are dear reader. Are these your memories too?

Olive Hamer's Story

Olive Beadle was one of the first girls to attend the Beckenham County School under Miss Fox, having started there in 1922, three years after the school opened in 1919.

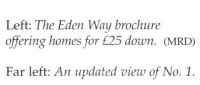

Left: *The Eden Way brochure offering homes for £25 down.* (MRD)

Far left: *An updated view of No. 1.*

Below: *An early view down Eden Way from No. 50. Building started at No. 1, at the far end of the row on the right, the house of builder Edward Barr.*

Olive's brother, Ernest Beadle, joined the West Wickham AFS in the Second World War and was one of 21 local firemen killed on the night of 19/20 April 1941 when 34 firefighters died as a result of a direct hit on Old Palace School in Poplar while they were mustering for their turn-out orders. For Olive it was a double tragedy, her husband Norman Mountjoy being killed by the same bomb. Of the 21 casualties, 11 were from West Wickham, five from Elmers End and five from Stanhope Grove AFS. The entire route from the parish church to the Beckenham Cemetery was closed for the procession honouring the firefighters, 19 of whom were buried in a mass grave at the cemetery. The other two men, Ernest and Norman, were buried in the churchyard of St John the Baptist, West Wickham, their grave next to that of five men from the Coney Hall AFS, who had died on their way to East End fires a month earlier when their fire appliance was destroyed by an explosion.

At the time of writing Olive lives in Altyre Way, near where her second husband, Stanley Hamer, ran his pharmacy at No. 172 Upper Elmers End Road. Olive was a gifted needlewoman and a keen supporter of St James' Embroidery Guild. She made the tapestry kneeler used for marriages and the communion-rail kneeler in the Lady Chapel, along with many other items.

Barry Jackson Remembers the Fair and Flitch

Every year from the early 1930s the Fair and Flitch,

This house in Lodge Gardens has many original features, including the name 'Joyrene', after the daughters of the original owners.

an event to find the married couple who had managed to last a year and a day without a cross word, was held in Blake's Recreation-Ground with the prize of a side of bacon (the flitch). It was a village enterprise run by the local community – churches, shops, scouts, etc. The occasion was preceded by a special shopping week in West Wickham with various competitions in the shops. Children were invited to find objects that did not belong, such as cotton reels in the butcher's shop window. When the great day arrived the ground was packed with sideshows such as coconut shies and roll-a-penny. In the last year before the war the flitch was shared between the Marchants and the Alexanders, the Court of Married Happiness unable to decide

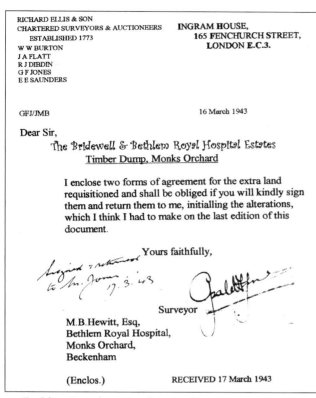

RICHARD ELLIS & SON
CHARTERED SURVEYORS & AUCTIONEERS
ESTABLISHED 1773
W W BURTON
J A FLATT
R J DIBDIN
G F JONES
E E SAUNDERS

INGRAM HOUSE,
165 FENCHURCH STREET,
LONDON E.C.3.

GFJ/JMB   16 March 1943

Dear Sir,

The Bridewell & Bethlem Royal Hospital Estates
Timber Dump, Monks Orchard

I enclose two forms of agreement for the extra land requisitioned and shall be obliged if you will kindly sign them and return them to me, initialling the alterations, which I think I had to make on the last edition of this document.

Yours faithfully,

Surveyor

M.B.Hewitt, Esq,
Bethlem Royal Hospital,
Monks Orchard,
Beckenham

(Enclos.)   RECEIVED 17 March 1943

Bethlem Royal Hospital grounds were requisitioned for a timber dump in the Second World War. (BE)

between them. The day ended with fireworks and, after the war, with square dancing, made popular by Princess Elizabeth and Prince Philip on their Canadian tour.

Living at the top end of Eden Way, Barry Jackson joined the West Wickham Yew Tree Youth Club who played their football and cricket at Mac Andrews (a playing-field at West Wickham named after a local man) and in the 1950/51 football season were in Division Two. This remained a youth club because conscription caused a cut-off point.

After a short time at St David's College, where his teachers were Miss Jupp, Mrs Cousens and Mrs Burgess, he moved on to Eden Park School with Mrs Mallick. His friends there included Keith Adams, Peter Ball, Colin Curtis, David Elgar, John James, Ralph Lampard, Richard Lane, Ian Law, Albert Parr, Christine Stenning, Gill Taylor and Hilary Whybrow, most of whom can be seen in the photograph on page 65. Do any of them seem familiar?

Barry went on to the Beckenham and Penge Grammar School for Boys, where he revelled in the sports. He remembers a visit by Sidney Wooderson, the Blackheath Harrier. Later the school's idol was old boy Derek Underwood, the Kent bowler who made his debut for Kent in 1962 aged 17.

Derek Eldridge of Eden Way

Wilfred and Beatrice Eldridge bought their house at No. 26 Eden Way as new – Derek found the original

Edward Barr sales brochure amongst his parents' papers. A deposit of £25 reserved a house with a completion payment of £75 and weekly payments of £1.13s. for 16 years. Those who took up this option would not have paid for their house until the start of the Second World War! They shut up the house and evacuated to hopefully safer parts – like the Eldridges, who moved for a time to Wales. The house has retained most of its original features, including the stained glass and overmantels, and has stayed in the same family since it was built. In the early days Upper Elmers End Road was not as wide, the houses then having longer front gardens.

At one side of No. 26 is the access road to the alley where most of the houses have garages. Derek remembers the articulated lorries that managed to negotiate the narrow way, taking timber from the Pool of London to the timber dump in Bethlem grounds – a safety measure of the war.

Derek also had a copy of a national newspaper dated 16 July 1944, saved by his mother, in which Beckenham was dubbed part of 'doodlebug alley'. On the front page was a picture of air-raid warden W.C. Field looking for V1s and, inside, pictures of the people of Beckenham going about their business.

The Williamsons moved into No. 24 Eden Way, on the far side of the road accessing the alley which ran along the back. Few of the houses had garages as few people had cars – Brian's father being one of the few. Their favourite car was a Wolseley with leather seats and an illuminated badge on the front. Before that they had a Morris Cowley and a Morris Minor with the registration AKP 1. For children, the alley was also a way into the Bethlem parkland – a playground for them and generations to follow.

Brian married into the Beckenham family which owned the garage on the memorial roundabout – still there trading under the name Deen, a contraction of the Southern Irish name Dineen.

To complete a trio in Eden Way, Shirley Morris (wife of footballer Frank Morris, see Chapter 9) lived at No. 21 from 1970–2002 and believes the alleyway to be the original access road to Monks Orchard mansion from the lodge in Upper Elmers End Road.

A Family from Eden Park

Sheila Bates grew up in Eden Way, where her parents signed the contract for No. 172 on the day the rocket fell on Harvington! Like Pam Wardell (see page 74), she remembers the thriving shops at Eden Park. Sheila attended Beckenham County School and took part in activities such as the Youth Fellowship at St John's in Eden Park Avenue, where she met her husband, Derrick Meakins. She is another of our contributors who remembers the dances on Wednesdays and Saturdays at the Eden Park Hotel. Sheila always thinks of those days if she hears 'Blue Moon' – the favourite song of the lady vocalist married to one of the band.

*Andy Meakins with his wife Ruth and
their three children.* (SM)

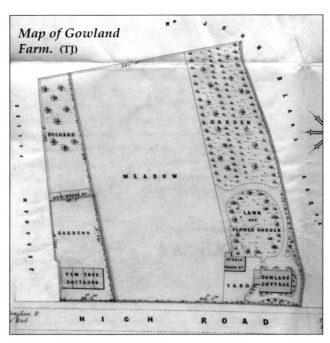

*Map of Gowland
Farm.* (TJ)

An important member of St John's Church was Miss Petley of Manor Way, who ran the Sunday school and events such as the popular annual flower show. Sheila's third child was born handicapped and could not go to Sunday school, so Miss Petley would invite her to tea in her garden instead.

Sheila is still a keen church member even though life has not been easy for her. Three of her four children, Andrew, Jane, Mary and Peter, born between 1953 and 1960, are no longer with us. Mary died as a six-year-old, Peter in a motorcycle accident when he was 22 and Andrew as the result of a plane hijacking in 1996.

Andrew (Andy) was confirmed at St John's and grew up a committed Christian. After working extremely hard at Hawes Down he studied at City University in London and became a civil engineer. He worked for two years as a missionary in Ethiopia, capping springs, drilling and bringing water to villages previously without. After returning to England for further training in this field, he was sent to Asmara in Ethiopia to help with a big irrigation system. He joined the TEAR fund as a missionary concerned with water development and was appointed co-ordinator in Addis Ababa. In this capacity he flew to Nairobi on 23 November 1996 when his plane was hijacked; he was one of the 123 killed when the Boeing 67 ditched in the Indian Ocean. Andy's Ethiopian wife, Ruth, was left with three children, Caleb (seven), Lydia (five) and one-year-old Abigail. Ruth's story has recently appeared in *Salt of the Earth* by Walter Dirks, in which she describes their life together and the circumstances of the tragedy, survivors of which reported that Andy was comforting passengers right to the end.

At the time of writing Jane and Ruth live next door to one another in St David's Close where Jane's children, Catherine and Jonathan, are near not only their cousins but also their grandmother, Sheila, who lives in South Eden Park Road. As a memorial to Andy there is a plaque on the north wall of St John's Church, where Sheila, a qualified flower arranger, enjoys taking part in the flower rota.

Rob Copeland's Nephew, Tony Johns

Anthony (Tony) Copeland Johns is the son of Olive, who is in turn the sister of Beckenham historian Rob Copeland. Tony's uncle lived at No. 114 Bromley Road, now a residential home. Both Tony and Bob Monkhouse attended St George's School in Albemarle Road (formerly St George's Preparatory School, St George's Road, started by the Egertons as early as 1914), run by Miss Woodham. They would go home together, often playing at No. 114 before Bob moved to No. 168 Bromley Road and Tony to No. 9 Village Way. Bob was only about five years old but even then was always wisecracking – his teachers had to turn away to hide their amusement. Many remember Bob at Elm Road Baptist Church where, about age 15, he would take over the youth club and try out his jokes.

Tony's home in Village Way was next to the first site of the Roman Catholic church before St Edmund's was erected on the opposite side and No. 9 demolished. His father knew the superintendent of Beckenham baths, who would let a group of about 12 use the pool when the baths were closed. The group called themselves the Arctic Swimming Club as, whatever the weather, they would run round the Technical School running track in their trunks after their swim.

Another of Tony's 1930s memories is of buying eggs from Mrs Petley's farm in South Eden Park Road, and the cobbles of the farmyard.

The family moved to Forest Ridge as the roads were built off Village Way and had a pet bull terrier called Grip. Tony Johns had a pal across the road, Tony Leeks, who had a sister, Mavis, and a brother Roger. Mavis came over to call her brother Tony to dinner one day, slamming the gate as she shouted several times. The dog was incensed and charged at

Eden Lodge. (RB)

the gate, leaping a clear five feet to bite Mavis on the arm! Pat Manning knows Mavis survived because they were in the same class at the Beckenham County School for seven years!

When Tony married Jean Hills (another Beckenham County School girl) in 1952 they moved into one of the pair of cottages that made up Gowland Cottage, which belonged to his uncle and was originally Gowland Farm, stretching from Croydon Road to Clockhouse. Eventually Rob gave Tony his cottage, a survey when the pair were sold in 1982 indicating

that they were sound. As they were being renovated, however, they had to be propped up and eventually demolished, and are now remembered only in the name of the road. Tony has three deeds dating between 1861 and 1871 relating to transfers of the property from William Fuller to Richard Glass, on to Sir George Gibson and then to Cornelius Lea Wilson the 'Squire of Village Place of Beckenham'. Each deed has a map of the land opposite the Eden Park estate between the 'High Road' and where the railway runs today. In the 1841 census we see Fuller's Place on farmland owned by Abraham Fuller. Robert Borrowman, in his book *Beckenham Past and Present* (1910), describes the five cottages as picturesque but in 1848 nearby Fuller's Row (approximately where Azelia Hall is at the time of writing), with its piggeries, was deemed insanitary by the Poor Law Board.

The Wheller family outside the George Inn.
Left to right: William, Jas Geo, his wife Martha,
Nell, Jas J., Alfred. (RB)

The cottages behind the George Inn after the 1878 flood.
These people were flooded out. (RB)

*Looking down Beckenham High Street
past the George Inn.* (RB)

*Above: Jas. Geo. Wheller
and regulars outside the
George Inn showing off
the old drinking pot
which bore the stamp
of William III.*

*Left: Brook Place from
Thornton's Corner in
1909.* (RB)

**The Wheller family
outside the George Inn.
Left to right: Arthur,
Nell, Alfred, Charles,
Alfred junr, Florence
and Jim.** (RB)

A mounted policeman (left) *outside Farnborough police station (the comb on the helmet pinpoints the 1850s date) and Ray Burden on Fred* (right) *in the same spot outside what was by then Hamptons Estate Office, 1990s.* (RB)

Tony has an interesting story about the ancient lych-gate at St George's Church. His uncle Rob tells of it being replaced and of T.W. Thornton using it to make a memorial to his two sons, killed in the First World War. A hexagonal coffee table was made from the timbers with yew wood for the beading. The coffee table was passed to Valerie, Thornton's granddaughter, who married Ric Sheldon. Valerie and Tony are second cousins through the marriages of the Freeman sisters, one to Tom Copeland and the other to T.W. Thornton!

Ray Burden's Beckenham Ancestors

Ray lives with his daughter Caroline in Eden Park Avenue and walks his Jack Russell on the Harvington estate. On many occasions he would meet Miss Vera Cook of No. 104 Manor Way, a house that her father had had built. Vera was an actress, mainly in rep, and before the war had toured with Robert Newton (famous for his role as Long John Silver in the Disney film *Treasure Island*). Vera knew the Campbell family who lived in Eden Lodge and supplied Ray with the photograph on page 83 – just one of his large collection. He is the great-great-grandson of the Whellers from the George Inn in the High Street, the earliest reference to which is in 1662 when Richard King paid hearth tax at the 'Sign of Ye George'. Thomas Cronk, parish beadle, was its landlord until his death in 1831, when James George Wheller succeeded him.

James assisted the introduction of gas lighting in Beckenham and was a member of the first sanitary authority. The family grave of the Whellers is on the south side of St George's Church – the gravestone is in two pieces but the names are still legible. The Whellers not only kept the George in the High Street but also owned the cottages behind. These were flooded when the heavy rain of 1878 caused such a

build-up of water in the manor lake that the wall on Church Hill burst open. The cottages were eventually sold to the telephone company. The telephone exchange now stands on the site occupied by Brook Place. Its auction papers had a picture of Brook Place on the front, in a view looking across from near the bottom of Church Hill. A cart and horse conceals James Crease's greengrocer's shop (later Furley & Baker). James George Wheller's granddaughter, Florence Edith Wheller, married Henry James Burden; they were Ray's grandparents.

Ray became a local policeman at Catford in the days when the section included Beckenham and Penge, all as part of Kent reporting to Maidstone. He was part of the mounted force at Westminster from 1967–85 with the remainder of his service spent patrolling our streets and parks on horseback until his retirement in 1996. His horse was Fyddlon, meaning faithful in Welsh, known to Ray as Fred. He became well known in Kelsey Park, Harvington, Spring Park Woods and elsewhere. Although the Met started in 1829, there were mounted policemen in the Bow Street horse patrol from 1805, funded by the Home Secretary from 1813. They wore blue greatcoats and trousers, red waistcoats, a stock round the neck, white leather gloves, Wellington boots with spurs and top hats.

One of Ray's favourite duties was to visit Oak Lodge School with Fred to show him off to each new intake and to describe how they spent their days.

Cliff Watkins Strikes It Lucky

Following demob from National Service in 1961 I resumed as secretary of Alexandra Park FC. After a season or two our first team reached the Premiership Division of the Beckenham Football League and I changed our home ground from the small and often

Local swimmers on their marks

Above: *Mayor William Duncan presents the 200yd breast-stroke championship cup to Olympic swimmer Chris Walkden, September 1955.* (M&AD)

Above: *The Manning boys of Beckenham Swimming Club – David, Peter and Philip, 1966.*

Left: *Beckenham Swimming Club national water polo winners, 1970. Left to right, back row: Bill Williams (trainer), Ray Cook, Mike Rushton, Peter Dixon, Roger Looker; front row: Martin Adderley, Chris Ayling, David Harris, Philip Manning, David Manning.*

Left: *BSC water polo team in 1980, before they split up. Left to right, back row: Philip Manning, Philip Saunders, Jerry Birmingham, Dave Hibbins, David Manning; front row: Graham Downes, Peter Mole, Peter Manning, Colin Kirkwood.*

Right: *David Manning moved on from water polo to become an international squash player.*

waterlogged pitches of Alexandra Rec to the wide, well-drained open space of the superb pitch of Blake Rec.

Our teams assembled at Penge East Station in 1967. While waiting for everyone to turn up, a player was running through the Grand National card. He announced that a Mr C. Watkins owned a 100–1 outsider, Foinaven. Challenged by this news, I had a shilling each-way bet before we left for the match.

It was a fairly easy match and one of our players, on the sidelines through injury, was repeating the commentary on the National from his transistor radio. He told of the amazing race where virtually every horse had fallen and a rank outsider had won the race. I was running the line on the far side of the pitch and could not believe it when the news was relayed from player to player and thence to me that my horse had won.

Friends and family told me off after my Grand National success. Why had I not bet £1 each way! Money was tight then. Veronica and I were trying to pay off the huge mortgage of £2,700 on our first home, No. 54 Eden Road. It was one of the terraces of two-up, two-down former agricultural workers' cottages where a couple of homes were, even then, still lit by gas lamps! We were both working and my contribution to family life was to do the weekly shop on a Friday night at the newly opened Sainsbury's in West Wickham, staying on the train instead of getting off at Elmers End. I would get a No. 194 bus home that conveniently stopped by the William IV pub opposite the end of my road.

One evening I had overspent and, sitting on the bus searching for change, I found to my great embarrassment that I did not have enough for my fare! Bravely, I asked the conductress if I could pay with postage stamps. She looked at me, saw my five Sainsbury's carrier bags and was duly impressed. She told everyone on the bus that as I was doing the shopping she would let me finish the journey without paying!

Howard Smith: Local Football Guru

Born in 1942, my earliest memories are around 1945 when my mum, nan and I returned from Cornwall, having gone there during the war. My parents had moved into Ernest Grove, the family home until 1962, when we moved to another part of Beckenham.

I went to Holly Lodge School in 1947 and remember walking to school in my red uniform and cap with my mum. Mrs Mallick was a stickler for the correct dress and woe betide those of us who didn't behave. She had a mean line in caning but the school was the best in the district. We were miles ahead when we went to senior school, having learned Latin and algebra at the age of ten. I remember going to watch Eden Beck football and cricket teams in the ground at the end of Ernest Close, now the home of Beckenham Town FC. We would climb the fence, sit amongst the allotments which had been dug round the edge of the ground in the 'Dig for Victory' campaign, watch the games and eat fruit from the allotments.

I believe we were the first family to have a car in Ernest Grove, a Ford Popular. DOY 510 was the registration number and my father bought it with the money he saved after giving up smoking.

As we grew up all our waking hours were spent in the recreation-ground in Stanhope Grove. We played football and cricket and the games lasted from dawn 'til dusk and were very competitive. As we grew up we wanted to play for Beckenham Town Football Club but the club felt that we weren't for them. Our saviour was the games warden at the time, Pat Quinn, who spent so much time with us boys. He went on to do similar wonderful things to help youngsters when he moved to Chatham. How we could do with someone like him now. He persuaded us to form a football team called Stanhope Rovers FC and in 1959 we played our first competitive match in the Beckenham League.

The club went from strength to strength and when the original Beckenham Town Football Club folded, ironically due to lack of members, Stanhope Rovers took over the name and now play as Beckenham Town FC in Eden Park Avenue.

Our social evenings were spent at the Rising Sun pub – the publican, Frank Tarbard, had lived in Ernest Grove. I remember when I went to Beckenham and Penge County Grammar School for Boys, Mr Tarbard would take us to school. We would meet in the public bar, which was a good start to the day, and he would drive us to school.

Days in Eden Park were good. There was little crime or vandalism, local shops were vibrant and life was without the hustle and bustle we have today. Whilst progress is vital, those days were good. We were taught good behaviour and good manners and have seen the benefit throughout our lives.

Olive Rippengal

Olive Rippengal is certainly one of the oldest residents of Upper Elmers End Road. Her family moved into the newly built Sunnycroft (No. 373) in September 1927, when the houses faced the open fields of Monks Orchard and before the construction of the Bethlem Royal Hospital. They could walk to Orchard Way to collect windfalls and in Olive's garden are three lilac trees dug up as saplings from the Monks Orchard estate! Also in Olive's garden there is still an air-raid shelter built by her father, Oscar, where the family slept during the Blitz in 1940.

Instead of attending Elm Road Baptist Church Olive went to St John's, where Sunday school was held in the open air. On 8 April 1939 Olive's sister Doreen was married at St John's and went to live in Eden Park Avenue. The Rippengal family were well established in Beckenham and Olive's great-grandfather was on the Parish Council. He ran a greengrocer's in Bromley Road next to Copeland's and another in Albemarle Road which was destroyed by a doodlebug in July 1944.

The Lewisham Train Crash

In these days of mobile phones and immediate news-flashes on TV, it is hard to contemplate the anguish and anxiety experienced on the night of 4 December 1957 by families wholly dependent on the radio for news. During the evening, one of dense fog, news began to filter through of an accident at a bridge near St John's and the magnitude of the crash gradually became apparent. The stationary 6.15p.m. Hayes train from Charing Cross had been hit by the steam train from Ramsgate, the tender of which had risen up and brought part of the bridge down onto the carriages. Felicity Edden's family were convinced that she had perished, especially as the first body brought out from the first carriage was her friend, the wife of Jane Fabb's uncle George, Margaret Webber. Felicity had survived the crash but was assisting one of the wounded while waiting for the emergency services to reach the scene through the dense fog.

Barry Jackson was working in central London and usually caught the 5.18p.m. train. When he reached Charing Cross it presented a chaotic scene, with timetables abandoned because of the fog. Eventually he caught a Hayes train that crawled home. Once there, he began to worry about his father, who also worked in central London but normally caught a later train than Barry. During the most nerve-wracking night of Barry's life, each thought the other had been killed. To the intense relief of the family, Mr Jackson reached home in Eden Park very late in the evening, having walked the last two miles and avoided a close encounter with a bus in the thick fog. They had both been very lucky. Barry had caught the last train before the crash and Mr Jackson had had the barrier closed in his face as he ran to catch the ill-fated Hayes train.

Many others from the area were not so lucky. Of the 90 fatalities, seven were from Eden Park. In addition to Margaret Webber, who left three daughters, there were Rosemary Ashley (age 19) of Hillcrest View, Vernon Henry William Newland of Eden Park Avenue, Richard Arthur Baker of Stonepark Avenue, Charles Edward Rowson of Stanhope Grove, Barbara Mary Hubbard (age 20) of Eden Way (girl-friend of Bob Pack) and Edward Phillips of Abbots Way, who died some days after the crash.

Bob Pack, like Barry Jackson, had caught the previous train. There were 265 notified injured, of whom six came from the Eden Park area. A third train narrowly missed adding to the carnage – the 5.22p.m. from Holborn Viaduct was on the overhead line when its power was cut off by the first accident, which prevented it from starting across the bridge and plunging to the tracks beneath.

Miska, Sasha and Nipper

At the time of writing Miska has just had her 20th birthday. She lives in a paddock at the bottom of the garden of a bungalow in Orchard Way. Every week she enjoys about eight pounds of apples, ten pounds of carrots, new-mown grass and lots of hay. She also likes leaves from the grapevine, for Miska is a pony.

In the early 1980s, Patricia and Ken Baxendale saw a pony advertised for sale at a house off Addiscombe Road. Curious as to how a pony could be kept where the houses were so closely packed, they went to investigate. The pony hardly had room to turn round and a pile of manure occupied most of its space. A youngster was put up on her back, and the kicking and mane-pulling that followed was enough for the Baxendales to make a decision. Miska had a long walk from Addiscombe to Orchard Way where she has lived in comfort ever since!

Miska is not the only animal in the household – there is also a black and tan German shepherd called Sasha for company.

And what about Nipper? This adopted fox appeared on the lawn as a tiny motherless cub of about four weeks. At the time of writing she lives under the shed at the bottom of the garden and has had three litters. In spring 2003 the grown-up offspring from previous years were still coming to the garden to feed on chicken wings while their mother was off caring for her new litter. She does not reappear until the cubs are weaned at eight or nine weeks, having spent the intervening time probably in the grounds of the Bethlem Royal Hospital. Many thanks to the Baxendales for this lovely story.

Miska, the rescued pony. (PB)

CHAPTER 3

Businesses

Eden Park Garden Centre

Ernie Bartholomew was in the Army throughout the Second World War while his family lived in Beckenham. Originally at Queensway, they moved to Clockhouse and then to Albemarle Road above the Post Office. They were away visiting Ernie when the doodlebug fell at the High Street end of Albemarle Road, killing three people. They then moved to the requisitioned No. 75 Merlin Grove, which was where Ernie came when he was demobbed. He bought a motorbike and sidecar, which had a box for his tools, and rented the piece of land near Eden Park Station for £2.10s. a week to put up a board advertising landscape gardening.

When he was given an unwanted greenhouse he started growing his own plants and in 1949/50 the Eden Park Nurseries was born. Now it is known as Eden Park Garden Centre, and is owned by Ernie's son, David Bartholomew, helped by his son Tony.

Below: *The tunnel to Eden Park Station.* (BR)

Ernie Bartholomew at his greenhouse below Eden Park Station. (EN)

Ernie's wife Sheila in the snow at the Eden Park nurseries. (EN)

A lorry from the nurseries unloads at Marble Arch. (EN)

The Bartholomews collecting turf – Barbara is driving the tractor and David is holding baby Tony, 1963. (EN)

Henry Tinsley

After starting work as an errand boy at the age of 11 and later becoming a clerk, Henry became interested in things technical while browsing in the Guildhall library. He trained for nine years at Muirhead & Co, the scientific instrument makers at Elmers End, leaving there to work for Cambridge Instruments and R.W. Paul & Co. before founding his own pioneering design business in 1904. He was living at Penlee in Elmers End Road, equipped with little more than a lathe in his small workshop at home. Penlee was between Witham and Marlow Roads, just past the cemetery.

The business expanded rapidly and by 1916 Henry had taken over Werndee Hall, South Norwood, where the firm was to stay for nearly 70 years.

This is where Olive Hibbert comes into the story. She worked at Werndee Hall for 20 years wiring test consoles for underwater cables and equipment for Concorde. At the time of writing Olive enjoys walking her German shepherd, Goldie, in the South Norwood Country Park, and is still well informed on Wheatstone bridges, galvanometers and capacitors – knowledge that for most of us has disappeared into the mists of time.

An expert gardener, Olive grows bedding plants from seed saved year on year, making the most of her small garden on the corner of Balfour and Werndee Roads, where Henry Tinsley established his business.

The Latham Story

The success of the Latham family lies squarely on the shoulders of Emily Smith, who married Alf Latham between the wars. They had five boys – Ronnie, Ken, Peter, Donald and Roger – with one daughter,

Olive Hibbert of Tinsleys in her garden.

Jeannie. In 1936 Alf, in his early forties, died from a brain tumour. Living in Ancaster Road at the time, the family were thrown out by the bailiffs and made their way to the 18-room Holmhurst in Upper Elmers End Road. It was here that Emily, holding her family together, started the family business with the purchase of a lorry.

During the war Ronnie, later with Ken, drove to Norfolk to work on the airfields parking planes. As the war came to an end they went on to moving coal, sand and ballast. They kept several lorries at the back of the house, where there were stables and an orchard left over from Home Farm, and dismantled Anderson shelters at £6 a time before expanding into the rubbish-clearing business. At the time of writing it is rare to venture onto the roads of the area without seeing a smart Latham skip lorry.

In 1961 they left Holmhurst for Marlow Road and

Looking towards Elmers End, 1885, with St James' Stream and Eden Park Farm on the right, and the Rising Sun on the left, with the industrial estate in the centre. (J&B)

Above: *Latham's fleet of lorries lined up at the back of Holmhurst.* (CL)

Left: *Front view of the house.* (DS)

Looking down Elmers End Road from Holmhurst, with Abbots Way on the right. (DS)

Holmhurst and remembers the horses that her uncles kept in the stables. They exercised them in the London Transport ground at Hawksbrook Lane. Unbelievably, grandmother Emily would take all the pillows apart in the spring and wash the feathers and ticking, reassembling them when they were dry – Chris enjoyed the wonderful fresh clean smell and played a fine game with the floating feathers. In winter there were enormous logs made from old railway sleepers in the massive fireplaces and always the sweet aroma of baking coming from the kitchen, where the Misses Robinson and Grant helped out with the cooking.

A snooker room had been added to the side of the building and Chris remembers her uncles lifting her onto the table, where she would run down the green baize that seemed to go on forever.

Emily had a firm head for business. When her mother had trouble paying the rent on her house in Kimberly Road Emily bought the landlord out, along with several adjacent houses, all of which have the same wrought-iron gates. Emily had 28 houses in Beckenham when she died, leaving them all to her daughter Jeannie, who now lives in Winchelsea.

Jeannie's brother Ronnie married Julie Oult but was electrocuted in an accident when working on a lorry in the yard at Holmhurst. Only 27, he left two children, Ronnie and Carol. Roger also died young, at 28 of leukaemia, leaving three children.

Peter built up his own tipper lorry business at Biggin Hill, where there is a road called Latham's Close, so named when the developers, Falcons, settled their debts to Lathams with several houses. Peter died during the 1990s.

in 1999 started their recycling plant in Kangley Bridge Road, with efficient new machinery in a complex layout for the sorting of soil, metal, wood, paper, plastic, pots and clinker, etc.

What became of Emily and her children is best told through the memories of her granddaughter, Chris, eldest of the three children of Ken, Emily's second child. For seven years Chris taught blind children, and at the time of writing has worked as the company secretary for 25 years. She was born at

Chris has two brothers, Kenny and Steven. Kenny is the mainstay of the firm and drives in from Yalding every weekday at 5.30a.m. He has not taken a holiday since he was 15 years old but spends his weekends with his horses, especially the pacers. In 2003 Chris arrived at work to find a border terrier pup from Kenny waiting in the kneehole of her desk. Called Ollie, he goes to work with her every day.

Chris, Kenny and Steve have six children between them (Christian, Dee, Ryan, James, Toby and Emma), five boys and one girl – just like the family of their great-grandmother, Emily. It was Chris' boys who played for Brookside by Elmers End Station in their Latham red-and-white strip sponsored by the firm.

How proud Emily would have been of her great-grandchildren and the united family business of Latham & Sons established in 1942. It is a company based on reputation, though it is obvious that the mutual respect and loyalty among family members is the real reason for its success.

Stoneham's: The Car People

Sitting in the comfortable, airy conservatory of David Stoneham's beautiful house at Keston Park, I (Pat Manning) reflected on the success story achieved by this family in just one generation. Without a doubt the main factors were their determination, their enthusiasm for establishing their own business and their capacity for hard work.

When David's grandfather died just a year after retirement, he left enough money for his son Ron, aged 16, to take on the tobacconist's and sweet shop at Elmers End. In practice, being where the buses terminated, it was more a café where all 536 of the bus crews could take a break.

Most afternoons Ron would play cards with three regular customers for the £5 or thereabouts accumulated in the kitty. This kindled interest among the other customers and they began a friendly business at the café of betting by phone. The war put an end to this when Ron's friends were called up, although his childhood polio meant he was left behind. Joining forces with Alfred Dyer, a bookmaker at the New Cross greyhound stadium, Ron opened a betting shop at No. 115 Upper Elmers End Road.

Then came the step that took Ron into the car trade. A failing garage nearby, Vincent's, caught his eye and, together with Don Mason, Ron went into business selling petrol, working from 7a.m. to 11p.m. A lucrative contract came their way – supplying the wagon which drew the Midland mobile bank to agricultural shows. Their next venture, in 1952, was to use their three-year-old Morris Oxford to start a self-drive hire service when new cars were still hard to come by.

Ten years later they were successful enough to finance the building of a completely new garage, using the architects Alan Jones & Allerton. The winter of 1962/3 was exceptionally hard, with snow lying for months from just after Christmas, but it did not prevent the garage being built on the site of the old cottages near the Rising Sun. Don Mason was the service manager with Mrs Knowles and Mrs Windsor as bookkeepers, Mr Pat King as forecourt manager, Peter Collins as driving instructor, Les Barnes as bank wagon driver and Vic Howes in charge of the breakdown vehicle and coach building. Ron's wife Betty ran the self-drive hire and driving school, and also played a vital role in the management of the entire business. Eldest son Peter managed the branch in Copers Cope Road after working his way up from the workshop, grease-bay and petrol pumps. When he was only 15, second son David started in Stoneham's grocery store in Avenue Road, where he learnt everything about he needed to know about running a business.

When Ron retired in 1976, it was David and his wife Elizabeth who became the main shareholders of the three parts of the business – the main garage in Upper Elmers End Road, its subsidiary on the opposite side (now Bromley Mitsubishi) and Copers Cope Road, which is mainly repairs. In 1972 when the firm was relaunched the name was changed to Masters, the original Vauxhall franchise becoming Renault, and in 1979 the Chinese Garage was added to the group.

David is now retired (2004) and has handed the reins to his sons, Christian and Scott. There are five grandchildren – Christian's son Oliver with twins Alison and Alexander and Scott's two sons, Lewis and Joseph. It looks as though we shall continue to see Masters in Beckenham for many years to come and we are delighted with all the photos and encouragement that David Stoneham has given us.

The Chinese Garage

In the 1920s, as cars became more popular, societies such as the AA, RAC, the Preservation Trust and the Horticultural Society became concerned about the ugliness of arterial roads and their petrol stations. It was suggested that the roads should be planted with trees and bordered with flower-beds and rock gardens. A competition was announced in the *Daily Express* for 'Brighter Petrol Stations', the preliminary judging was done through the submission of photographs, either by the proprietors or by members of the public, by Monday 22 July 1929. A special prize of £10 was offered and the winning petrol station was to receive a handsome gold cup, worth £50.

The summer of 1929 was exceptionally hot with drought conditions, but the light was excellent for photography. It was also the right time for Park Langley Garage because Taylor Brothers, under the architect Edmund Clarke, were on the point of completing its construction. Coloured lanterns hung from the roof and a red flaming torch crowned an ornamented turret. Liveried staff in peaked caps and plum-coloured uniforms supplied petrol and the

Left: *The Rising Sun cottages, with sunflowers in the front gardens.* (DE)

Right: *The young Ron Stoneham outside his café at Elmers End. Note the poster for the Rink cinema and the sign for 'Wild Woodbines'.* (DS)

Left: *Stoneham's petrol station in the 1950s.* (DS)

Below left: *Ron Stoneham on his birthday, 21 June 1992.* (DS)

Ron Stoneham Ltd.

GARAGE

UPPER ELMERS END ROAD, BECKENHAM

★ CAR SALES AND SERVICE
★ SCHOOL OF DRIVING
★ REPAIRS · MECHANICAL AND BODY
★ SELF DRIVE HIRE
    All new cars at competitive prices

LARGE STOCKS OF NEW AND REMOULD TYRES

TELEPHONE. BECKENHAM 0782

See local directory for new number after January 1963

Watch it grow · Rebuilding June 1962

Ron Stoneham's petrol station.

A 1920 postcard, owned by Mr Stanley Mitchell of No. 31 Greenways, showing the lampposts which gave Park Langley its Oriental feel (at the time perceived as Japanese). Tony Johns remembers the lamplighter walking along to light these gas lamps in the evenings. The lamppost on the central island has the mirror of 'looking-glass corner' hanging from it and on the left, set into brickwork in the wall of the estate agent's bungalow, is a letter-box that could also be considered Japanese in style – a similar one is still in use in Wickham Way. At least three of the lampposts survive in front gardens at No. 3 Wickham Way and Nos 5 and 27 Hayes Way. The brickwork of the letter-box has survived, as has the adjacent post which has hooks for the estate agent's board. (SM)

breakdown 'truck' was a Rolls-Royce.

The results were announced in the *Daily Express* of 23 August 1929. The Park Langley petrol station had scored a near miss and was awarded a silver cup. The winner was Captain Peaty's Coombe Bridge petrol station on the Kingston bypass. The judges were Colonel Wilfred Ashley MP, Mrs Philip Runciman OBE (chairman of the National Gardens Guild), Mr Gilbert Jenkins FRIBA and Mr Gerald Butcher, the horticultural expert. Left to Mrs Runciman, the Park Langley petrol station would perhaps not have scored so high. She praised the winner, saying 'there is nothing garish to stun the sensitive seeker of petrol', but of the Park Langley station said:

showed too much elaboration and the English half-timbered walls and the leaded windows did not seem in precise harmony with the Oriental aspect of the roof and garden.

In contrast to the so-called flamboyance of Park Langley, Coombe Bridge was of red brick and tiles against a background of tall trees with a rustic bridge over a small stream and beds of roses and lupins. The Thiristane garage was a study in black and white, with clipped box hedges, golden privet and hanging baskets of geraniums.

The Burmese (thus described by the press) pagoda and Japanese garden of the Park Langley petrol station must have presented a striking contrast to more traditional entries and over 70 years later it is little changed except for its name (now the Chinese Garage), and is a Grade II listed building.

As to why the Oriental design was chosen and whose decision it was, Doug Worgan, the owner/manager in 1946, wrote as follows in his advertising material:

Built in 1929 its Japanese architecture was in keeping with the surrounding area as the then Lord of the manor

was a Japanese fanatic and lived in what is now Burroughs Wellcome. A man was brought from Japan to design the complicated roof bearers and the tiles were made specially by the Marley Tile Company.

Henry Wellcome owned Langley Lodge. Could he be the 'Japanese fanatic' and 'lord of the manor'?

Doug Worgan goes on to say 'the lampposts and even letter-boxes in the area were of Japanese design.' Since builders Taylor Bros of Lewisham and architect Reginald Fry were developing the area, was the 'Japanese fanatic' associated with them? The front page of the *Beckenham Journal* of the first week in September 1929 shows the garage and a photograph of Stone Farm taken in 1928 by Mr Lester Martin, who added that Cullen's the grocer's was built on the Stone Farm site.

Perhaps there is a better candidate. An article by Mary James in the *Kentish Times* of 26 October 1989 suggests that the person with Japanese interests was J.L. Bucknall. James Loyd Bucknall could certainly have been considered 'lord of the manor'. He had lived at Homewood in South Eden Park Road from 1874 and in 1886 had had the old mansion of Langley Farm replaced by Langley Court, where he lived until his death in 1917.

Mary goes on to say that so great was his influence locally that the street furniture of the Langley estate was in Japanese style – confirmed by the postcard of the old road junction (see above).

Whittingham's: The Eden Park Grocers

Ron Whittingham was the elder of the two sons of Nellie and Bill Whittingham, who came to run one of the first shops at Eden Park in 1932.

The top of Upper Elmers End Road was undeveloped then and 12-year-old Ron remembers picking flowers for his mother in what, at the time of writing, is Links Way. At that time it was possible to walk up

PARK LANGLEY
GARAGE
(Beckenham) LTD.

AUTOMOBILE
ENGINEERS

AUSTIN AGENTS

All makes of Cars supplied
New and Secondhand

★

WICKHAM ROAD,   BECKENHAM
Telephone: BECKENHAM 3466   5 Lines

Top and above: *Park Langley Garage in 1929 with the original pumps and plum-liveried staff. Petrol brands then were BP and Pratt's.* (DS)

what became Hawksbrook Lane to the old farm buildings, one of which must have been a smithy because there was an old anvil there which must have weighed a ton! One large barn was used by a firm making firelighters and there was great excitement when it went up in flames, with the children chasing after the fire engine on their bikes. The barn had been described in the 16 October 1909 edition of *Queen* as a:

very fine barn with magnificent oak timbers and braces which it is hoped will be turned into a hall for concerts and dances while retaining its old timbering and appearance.

Although Ron was destined to become a versatile engineer, his early years at Eden Park were spent helping in the shop, stacking shelves, taking orders and delivering them on the shop bike – his brother Keith would sit on a cushion, legs dangling over the front of the bike, while Ron pedalled the orders to the customers.

At Marian Vian School Ron enjoyed woodwork, almost completing a cabinet which remained part of

the family furniture, even though Ron had to finish it off at home. He enjoyed Mr Millican's science lessons and was awarded a prize – *The Age of Machinery* – which he has to this day. Sadly Mr Millican died in Somerset whilst trying to save a child from drowning.

Ron sang the *Messiah* in St John's choir and when the organ failed one day he repaired the sheared bolt with a part from his Meccano set!

Ron used to go to the sports grounds behind Eden Way to ride his bike in the woods or to play darts in one of the pavilions. He watched the maiden flight of the Hindenburg while playing in the Bethlem parkland. Before the war there moved next door to the Whittinghams a young man with an open-topped Austin car. Interested in electrics, he became a friend, and sold out to Mr Fisher, who charged the accumulators needed to run the wireless. Ron helped Mr Fisher install the dynamo and shelves

For Groceries & Provisions
COME TO
W. M. Whittingham
(trading as J. H. SCHOFIELD)
527, UPPER ELMERS END ROAD, EDEN PARK
PERSONAL ATTENTION
'Phone your orders to BEC 2569

Top: *Remember YoYos?* (RW)

Left: *Bill outside the shop when it became Whittingham's and* (above) *when it was still Schofield's.*

The Tilling bus No. 217, registration LF 9028, from the Thomas Tilling garage. (DE)

Above: *Ron, Nellie, Keith and Bill on a trip to Hastings in 1936, sitting on the stones in their best suits.*

Right: *Ron Whittingham's science prize, 1934.* (RW)

and gradually took over the charging and delivery of accumulators. The shop was an agent for Meccano and at Christmas ran a Hornby train in the window.

On Sundays, four bus companies – the General Omnibus Co., Tillings and two brown buses, Birch and the London City Omnibus Co. – vied for custom in Upper Elmers End Road, overtaking to try to get ahead. During the week, No. 78 was supposed to run every 7.5 minutes from Shoreditch to West Wickham but the raising of Tower Bridge for river traffic made its arrival unpredictable! By 1931 the buses had started to work together and at the time of writing the Shoreditch–Bromley–Farnborough route (No. 47) still runs.

The double-storey red-brick stationmaster's house next to Mr Fisher's had open land up to the station, where there was a large pond always covered with green weed and known as the 'stink pond'. By 1954 it had shrunk to little more than a puddle.

In 1935, Les Foulgar of Merlin Grove, who worked at Wellcome's, started up a branch of the Red Cross. Ron's father joined and a year later, when he was 16, Ron became a cadet. They bought an old ambulance which no-one could drive and recruited Mr Field from the undertaker's opposite to drive it round the roads drumming up support. In the 1938 crisis they were asked to volunteer for service in the event of a war. Ron received his call-up into the Red Cross on the Wednesday before the outbreak of war on 3 September 1939 and was stationed at Churchfields depot and Beckenham Baths. The unit was made up of Rover Scouts, the ARP and Red Cross trainees. Some may remember the Christmas party run by Rover Scout leader Slim Wall for the children of Churchfields School in 1940.

Joining the RAF brought Ron the greatest satisfaction in his life and was the cause of him leaving Eden Park forever. He now lives in Kenya. Thanks must go to Ron for these memories.

Lampard's: The Beckenham and West Wickham Bakers

According to the stone above the Post Office, the Croydon Road parade of shops was built in 1930 and contained a complete complement of butcher, baker and candlestick-maker with greengrocer thrown in. Today only the baker remains and that because of the efforts of Cyril William George Lampard & Sons.

C.W. Lampard (called John) bought the business from its original owner in 1939 when his sons Ralph and Philip were aged six and 12 months respectively. Both boys and their sister Patricia Ann attended Eden Park School. Ralph went on to St Dunstans and Philip to the Beckenham and Penge Grammar School. Fortunately for the business, when their father was taken to hospital suffering from a duodenal ulcer, his wife Marjorie was able to take over, both the boys training at the Borough Polytechnic to be bakers. The recipes were all in John Lampard's head, though Ralph subsequently wrote them down, and all the bakery products sold in the shop are, at the time of writing, made on the premises. Before the supermarkets took over, Lampard's ran a home delivery service which included deliveries to the Robertson family of golliwog jam fame who lived on the Beckenham Place estate.

Early every morning, at the time of writing, you can see Philip Lampard carrying bakery produce to his van to stock the bakery's other shop opposite the baths in West Wickham. His brother Ralph sets the alarm for 4a.m. every day except Sunday in order to reach the shop by 5.15a.m. to start making bread. At one time they had a third shop in the Upper Elmers End parade, now the Patisserie, which they sold to Pole Alfonse Zymala.

In the Croydon Road shop are two models – one of the Lampards' horse and cart and the other of the muffin man with a tray on his head. These were fashionable in the trade in the 1970s and were promoted by

Ralph Lampard in the Croydon Road shop with (inset) the model of Lampard's horse and cart.

Spillers, the flour company. The horse and cart, at the time of writing the only one in a Beckenham baker's, cost £70, while the muffin man caught Ralph's eye at a trade exhibition at the Barbican and cost £200.

In 2004 Ralph is not only a member of the Langley Park Rotary Club but is also a vice-president of the Constitutional Club on Church Hill, where he enjoys a game of snooker. Both brothers are jazz fans and on Friday afternoons Ralph goes to listen to jazz near Charing Cross.

Every Easter the window is filled with displays of chocolate Easter bunnies and at Christmas there are rows of delectable Yule logs, all made by Ralph

Lampard. Which are most tempting – the appetising sausage rolls, the crisp, well-baked rolls or the delicious Friday fruit bread dusted with icing sugar? Many of us as children depended on a bag of yesterday's buns to allay hunger pangs after swimming.

What makes Lampard's special? It is a friendly local shop in touch with its customers and reminds us of how things used to be.

Hazelton's: The Hardware Store

Frank Hazelton had a hardware shop at Elmers End that was later run by his son John as a butcher's shop.

Frank was a member of Beckenham FC in the 1930s. In the Stanhope Grove days John also managed a football team, the Magyars, among whose members were his younger son, Mike, and friends. At the time of writing John lives in Lloyd's Way, where he and his wife Pat are keen gardeners.

Frank Hazelton's hardware shop (above), *and John Hazelton's butcher shop* (right). (JH)

CHAPTER 4

Schools

Kit Bailey and Marian Vian

Generations of children will remember Mrs Bailey at Marian Vian School, where she was a teacher from 1939–75, having already served a year there in 1933. She preferred teaching to admin, although she occasionally took on the job of deputy and acting head. Now a lively 91, she entertained us for two or three hours at Andon Court in Croydon Road with tales of life with her husband Bill and of her work at school.

Kit has some amusing tales. There was a boy called Quickenden, who swallowed a glass alley (marble) for a sixpenny bet and was merely sent back to his lessons. What would happen today? When 'caps' and 'bombs' were the rage amongst the boys one was dropped during the visit, in all his regalia, of charter mayor Sir Josiah Stamp, who fell up the steps, his mayor's hat flying. A boy called Ian picked it up and was upset that the shocked mayor did not thank him for his trouble!

Not long afterwards Sir Josiah Stamp and his family were killed when a bomb destroyed their house, Tantallon Park, at Hill Road, Shortlands on 16 April 1941.

The children were disappointed at a visit by Rear Admiral (later Admiral) Philip Vian, nephew of Marian Vian, when he arrived in a pale grey lounge suit instead of resplendent in his uniform. They had followed his exploits keenly throughout the war.

One of Hugh Bean's earliest public performances on the violin was at a prize-giving at Marian Vian, which was his primary school.

When Kit joined the staff the deputy head of the juniors was Miss Hayes, who had joined the school in 1911 after having taught, straight from college, at the village school of St James'. In her book *Peace and War in Elmers End, Beckenham* she writes of the school 'set among green fields with elm trees to shelter under and little rivers running through the meadows', and remembers Fred Hards who became chauffeur to the Earl of Suffolk and who was killed by a bomb in the Second World War, as was the Earl who was trying to defuse it. She kept a meticulous record of all the alerts in her diary – by May 1940 there had been 531. In 1942 a former member of staff, Mr Holehouse, was killed at the wheel of a convoy in Tunisia. Not only was the school damaged several times during the war but it was also used as a rest centre for those bombed out. Miss Hayes finishes her book triumphantly with a report of a memorable visit in 1946 by Captain Williams of the SS *Tongariro* – 'our ship' – in a link with the merchant navy forged through the ship adoption society. Captain Williams brought a 10-foot New Zealand spear and was given a scale model of his ship made by the boys under the supervision of woodwork master Mr Jones.

The headmaster of the senior school, Tom Telford, was the grandson of Scottish civil engineer Thomas Telford (1757–1834), builder of the Caledonian Canal, the wrought iron Menai suspension bridge and St Katherine's Docks in London. He was in every way a First World War Army man, always smart and with an officer's cane. When a basket of apples intended

Alice Maud Hayes' 99th birthday tea. (JL)

'Doc' White, Alderman Duncan and Mr Gully examine the cups at the Beckenham and Penge Grammar School for Boys. (M&AD)

The Beckenham and Penge Grammar School for Boys rugby team, 1945, trained by Bill Bailey. Left to right, back row: Peter Stewart, ?, Martin Lambert, ?, Colin Gordon-Smith; third row: John Stoddart, Pete Cannon, Donald Hardie, John Pinnock, David Rands, Ken Pleant; second row: Bill Bailey, Bob Pope, Norrie Pedgrift, headmaster 'Doc' White, Maurice Britton, John Tonge, Gordon Price; front row: John Brewer, Alan Mead. (T&NP)

for the girls' cookery lesson was raided by boys and he used the school cane on all 20 of them, they loved him in spite of it. He did not cane the girls, of course – that was the job of the deputy head, though in Kit's time as deputy head she was never asked to cane a girl.

Bill Bailey started teaching with Kit at Marian Vian before going on to specialise in English at the Beckenham and Penge Grammar School for Boys, where he remained until his death from a heart attack while invigilating an exam at the school at Park Langley in 1970. He was an old boy of Chatham House, Ramsgate, Ted Heath's school. Kit's school was St Olave's.

Bill was a keen sportsman and although really a footballer he learned the rules of rugby and ran the school's rugger team for years. He played cricket as a fast bowler at the Elmers End CC near the industrial centre. Today it is the Wren housing estate, where all the roads, such as Kingfisher Way and Wagtail Walk, are named after birds. The match against NW Surrey was always for a barrel of beer and cricketing brothers Dennis and Leslie Compton were on the visiting side in their younger days. The best pitch in those days was the Standard Bank of South Africa ground in Stanhope Grove, now Amida, where the South African test teams practised when in England. Josie Wait, who has lived in Stanhope Grove since 1966, says how beautifully kept the

ground was and recalls the Bluett Smith insurance and Sunset companies having sports days there.

Fondly remembered by the Baileys was the family of Norrie Pedgrift, who stooked the corn and hoed the turnips at the harvest camps during the war. The Pedgrifts had lived in Ambleside Avenue for a while, the eldest of the three sons, Gordon, attending Marian Vian in the early 1930s. When Bill Bailey bought a car after the war, he sold his trusty bike for £2 to Norrie, who still uses its red rear reflector to mark the end of his garage in the dark.

Thelma and Norrie Pedgrift of Bridge of Earn, Scotland, 2001. (T&NP)

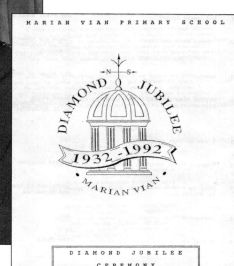

Above: *Alderman William Duncan handing the Beckenham Schools Trophy to Marian Vian's school captain, Janet Dallimer, December 1955.* (M&AD)

Pam's class at Marian Vian. Left to right, back row: Pat Cashman, ?, Janet Fookes, Margaret Else, Carole Saunders, Miss Bootes, Julia Meekins, Carole Brakefield, Murial Crompton, Rosslyn Parkin, Pam Holland, ?; middle row: Sandra Hall, Janet Rampling, Brenda Pollard, Gillian Robinson, Susan Sparrow; front row: Maureen Bullock, Annette Howard, Marilyn Scott, ?, Jean Johnson, ?. (PW)

Above: Elmers End Cricket Club teams, in the 1920s (left) *and with Tony Spencer as captain* (right) *in 1946.*

Below: The deed for Elmers End Cricket Club. (JHU)

Norrie married Thelma Flack, daughter of the third Henry Flack, manufacturer of French polish, lacquer and varnish at Elmers End. The firm was started in Southwark in 1860 by the first Henry Flack, moving to Elmers End in 1926, where it was eventually incorporated into Bolloms. Thelma did her teacher training at Marian Vian and her father played cricket at the Elmers End Cricket Club. Norrie and Thelma have spent much of their married life in Bridge of Earn, Perth, Scotland where Norrie has taught geography at a school in Strathallan.

Stan Kelly started at Marian Vian at the same time as the Baileys, followed in turn by his two children. Stan went on to the Balgowan Central School and became a plumber and decorator with his own business. In 1946 he paid an unbelievable £695 for 48 Aylesford Avenue when it was 12 years old!

Another past pupil from Marian Vian became its headmistress. Pat and Shirley Willis both went from the juniors to the Beckenham County School but Shirley returned to Marian Vian in 1954, teaching there for 14 years, and was headmistress in 1981/82, when infants and juniors ceased to be separate. As a pianist she was always in demand and played 'Jerusalem' at the school's diamond jubilee celebrations in 1992. Ian Muir remembers the play she produced in which he had one line as a gipsy.

Soon after Shirley started at Marian Vian, in April 1939, lessons were held in various local houses while air-raid shelters were built at the school. She lived at 64 Dunbar Avenue and had her lessons with Miss Stubbs at No. 36. Eric Smith, who now lives in Tonbridge, had his lessons in a room at the Eden Park Hotel, close to his home at 360 Upper Elmers End Road.

Jim Hurley, a friend of Eric Smith, provided an interesting snippet about the Elmers End Cricket Club: Tony Spencer, a friend, had given him a copy of a deed dated 16 March 1921 in which the cricket ground of some 5.2 acres was bought from a farmer for £742 including expenses, in the names of a large number of trustees each donating between £2 and £100, but mostly £5 or £10. (One of the subscribers, J.H. Hurley, was a relative of Jim's.) The ground was to be used primarily for cricket, although football could be played there, and its formal name was the Elmers End (Alfred Inglis) Sports Club, known as the Elmers End Cricket Club.

The Oak Lodge Estate and St David's

It seems that we have John Wilson Davis to thank for the name Oak Lodge. Born in Deptford in 1773, he came to West Wickham soon after 1820 and acquired half of Ridle Meadow. At that time the house there was called Wickham Hatch. The 1840 tithe map, however, shows the field (now Blake's Recreation-Ground) as Oak Tree Field. Shortly afterwards Wickham Hatch became Oak Lodge and John, employing five men, farmed the land until at least 1851.

By 1854 the Grippers were living at Oak Lodge, staying there for around 36 years – the hill up South Eden Park Road was known as Grippers Hill and the family was well known socially.

Subsequent occupants of Oak Lodge included E. Fyffe of the banana company, who lived there for three years. The famous Fyffes blue label was introduced in 1929 to defend against competition from the Jamaica Producers Association.

William Shoebridge was resident in 1904,

Miss Davies (middle row, third teacher from the left) *with her school, 1933.* (AB)

followed by Ernest Bliss for seven years and then Mortimer Justin, who rented the property in 1913, eventually (at the time of the Monks Orchard sale of 1920, Oak Lodge Farm being listed in the brochure as covering about 62 acres) buying the house and estate in the name of his daughter Winifred, wife of Arnold Schove. Mortimer and his wife Louise continued to live there until their deaths.

St David's College now enters the story. Gwenllian Davies lived with her husband at St David's House, subsequently 29 Eden Park Road, where they started a kindergarten for children between the ages of five and ten. In 1925 Mr Davies had bought the building plot intending to build a house in which one of the rooms would be used as a schoolroom. The electrification of the railway in 1925 led to a housing boom, with professional families needing private schools for their children. By 1931 there were 32 pupils on the roll, more teachers and other rooms in the house were being used for teaching. For play they used the field at the bottom of the garden, which belonged to the Schove estate and which was also home to a herd of Jersey cows.

Meanwhile, the large field called Oak Tree Field, on the West Wickham side of the house, was sold to the Beckenham UDC and opened in 1932 as Blake's Recreation-Ground. William Blake, a much-loved Irishman, was the village doctor but, more than that, was medical officer at the Warren and at the German prisoner-of-war camp and chairman of the Community and Parish Councils. He drove his Model T Ford as if he were the only road user!

The foundation-stone for the present building, Justin Hall, a lecture hall and spiritualist church, was laid on 28 March 1933 by Louise, Mortimer Justin's widow. The kindergarten was still held at No. 29, where Aline Nisbet (née Wilson) wore the familiar brown uniform as a three-year-old in the late 1940s. Aline went on to Woodbrook.

During the 1930s various improvements were made to Oak Lodge and during the Second World War Derek Schove taught older pupils mathematics and physics there before joining the RAF as a meteorologist. His sister, Mrs Betty Ramsden, ran the school with Miss Jupp in his absence. Justin Hall was hit by a bomb and after the war was rebuilt as it is today (2004). In 1946 Derek married Vera Mitchell who with her eldest daughter, Mrs Ann Wagstaff, is principal at the time of writing. Derek died in 1986 shortly before the school's diamond jubilee.

Members of the Schove family continued to live at Oak Lodge until 1964, when it was used by the school for speech, drama and music lessons as well as being an office for Dr Schove's academic studies. Plans to demolish the buildings by buyers in 1988 fortunately were rejected by Bromley Council and English Heritage advised its conversion to spacious apartments. The building is Grade II listed and the dairy next door has also been converted into attractive living accommodation.

Houses at the school are Justin, David and Oak, which compete with each other at events such as sports day. In 1982 the school was used as the location for a TV film entitled *A Childhood* and its success in speech, drama and music has been outstanding. The school hymn was composed by one of the few male teachers, Mr Want, and the school runs both Cub and Brownie packs.

In 1952 work was started on a new primary school in another of the original Oak Lodge fields, West Lees, one-time pasture of the Jersey cows. Although it was planned to be called Spring Park School, it opened in 1954 as Oak Lodge, thus perpetuating a name over 150 years old. The official opening was by Col F.W. Chamberlain CBE on 10 July, although the school had started on 1 February with 151 pupils, four permanent teachers and headmistress Miss Shilling.

As numbers increased, the school was divided into four houses named after men of Kent – William

Pitt, William Wilberforce, General James Wolfe and Charles Dickens.

The year 2004 marked the school's half-century and among the celebrations planned were a balloon release in January to mark the start of the celebrations, a grand ball in May, a fête in June and a sports day in July. A tie bearing the 50th anniversary symbol was produced to mark the occasion.

The release of green and yellow balloons on 16 January at 13.30 was an amazing success. The chosen day was bright and breezy. Forget the balloons that reached Sevenoaks and Deal – in the next fortnight balloons were reported in Belgium, Germany, the Czech Republic and Belarus, east of Poland, a distance of some 6,000 miles.

Among past pupils who have made the headlines are shot-putter for Great Britain Judy Oaks, still competing in 2000, and high jumper Tim Foulger.

Edenham School

Edenham is one of the most recently built schools in the area, having been opened in September 1977 under the headship of Mr Jones, who stayed for 19 years. The school's name was chosen from a shortlist of four; Carmo Manor High (from Harry Cameron, known as the Great Carmo, the circus owner who overwintered his animals on the land), Ham Farm High (the farm on the fields on which the school was built), Burrell High (from the landowners of the Langley and Kelsey estates) and Edenham High (from a Lincolnshire village).

The connection with Edenham depended on the

Justin Hall foundation-stone.

Dr Schove with three pupils, three ice-creams and the mayor, Alderman William Duncan, 1955. (M&AD)

Children racing at St David's sports day, late 1930s/1940. (STD)

Arnold Schove and wife in the woods at Oak Lodge. (AW)

The sitting room at Oak Lodge. (AW)

love affair between young cricketer Peter Burrell and 17-year-old Priscilla Barbara Elizabeth Bertie, born in 1761 at Grimsthorpe, two miles from Edenham village. She was descended from an ancient family that can be traced to the Berties of Bertiland in Prussia. The town of Bersted, near Maidstone, may have been a gift to them from Saxon kings but what is certain is that Richard Bertie married Catherine Willoughby de Eresby in 1553 and that they named their eldest son Peregrine.

Peter and Priscilla married in 1779, by which time Priscilla had become joint holder with her sister Georgiana Charlotte Bertie of the family title of Lord

Above: *A wartime application form for St David's.* (STD)

Left: *The choir with Mr Want, who composed the St David's school song.* (STD)

Junior children at St David's. (STD)

Great Chamberlain of England. Peter became the first Lord Gwydir, as befitted the husband of a titled wife. Priscilla inherited the ancient Willoughby title in 1809 and became the 20th Baroness Willoughby de Eresby.

Their son, Peter Robert Burrell, graduated from Cambridge in 1801 and in 1807 married Clementina Sarah Drummond, only daughter of Lord Perth, in Edinburgh. He changed his name to Drummond Burrell and became the owner of Drummond Castle. On the death of his father in 1820 he became the second Lord Gwydir and took his seat in the House of Lords. When his mother died in 1828, he inherited two more castles, Gwydir Castle in Wales and Grimsthorpe Castle in Lincolnshire, and became the 21st Baron Willoughby de Eresby, changing his name to Drummond Willoughby.

He introduced many improvements to the Grimsthorpe estate, the most exciting of which was the Edenham Branch Railway opened in 1855 when he was 73. The line, known as Lord Willoughby's Railway, was 6.67 kilometres long but its life was short and it closed in 1873 – eight years after the death of Baron Willoughby.

Peter and Clementina's daughter married Sir Gilbert Heathcote, first Baron Aveland, their son's titles being impressive indeed. He was called Gilbert Heathcote Drummond Willoughby, the second Baron Aveland, first Earl of Ancaster and 24th Baron Willoughby De Eresby! The title Ancaster dates from another Bertie title of 1715. Various roads are named

from these historical connections: Burrell Close, Ham View, Peregrine Gardens, Eresby Drive and Overstone Gardens.

The children at the primary school in the village of Edenham were delighted that the name of their village school was also to be the name of a school in the London Borough of Croydon, especially as it corresponded with their centenary – 1873–1973.

The school badge was designed by Mr Jones to avoid any heraldic charge and has no special historical significance. It was intended to be simple and easy on the eye with its three small white shields, each with a blue cross within a larger one. The blue uniform was chosen partly because no other school in the immediate vicinity was using the colour and because in it the children looked attractive and distinctive. After some years the compulsory wearing of a blazer has, at the time of writing, been reintroduced. For their first three years the children wear a grey and silver striped tie and thereafter a black tie bearing the badge.

Monks Orchard School

The first schools in the area were run by St John's Church but by the 1930s a school was needed for the children of the Monks Orchard estate. The new school was opened on 27 October 1936 with Mr R.B. Darby as headmaster and four members of staff to teach the 128 children on the roll. As numbers increased a house system was introduced and, with no local personalities deemed worthy, they were named after the poets Browning, Longfellow, Tennyson and Wordsworth.

The crisis year of 1938 brought the prospect of evacuation, with 152 of the families in favour to 61 against. On 4 September 1939, six teachers and 102 children left East Croydon for Whitehawk School, Kemptown, Brighton. It did not sound so bad, with mornings spent on the beach and afternoons on games and rambles. There were half-day lessons at St Mark's School but at Christmas they went to the pantomime and visited the pier. By the summer of 1940 most of the party had returned to Monks Orchard. Although another group went to Braunton in North Devon in June, Monks Orchard School remained open throughout the

Mounted policeman Ray Burden visits Oak Lodge School, 22 June 1994. (RB)

Right: *Aerial view of Monks Orchard School.* (VW)

Below: *The children of Monks Orchard School in a 50th anniversary photo, 1987.* (VW)

1940/41 Blitz and for the rest of the war. In the summer of 1941 the Monks Orchard Home Farm Enterprise was started with two rabbits and by the end of the summer there were five breeding does as well as 11 hens and a haystack in the corner of the school field. The only damage to the school was by incendiaries in March 1944, when two of the infants' classrooms were burnt.

The end of the war was celebrated by two days' holiday and, in 1946, a grand celebration, with fancy dress, races, tea, Punch and Judy and a visit by the mayor to present medals and prizes. Numbers rapidly grew and both buildings and fields were extended to accommodate the 12 classes of children. The opening of Orchard Way Primary School in 1969 relieved the load on Monks Orchard. A glance at the school logbook shows that Monks Orchard was not merely a school. Extra-curricular successes for 1983 included 'Top of the Form' champion in Croydon. The five-a-side football team was champion for the Croydon schools and also in the Metropolitan Police Z Division held at the 'Warren', Colney Heath. Four girls sang in the choir at the Fairfield Halls for HM Queen Elizabeth's visit during Croydon's Charter

A Monks Orchard class on an outing to Penhurst Place, 15 July 1988, including Stephen Pike, Peter Davis, Peter Barnett, Mark Clements, Daniel Payne, Rachel Dyson, Debbie Clarke, Delwynne Miller, Michelle Cole, Tammy Strudwick, Ross Harrison, Gemma Dines, Kelly Gardner, Jerome ?, Jeyda Suleyman, Sarah Harrington, Lynne Barker, Louisa Williams, Angie Meadows, Georgina Jakeman, Andrea Saunders, Kelly Gibbs, Steven Barnett, Andrew Scott, Matthew Walford, Rachel Dodgson, Ceri Williams, Kristian Wyatt, Richard Davis and Kevin Duckering. The teachers were Mr Turtle and Mrs Ogden. (MC)

EDEN PARK SCHOOL
204 UPPER ELMERS END ROAD
BECKENHAM

Preparatory: Boys 5 years to 11 years
Girls 5 years to 16 years

All Public and Grammar School Entrances and
Scholarships

MUSIC :: ART

New **Commercial Department** for
SENIOR GIRLS 13 to 16 years

Shorthand, Typewriting, Book-keeping & Languages
External Pupils received

Principal: Mrs. A. MALLICK, B.A.

Janet Starr's class at Eden Park School. Left to right, back row: Miss Cousins, Marjorie Saunders, Christine Bess, Sheila Holland, Margaret Ellery, Sandra Parsons, Hazel Neable, Mrs Mallick; third row: ?, Alan Griffiths, Peter Cuthbert, Peter Ledger, David Gorrie, ?, Ronald Ward; second row: Anne Bashford, Felicity Edden, Gretel ?, Tessa Agutter, Pauline Cole, Janet ?, Margaret Doughty; front row: Brenda Mitchell, Margaret Price, Maureen Rickaby, Janet Millegan, Jill Player. (JS)

Centenary; the cricket team won the Primary League final at Sandilands and played in tournaments at Old Trafford and the Oval, and musicians from Monks Orchard School played at the Carol Service at Croydon Parish Church.

The mid-1980s saw Marie Cahill appointed as headmistress in time to celebrate the school's golden jubilee in 1987. Jubilee week opened with a balloon launch, with balloons reaching Cambridgeshire and Hertfordshire. Clare Stammers won a Jubilee Badge competition with her design of bees and beehives and an exhibition of work and memorabilia was opened by famous ex-pupil John Surtees. The week ended with the children all enjoying a teddy-bear's picnic organised by the parents.

As of 2004, this is truly a family school with teachers, parents, governors, children and friends all working together to make Monks Orchard School the exciting place it is.

Eden Park School

Eden Park School began in one of the houses further up the road at the start of the Second World War, with Mrs Mallick soon taking over Holly Lodge at No. 204 Upper Elmers End Road, which dates from at least 1881 and probably earlier and at one time belonged to Eden Park Farm, across the road.

Many of our contributors have fond memories of the school, although everyone comments on how strict Mrs Mallick was! It is a tribute to the school that, even when late headmaster Mr Mallinson became ill and decided to sell to developers, the school continued to flourish at Wickham Court in West Wickham. When the building was finally demolished in 2002, it collapsed in two parts, the older walls falling separately from the more modern extension.

Memories of former pupils can be found in Chapter 2.

School cups from Eden Park School.

✦ CHAPTER 5 ✦

Leisure

Racecourse, Golf and Playing-fields

When we go to Bywood Avenue and see the expanse of football pitch between Long Lane and Woodmere Avenue it is hard to imagine all the changes that have taken place there during the last 150 years. By the 1860s the land of Ham Farm had been transformed into the Woodside racecourse and when Woodside Station opened in 1871 racing enthusiasts crowded to the area. Queen Victoria's golden jubilee was celebrated there on 22 June 1887 with many important citizens attending but the racecourse had become a honey-pot for all kinds of sharp practice. Its last steeplechase was held on 26 November 1890 before the racing was moved to Gatwick. Brighton later became the venue, where the Woodside Stakes was run in memory of the years at Long Lane. For the next 60 years the land was leased to Beckenham Golf Club, until the outbreak of the Second World War led to another change of use.

Before the Second World War Margaret Neech, later widowed, lived almost opposite the fire station in Long Lane. She would go with her grandfather to see the bluebells in Long Lane Wood, although it was then private property and not as accessible as it is today – at the time of writing, however, there are more brambles than bluebells. Her grandfather was from a farming community in Cornwall and had joined the Army as a young man to gain an education, falsifying his age by a year. His release papers gave his age as 25 but when he subsequently married he was only 24! He became one of the superintendents of the Brighton and SE coast railway at Norwood Junction.

The golf course was in regular use until the war, when an ack-ack battery was stationed there and doodlebugs fell where the River Chaffinch flowed through the site. In 1950 the pavilion was used as extra schoolrooms for Ashburton while the new school was being built and eventually a council estate was built opposite Margaret's old home, the roads all having names with a literary connection: Coleridge Road, Chaucer Green, Keats Way, Swinburn Crescent and Delamare Crescent – Walter de la Mare had lived locally in Ravenscroft Road. Margaret moved to the other side of Ashburton playing-fields, to secluded Round Close with its own green island of trees built on land once belonging to Ham Farm. At the time of writing she lives in East Preston, near the sea.

The source of the River Chaffinch on Addington golf course is marked by lines of trees across the fields, although these days (2004) the river bed is usually dry. New housing in Shirley resulted in most of the water from the tributaries of the Chaffinch, including that from Stroud Green, being diverted underground. It does not seem so long ago that a bridge was needed to cross the river and Bywood Avenue was inundated during flash floods.

At the time of writing Woodside Station is a sorry, boarded-up reminder of the railway, although the Tramlink, using the destitute line, provides a pleasant, easy ride from Beckenham to Croydon, skirting the land that has seen so many changes.

Margaret remembers how, aged about eight, she would sit twice through cinema programmes at the Regal, totally entranced by Richard Talbot in *Land of Smiles*, the Western Brothers live on stage and the cinema organ that came out of the floor. Her friend left after the first performance so she travelled home alone on the No. 54 bus to a mixed reception!

Margaret got to know Tony Johns through their respective spouses, Nick and Jean, who both worked part-time at the Kingfisheries aquarium shop in Croydon Road. It's a small world!

At the time of writing, Audrey and Michael Flynn are friends of Margaret Neech and live round the corner at the end of Woodmere Avenue, where developers have had an eye on the long gardens of the bungalows and Pellings have at last persuaded the owners to sell. The Flynns' bungalow will disappear under a new road.

When Michael was a youngster he lived in one of the first two houses to be built in the Rosery, where the Chaffinch Brook ran past the summer-house at the bottom of the garden. His aunts with their flowery names all worked at the Shirley Schools. His father was the plumber for the new houses built in the 1930s on the Ham Farm site. Michael has two striking memories of the golf course. The first is of a small plane landing there before the war – quite an event in those days – and the second is being machine-gunned by a German plane in which he could see the pilot. What did he do? He just ran! Several others had a similar experience – Mary McInally was in Beckenham Place Park and, luckier than Michael, was able to jump into a convenient ditch, and what may have been the same plane flew past Balmoral Avenue, where Pam Evans saw the distinctive black cross and the pilot before it disappeared over Marian Vian School, machine-gunning the playground.

Audrey worked for the electricity board from

1948–56, at their three buildings in South Eden Park Road – Chalfont, Homewood and Harvington. She remembers old Ben the gardener and how beautiful Harvington was, although staff thought it was haunted (leaving work late and switching off all the lights only to see, on looking back from the gates, that one had been turned back on!).

Nestanglo

Few of us will remember what or where it was, but Nestanglo was the name given in 1929 to the playing-fields beside Balmoral Avenue, later called the Coop.

With Greta Garbo about to appear at the King's Hall and Jack Pickford at the Pavilion, a privately owned Tiger Moth landed through the mist at Elmers End, having lost its way to Croydon airport. The pilot and his woman passenger had been looking for the Crystal Palace towers to guide them but the mist was too thick. The residents of Wilmar in Upper Elmers End Road thought the plane was going to crash onto their roof as it circled twice over the houses, narrowly missing the wire fence, a cricket boundary post and the mower as it landed in the field. At the approach of two policemen, however, the pilot hurriedly took off!

Beckenham Town Football Club and Stanhope Rovers

The original Beckenham Football Club was founded at least as early as 1878. Affiliated to Kent County Association the club, in 1936, played in the Kent Amateur League (now the Kent County League) after being champions of the London League in 1926/27. They were three times finalists in the Kent Amateur Cup and in 1934/35 reached the final of the Kent Benevolent Shield. The club folded in 1938 but after coming out of the Navy in 1946 Eric Huggins was instrumental in starting the club up again. The name was changed to Club Beckenham FC and the team played at the Rifle Brigade Ground for one season in 1946/47. That ground is Eden Park Avenue, where Beckenham Town play today.

The club counts such well-known names among its presidents as the Rt Hon. Harold Macmillan. Officials for the 1949/50 season, when David Greg was patron, were Alderman Dr Edden OBE (former mayor) and active vice-presidents J.H. Atkins (also mayor) and C. Head. Hon. vice-presidents were Sydney Box (the film producer who shared an Oscar with his wife for the 1945 film *The Seventh Veil*), H. Buckland, M.H. Connelan, J. Ward Dais, W. Fletcher CBE MP, George Green, Percy Jones of Twinlocks, J. Lilley, A.C. Marsh, S.J. Megennis, E. Morgan, H.F. Moreley, Cdr R.M. Prior DSO DSC, F.C. Rogers, Squadron Leader J.S. Saxby and F. Tarbard, manager of the Rising Sun.

Records show that Beckenham Football Club played at the Rectory Field. Town also played at the former Anerwood United sports ground, where Abbotts Way is today. They also played on two grounds in Balmoral Avenue, one the former Nestanglo sports ground, where Mountbatton Close is today. Moving to Stanhope Grove in 1948, their present ground is at Eden Park Avenue.

On 2 October 1948, Beckenham played at Stanhope Grove for the first time:

Beckenham 5, Chislehurst Athletic 1
Bunny Copper has a day out
and scores 5 for Beckenham

The Kent Amateur League Premier Division played at Stanhope Grove on Saturday. Injuries and the unavoidable absence of centre-half Roberts led to positional changes which at the start appeared to throw the Beckenham machine slightly out of gear. In fact, the early stages of the game showed neither team to advantage.

Both sides took some time to settle down but the home team appeared to be more dangerous. In front of goal, Bunny Copper in particular was very active and it was his opportunism in the 13th minute that resulted in the first goal. Marron at outside-left had taken the ball well towards the corner flag and after beating a defender put in a centre which Copper collected to make no mistake with a rising shot. A really good ball lobbed in from the wing and Copper's head did the rest.

Some strenuous midfield play followed and an injury to the Chislehurst centre-half held the game up for a while. Beckenham, heartened by their previous success, continued to be the more effective team and Copper collected his third goal after 40 minutes play.

At the annual general meeting in 1951, after a long discussion, it was decided to change the playing colours of the club: 'As soon as practicable, players will wear scarlet shirts, white shorts and scarlet stockings instead of the familiar green and white quarter-squares.'

The following season Beckenham would play in the premier division of the London League, having played in the Kent Amateur League for four years postwar.

Mr Vic Keen, chairman of the management committee, said that Beckenham was one of five clubs accepted by the London League council for recommendation to the annual meeting in June:

If the recommendation is accepted, then the reserves will play in division 2 and the A team will continue in the premier division of the Beckenham League.

He went on:

Our first move was to accede to the request from Crystal Palace to become their nursery club. This will give the club first-class training and attention.

Beckenham Town FC, 1936. Left to right, back row: *A. Arnold, T. Humphreys, C. Bethnal, F. Hazelton, E. Walton, G. Cator, R. Brown, S. Richards, E. Lamb, M.H. Connellan;* front row: *T. Whitney, J. Stephenson, C. Wallis, B. Freemantle, E. Taylor (captain), T. Haywood, J. Britten, D. Whitney. The mascot was ? Smith junr.* (HS)

The second step was to win approval from the council for permission to charge admission to all games at Stanhope Grove.

Beckenham Town FC 1965/66
Pre-season game against Fulham FC

On that very hot day the spectators were in for a treat. Captaining the Fulham side was the legend Johnny Haynes. Ian Muir recalls:

Johnny was coming to the end of his magnificent career but played the game as if it was his first. I will never forget the sight of him going to the centre of the pitch to meet Town's captain and the referee.

Stanhope Rovers was founded in 1959, the brain-child of teenage footballers and friends Howard Smith and Geoff Ward, in association with Pat Quinn, who was head games warden at Stanhope

Grove. The team was formed from local boys who used the recreation-ground of the same name – they had offered their services to Beckenham Town FC but been turned down. The 20 or so boys, wanting to represent the borough and finding themselves without a game of football, formed Stanhope Rovers. They were so successful that five years later Beckenham Town approached them with a view to amalgamation. Stanhope was sufficiently satisfied with its own standard to decline the offer. The solid foundation on which the club was built owes much to the guiding hand of Pat Quinn. Both Geoff Ward and Howard Smith are still involved with the club in 2004.

Rovers competed in the fourth division of the Beckenham League in 1959 and in the following season were promoted to the third division. On promotion to the second division they won that too – with an unbeaten record.

Beckenham Town FC at Balmoral Avenue, 1946. Left to right, back row: *Hugh Cunningham, Derek Holyoake, Jimmy Hyett, Jock Graham, ?, Peter Austin, Ken Hyde;* third row: *Dennis Penston, Bob Niblock, ? Shreave, ?, Bob Price, Dick Stroud, Bob Percival, George Lewis, Nobby Clarke, Eric Huggins, Jim Gear, Bill Pizey, Peter Hennion;* second row: *?, Len Ralph, Doug Latter, Dickie Bates, Wally Dobson, Arthur Brereton, ?, Bill Barnes, 'Alec' Alexander, Fred Bower, Ernie Cross;* front row: *Cyril Leach, ? Ellis, ? Hicks, Bunny Cooper, Lewis Owen, Cyril Roberts, ? Leach, Ginger Marron, Fred ('Ticker') Walsh, Kenny Kingscote, John Telfer.* (HS)

Right: *The team leaves the pavilion led by their mascot, Charles Stevens, 1948. On the right is Alf Silver, who can still be found most Saturdays at Eden Park Avenue, and on the left is Dr Edden. The players include: ? Trinder, Jock Hunter, Derek Holyoake, Jimmy Banks and George Reeves.* (FB)

Left: *Beckenham Town versus Fulham FC.* (PF)

Right: *Beckenham Town play at the Stanhope Grove ground for the first time, 1948.* (ES)

Above: *Beckenham Town FC president Dr Edden presents the cup to a team from Wageningen, 1948.* (FB)

Right: *Johnny Haynes, Fulham FC.* (FFC)

The badge of Stanhope Rovers FC. (HS)

Stanhope Rovers FC, 1961/62. Left to right, back row: Pat Quinn, Mike Heppell, Rod Shulter, John French, Brian Agate, Dick Whatmore, Dixie O'Keefe, Terry Hodges, Bob Funnell; front row: Geoff Ward, Barry Woodley, Tony Dennett, Howard Smith, Cliff Darby. (HS)

5). The business of Stanhope Rovers F.C. were now terminated and the motion adopted that Stanhope Rovers Fc. now became Beckenham Town. Fc
The Secretary advised the meeting that perm sanction had been obtained from the following:-
L.F.A.
K.C.F.A.
Bromley Town F.C.
Bromley Council.

Beckenham Town FC, 1965/66 – the team that faced Millwall. Left to right, back row: Mick Irons, Ken Thomson, Shaun Tulley, Dave Wentworth, Graham Woodhead, Maurice Chilver; *front row:* Ray Headington, Ken Nash, Doug Meekins, Mike Howlett, Tom Richards. (BE)

Agenda notes from the last ever Beckenham Town meeting. (HS)

Stanhope Rovers FC in the Beckenham Hospital cup final, 1968/69. Left to right, back row: Paul Watkins, Brian Agate, Colin Wilkins, Terry Hodges, Michael Pyant, Howard Smith; front row: Paul Bartholomew, Roger Bartholomew, Graham Figg, Dick Whatmore, Rodney Shorter, Ian Kay.
(HS)

Wishing to improve their standard of football, they joined the South East London Amateur League's premier division. In 1961 Stanhope started a reserve side to supply the first team with players. At one time there were 40 playing staff. Members were kept informed of the club's activities by way of the club magazine, which kept players and officials abreast of social and footballing activities. In the first issue a report of a friendly game against Sittingbourne included the topic of Paul Bartholomew's much-travelled van, the team having arrived half an hour late for the game. Rovers won 3–1, the scorers being Muggeridge, Starmer and O'Keefe, who was making his debut. The first issue also reported that club founder Pat Quinn had moved to Chatham to take up the post of games warden for the local borough. In a 2004 letter Pat wished everyone well and, as president, donated a small sum to club funds.

During the successful 1962/63 season the club lost in the final of the Beckenham League Challenge Cup

(section B). The following season, ambitiously, they jumped to the premier division, reaching the quarter-final of the Kent Benevolent Cup – a feat they performed again in 1966/67, when they reached the final of the Kent Junior Cup (section C) and were invited to play in the Lewisham Charity Shield the following year.

During their time in the Beckenham League, ten Stanhope players gained representative honours.

The original Beckenham Town became defunct in 1969. Stanhope Rovers, having sailed through the Beckenham and South East London Amateur Leagues with consummate style and relative ease, had become the senior football team in Beckenham. It was therefore logical that they should apply for the name relinquished by their predecessors two years earlier. In 1971 their application became a footballing reality and Stanhope Rovers became Beckenham Town.

In the midst of its final death rattle, Beckenham Town signed its name and possessions over to

Beckenham League Football Clubs 1950/51

PREMIER	DIVISION ONE	DIVISION TWO	DIVISION THREE	DIVISION FOUR
Shortlands	Clockhouse	Fairfields	Penge Pioneers	Elmers End A
Waynes	Churchfields OB	George Green	Elmville	Cator Park
Elmers End	Penge Trades	Sanderstead	Kings Park Rovers	Elmville
London	Elmers End Reserves	Cooperville	Tablonians	Reserves
Transport	Wickham Park	Yew Tree	Catford College	Penge Pioneer
Beckenham	Eden Beck	Waynes Reserves	Fairfield Reserves	Reserves
Twinlocks	Muirheads A	Tredown	Aerograph	St James
Anerley	Christchurch	Wickham Park	Muirheads B	Kenilworth
Alexandra	Bromley Nat OB	Reserves	Coney Hall	Wickham Park
Edwards	Anerley B	Alexandra A	Londex	Reserves
Gardners	RAFA	Edwards Reserves	Christchurch	Columbia
		SEM	Reserves	Classics
		Twinlock Reserves		Swift Rovers
		Sydenham		

The Beckenham Town team, 1977/78, on the win against Hatfield which gained them promotion to the London Spartan Premier League. Left to right, back row: Dave Fitzgerald (manager), Glynn Garfield, Kevin Port, Terry Miller, Steve Kinchen, John Huggins, Micky Howlett, Willy Proud, Terry Ward, Tony Pettit, Dave Barker; front row: Terry Clark, Dave Wright, Tony Algar, Freddie Kay, Mark Hudson. The mascot is Terry Miller's son. (HS)

Beckenham Town FC, 1984/85. Left to right, back row: Simon Wood, Steve Jeacott, Peter Wellman, Steve Biggs, Steve Accott, ?, ?, John Collins (manager); front row: Gerry Dolke, Paul Mulhem, Mark Goldberg, Dave Burke, Lol Langdon, Martin Kennard. At the time of writing, Gerry Dolke is chairman of Bromley FC, whilst Mark Goldberg is a former chairman of Crystal Palace FC. (HS)

neighbouring Bromley Football Club. However, following negotiations between Stanhope Rovers' secretary Barry Starmer and the late Charlie King, Bromley's counterpart, it was unconditionally agreed that Stanhope Rovers would henceforth assume the name of Beckenham Town (1971). Simultaneously they claimed the red and white colours synonymous with Beckenham Football Club down the years.

As Beckenham Town, the club continued to compete with distinction in the South East London Amateur League, gaining intermediate status as they did, and it was perhaps fitting that they changed their home ground to Stanhope Grove.

Switching to the Metropolitan London League in 1973, Town achieved second place in the reserve Division One in 1974/75. On earning senior status in 1975, they made the quantum leap to the Spartan League for the start of the 1975/76 campaign, where they took their place in the senior first division.

Alan Drake (left) *and,* (above), *manager Bob Chilvers.* (HS)

Beckenham 3, Hatfield 0
The Proud men of Beckenham made sure beyond all doubt last Saturday that they would be playing in the London Spartan Premier League next season. Hatfield was given no chance and rarely threatened Town's goal. Goalkeeper Port was almost a spectator.

It was a sad day for Beckenham's Willie Proud who missed his first game for two years.

On gaining promotion to the premier division in 1977/78, Beckenham went on to achieve a creditable sixth position in the top flight. They consolidated their success by reaching the final of the London Spartan League Cup, where they were narrowly beaten by Welling United on penalties after a 3–3 extra-time result.

Beckenham's following two seasons in the premier division were less notable, with 14th position in the league being attained on each occasion, but they did manage to reach the final of the league cup again in 1978/79, only to lose 2–0 to Farnham Town.

Beckenham Town move to Eden Park Avenue, season 1980/81

In July 1980 Beckenham moved to their present ground in Eden Park Avenue, which they obtained from the London Borough of Bromley on a 25-year lease and, with an eye on the future they also formed a limited company.

On 16 August 1980 Whiteleafe claimed the distinction of becoming the first team to meet Beckenham Town in a competitive fixture at their new headquarters in what was Town's penultimate fixture in the Spartan League. Their final season in the league saw Town finish in eighth spot and, more significantly, reach the final of the Kent Senior Trophy, where they lost 3–1 to a powerful Fisher Athletic side at Bromley's Hayes Lane ground.

June 1981 – Willie Proud

Named as new Town manager, Willie joined the original Beckenham Town in March 1966 and remained until the club disbanded in 1969. After a short spell with Bromley Town FC he switched to Muirheads, who later changed their name to Polychrom. He became a Beckenham Town player again in 1974 when Stanhope Rovers took over the name of the defunct club. Three years before becoming Town's manager Willie had made his first venture into management with Polychrom. Town had always kept a link with the past and one dedicated servant was legend Dotty Morris, who played for Beckenham Town before signing for Crystal Palace, where he played over 70 first team matches. He was also a gifted boxer and became ABA Champion. At the end of his playing career Dot served the club as coach and was on the committee with his wife Shirley, who was treasurer.

Since moving to the Kent League in 1982/83, major honours have so far eluded Beckenham, although they did reach the final of the Kent League Cup in 1985, only to fall once again at the last hurdle, this time at the hands of Greenwich Borough, for whom Mark Gall (now Maidstone United) notched a heartbreaking last-gasp winner.

Over the years Beckenham Town has seen many players go on to become professionals and also progress to become chairmen of football clubs. In 1989/90 Beckenham achieved national recognition through their FA Cup first round qualifying matches against Barking of the Vauxhall League premier division. Following a remarkable 0–0 draw at Barking, Town lost the replay 1–0. The lack of floodlight facilities at Eden Park Avenue prompted Barking chairman Harry Redfern's statement that teams without their own floodlights should not be allowed to enter the FA Cup, or should be forced to replay their matches away, a debate which still rages in non-league circles.

Beckenham Town season 1986/87
Crocks crash to Town terrors!
Beckenham Town 3, Crockenhill 1
FOOTBALL'S a funny game! It is one of the sport's

most annoying cliches – and yet it was never better applied when Town beat title-chasing Crockenhill in the Winstonlead Kent League First Division at a muddy Eden Park Avenue.

Delighted Town boss Bob Chilvers told me afterwards 'you'll have to get me down from the ceiling! I have been saying for several weeks, that one of these days we would give a good side a hiding and today was the day!' Chilvers could not contain his emotions when Town scored their decisive second and third goals leaping on to the pitch to his jig of joy! And who could blame him after the sort of lean spell that Town had endured in recent weeks?

Loyal supporter Alan Drake was affectionately known as 'Mr Radio' – where Alan went his radio went too and he could always be relied upon for up-to-date score flashes from the day's top games. He lived with his parents in Beckenham and travelled home and away with Town – especially during the 1980s when a packed supporters' coach always used to run to the away matches. An enormously popular figure at Beckenham Town, he was delighted when selected to play for Beckenham against an All-Stars team in front of a bumper 1,600 crowd at Eden Park Avenue. Alan had a tremendous singing voice and his rendition of the 'Laughing Policeman' was a popular request at social functions.

The club now boasts an excellent set of flood-lights, hard-standing all round the ground, portable dug-outs – all the facilities required to continue in the Go Travel Kent League and to retain their status as a senior club within the football pyramid. Town has recently been given an improvement grant by the Football Foundation for a new pitch-drainage system and a perimeter fence to deter would-be vandals.

The official Beckenham Town Football Club website is www.beckenhamtownfc.co.uk.

A cold February night at the football ground in Eden Park Avenue. (HS)

Beckenham Football Club

★

Only Club in Borough playing in Senior Amateur Soccer

★

AETOLIAN LEAGUE – See Local Press for Fixtures

Local Players and Spectators welcome

GROUND: STANHOPE GROVE, BECKENHAM

Tel.: BEC. 3719

Edenstone Football Club

Formed in 1965, the founder members of Edenstone Football Club were Peter Gardner, Steve Ellingham and Michael Harrison, the club name deriving from Eden Park and Stone Park, where the three school-boys regularly met before taking the bus to Bromley Technical High School.

Steve's father, George Ellingham, became manager and secretary, the club flourishing under his leader-ship and strong principles of sportsmanship. In 1975 Jack Russell became chair-man, maintaining the high standards of management.

The headquarters and meeting place for all team members and supporters was the Eden Park Hotel and there would regularly be in excess of 20 Edenstone people at the hotel on a Friday.

In 1965 the club entered the Beckenham League fourth division, with barely a player over the age of 18, and played all their home matches at Croydon Road Recreation-Ground. In the second half of this first season several friends joined up to play in the team including two of the Hepburn broth-ers, David and Ritchie, the latter eventually playing in the veterans – a continuous playing record of almost 40 years. Alan Turney joined in the same year as did Ritchie Colley, who went on to become chairman. With this early influx of new players the club formed a second team who entered the Beckenham League fourth division in the 1967/68 season. The club's early success encouraged a number of good local players to join including Brian Russell from Croydon Amateurs and his younger brother Mike, Brian Huxley from Sevenoaks Town, Kent schoolboy Steve Sherer and Dave Hollick, Lloyds Bank's first-choice goalkeeper, enabling the club to climb through the Beckenham League. There was some strong opposition at this time, notably from Penge, Sydenham Gas, Alexandra Park, Thomas Ryan Print, Tower Bridge Police and Croyde – all competent teams playing in what was a very strong Beckenham League.

The quality of the Edenstone players was recog-nised by their regular inclusion in the Beckenham League representative side.

As few of the players had cars it was customary for teams to meet by the Beckenham Regal, where the pathway would be blocked for 20 minutes at a time by footballs and football bags.

Edenstone enjoyed tremendous success in their nine years in the Beckenham League, winning the third, second, first and premier divisions and twice completing the double. In the 1972/73 season they

Edenstone team in the 1972/3 season. Left to right, back row: *Les Clarke, Mark Ellis, Robert Hepburn, Bobby Elliott, Dave Hollick, Ritchie Hepburn, Michael Russell, Steve Shearer, Jack Russell;* front: *David Hepburn, Alan Turney, Brian Russell, Clive Reed, Brian Huxley, Paul Russell (mascot).* Inset: *George Ellingham of Edenstone FC.* (RH)

beat Thomas Ryan Print in the league cup final and won the first division; the following season (1973/74) they won the premier division and beat Sydenham Gas Reserves, having beaten their first team in the previous round, again in the league cup final.

In 1975 the club had what may be considered its finest moment – beating Fisher Athletic in the area final of the London Junior Cup.

The club continued to use council pitches, playing at Harvington, Blake's Recreation-Ground and Croydon Road until, in 1975, they took the opportunity to lease the Bromley Town and Old Bromleians ground off Hayes Lane. The cricket club required money up front, and through the commitment and excellent spirit of those football club members who came forward with financial loans, the use of the new ground was secured. Now with its own ground, the club was able to enter the Kent County League, which provided the challenges it wanted.

In the 1981/82 season Beckenham Youth joined Edenstone and the club continued to flourish, at its peak having five sides.

Honours attained by Edenstone

Beckenham League Third Division Winners
  1967/68
Croydon Junior Cup Finalists, Runners-up
  1968/69
Beckenham League Second Division Winners
  1971/72
Beckenham League First Division Winners
  1972/73
Beckenham League Cup Winners 1972/73
Beckenham League Premier Division Winners
  1973/74
Beckenham League Cup Winners 1973/74
Beckenham Hospital Cup Semi-finalists 1973/74
London Junior Cup Area Winners 1974/75
Joined South East London League 1975/76
South East London League Winners 1977/78
South East London League Cup Runners-up
  1977/78

Kent County Third Division Runners-up 1978/79
Kent County League Cup Finalists, 1978/79
Kent County Second Division Runners-up 1979/80
Kent County First Division Runners-up 1980/81
Bromley League Third XI Second Division
  Runners-up 1980/81

At the beginning of the 1980/81 season Edenstone had four teams playing:

Bromley League 2nd XI Charity Cup Finalists,
  Winners 1982/83
Bromley League 2nd XI Charity Cup Finalists,
  Winners 1983/84
Bromley League 2nd XI Charity Cup Finalists,
  Winners 1984/85
Bromley League 2nd XI Division One Runners-up
  1984/85

Above: *Alderman Crease opens Crease Park, 1936.*
Inset: *The opening of the new parks.* (FB)

In 2004 the club has two veterans sides, for over-35s and for over-45s, with a nucleus of players from the early days of the Beckenham league. The tradition continues of an annual dinner-dance, attended by current and past players and which, in 2005, will include the celebration of the club's 40th anniversary.

Memories of David Hepburn, Edenstone FC

I was born in 1947, about a year after my parents moved into their newly constructed prefab in Eden Park Avenue. Originally designed to last about 10 years, prefabs were a short-term solution to the postwar housing shortage. For the time they were modern, well equipped and comfortable, with a fully fitted kitchen including electric cooker, fridge and running hot water which, together with the modern bathroom with bath, basin and separate loo, made them desirable homes, with rent and rates of 18s.6d. I and my two brothers best remember the large garden backing on to Harvington playing-fields. In the early days I recall walking up to the rear fence to watch the cows grazing but within a few years the field was turned into a sports field, with football in the winter and cricket in the summer.

I spent many long summers with the other boys from the road, in particular the Russells, Turneys and Lowes, playing football and cricket or building camps and climbing trees in the woods behind the fields – an absolute paradise for boys of our age. Those summers seemed to go on and on, and the community spirit and friendships formed then were to last a lifetime.

We regularly attended St John's Church, just a few minutes' walk away, and were members of the choir and the Campaigners. Under the choirmaster, Mr Brookman, we would sometimes attend the church three times on a Sunday and during the spring and summer would look forward to earning extra pocket money by

Alderman Crease at the gate to Crease Park. (PT)

119

Left: *The Rising Sun, 1961.* (JF)

Drink a MANN'S BEER at

'The Rising Sun'

(Frank Tarbard)

OFF LICENCE
VAN DELIVERIES DAILY

*Fresh and Tasty Hot and Cold Snacks
always available*

Glasses Loaned for Wedding and Party Orders

Upper Elmer's End Road, Beckenham

BEC. 1738

Right: *The Dutch team from Wageningen celebrates their football win at the Rising Sun, 1948. Frank Tarbard (pub manager) is standing fifth from the right, wearing a dark suit.* (JF)

Left: *The estimate for rebuilding the White Hart in 1907.* (B)

Estimate
for
Pulling down & Rebuilding
The White Hart Beer House
West Wickham Kent.
for
Messrs Crowley, Brewers, Croydon.

September 1907

Above: *The White Hart in 1926.* (B)

singing at weddings on a Saturday.

The lads that used to meet at Harvington at that time represented the beginnings of what was later to become Edenstone Football Club. It is testimony to our outdoor upbringing that the club, at the time of writing, runs a team known as 'the Legends', which includes many of the 'prefab boys', now well into their fifties. The prefabs were demolished in around 1968/69, some 20 years after construction, but the friendships continue.

Our Pubs

The two pubs which most readily spring to mind are the Eden Park Hotel and the Rising Sun. Built in 1930, in the days when there were live bands on the wireless – Ambrose, Harry Roy, Carroll Gibbons, Geraldo, Charlie Kunz and that strict-tempo maestro of the dance band, Victor Silvester – the Eden Park Hotel has been used for every purpose imaginable.

For Eden Beck Cricket Club, from their ground on the left just under the railway bridge, it was the obvious post-match meeting place, and continues to be so for Beckenham Town FC.

In the Beckenham Charter Celebrations of 1935, Lionel C. Ixer's band played on Friday 27 September at the carnival dance – entry 2s.6d. single and 4s.6d. double, with prizes including carnival novelties. Saturday night and mid-weekly dances became a regular feature.

Civic dinners were held there in the years before the war and the hall was used for meetings of the Eden Park Ratepayers Association, which selected local candidates for council elections and urged the council to preserve open spaces amidst the extensive housing development of the 1930s. A report on the layout of Crease Park may explain why the toddlers' playground is in the middle of the park – it was thought that the children's voices would annoy the residents, especially those who were night workers, and trees were planted round the chutes and slides.

The association urged that there should be a bowling-green in Stanhope Grove Park and one Saturday afternoon in 1936 the Kelsey Park extension, Crease Park and Stanhope Grove Park were all officially opened – a great occasion for Eden Park. Peter Mordey celebrated his sixth birthday at the Eden Park Hotel in 1939, his parents being the proprietors.

In the first year of the Second World War evacuation was not considered necessary for the children of Beckenham, although those from Haseltine Road, in next door Sydenham, left by train for Sussex on 1 September 1939. Until shelters were dug at Marian Vian, pupils were taught in small groups in houses close to their homes. Naturally the Eden Park Hotel rose to the occasion and a class was held there.

In the 1960s Roman Catholic services were held in the ballroom at the back of the premises and in the spring of 1963 a motor club was formed by the schoolmates, workmates, customers and friends of Stoneham's garage, their first event being a Sunday treasure hunt in September. The proceeds raised by a rally and dance were enough for Stoneham's garage to provide the body unit needed for a new ambulance – Mrs Stoneham was Commandant of the New Addington Red Cross at the time. With meetings held at the Eden Park Hotel, the West Wickham Garage and Squires timber joined the motor club, renamed the Borough 19 Motor Club (when Beckenham and Bromley became London Borough 19) and affiliated to the RAC.

In the late 1960s and early '70s, when Jim Survey was manager of the hotel, world-famous pop groups came to play: the Zodiac Club with Alvin Lee on 28 March 1968; the Herd with lead singer Peter Framton on 9 and 30 May 1968. Peter, whose grandfather lived in Merlin Grove, had attended Bromley Technical High School. On 12, 19, and 26 February 1970 Mott the Hoople, Juicy Lucy and Quintessence played, followed by the group Free on 5 March. Mott the Hoople had a No. 1 hit with 'All the Young Dudes', written by David Bowie, and Free had hits

A civic dinner at the Eden Park Hotel, 26 October 1938, and left, Beckenham Town's Smoking Concert programme, 1950. (FB)

Elmers End Road, just a lane at the time, with Holly Lodge (centre) and the Rising Sun (right), c.1900. (J&B)

Above: *Tom Holden's car outside his greengrocery with the Eden Park Hotel in view.* (RW)

Inset: *The hotel sign, which in 2004 reads 'Toby's Carvery'.* (FB)

with 'All Right Now' and 'My Brother Jake.'

The inaugural dinner of Langley Park Rotary Club was another auspicious occasion, held at the Eden Park Hotel on 7 April 1975. Meetings were held there until the membership became too large.

Food has always been available at the hotel, which quickly became a favourite place for local workers to relax at lunchtime and for more leisurely celebrations – sixth-formers and staff from Langley Park schools especially favoured it!

With St John's Church nearby, the Eden Park Hotel was and still is the first place considered for wedding receptions and for reunions, nostalgia playing its part in erasing the intervening years. One of the more

recent groups to meet at the hotel is the Beckenham Round Table, founded in 1936 as member club 204. At the time of writing members meet monthly in the Toby Carvery for a meal and to plan charity events and support the Antony Nolan Bone Marrow Trust and WhizzKidz, as well as many local charities.

The Rising Sun is much older and is marked on old maps as a beerhouse, although not with its present name. The Acts of Parliament of 1828 and 1830 abolishing control of beershops resulted in a large increase in their number, and it is likely that the Rising Sun dates from at least this time. In the census of 1851 Milwood, with his family, was the beerhouse keeper. By 1861 it was called the Rising Sun, with retailers William and Mary Blazey. The proprietor in 1871 was Robert Eaglestone, with wife Ann and son Walter.

In the early 1900s the brewers supplying the Rising Sun were Mann, Crossman & Paulin Ltd who in 1958 joined Watney, Combe, Reid & Co. Ltd to

The White Hart on Mother's Day, 2004. (B)

become Watney Mann Ltd. It was Combe and Co. Ltd who took over from William Cator & Co., brewers of Old Street, London, in 1799, a French boarding party having killed William in the Bay of Bengal on his way to Calcutta. William was the brother of John and Joseph Cator of Beckenham – an interesting link with our early beerhouses. There could have been a beerhouse on the present Rising Sun site, supplied by William Cator, as far back as 1789, perhaps when John Cator, lord of the manor of Beckenham, was asked in the late 1700s to build four cottages at Upper Elmers End. Until the 1960s there were two sets of cottages in Upper Elmers End Road, those near the Rising Sun (known as the Rising Sun cottages) being a group of eight with the front doors in pairs and occupied by workers from surrounding farms. These were demolished in 1962, partly to make way for the extension to Ron Stoneham's petrol station. The second group was of four cottages, replaced by the blocks of council flats on the bend of the road. It is not clear which set of cottages, if either, was owned by the Cators.

The Rising Sun kept its name for 140 years. It is certain that the present building, for a short time called the Tudor Rose, is about 100 years old: in 1902, in the early hours of the morning, a fire, cause unknown, broke out and all seven rooms were completely gutted. An old building with seasoned timbers, the firemen, there within ten minutes of being called, could not save it from complete destruction. There had been plans for extensive alterations to the pub, which belonged to the Monks Orchard estate and had previously been let out on long leases.

The White Hart in West Wickham is probably older than the Rising Sun, having taken its licence from the King's Arms next door in 1821. The King's Arms was a coaching inn listed in the Licensed Victualler's registers from 1753–1816. It was reached by a bridge over the River Beck and in 1821 was acquired by Edward Little who renamed it Pond House, passing the licence to the adjacent beerhouse. Edward's brother William, a tailor from Vauxhall, sold Pond House in 1863 to Lewis Loyd for £1,130 in an auction at Garraways. It was demolished in 1946 after it suffered irreparable damage when a doodle-bug fell in the High Street. From the late 1960s the manager of the White Hart was a Mr Hart, whose two sons attended Hawes Down Secondary School.

Although the pond is filled in, the Beck continues its way through High Broom Wood and the White Hart survives. The 1821 beerhouse was pulled down and rebuilt in 1907 for Messrs Crowley, brewers of Croydon. Estimates for the work varied between £1,300 and £1,662 and the new building included a dovecot with seven compartments. The present White Hart, Eden Park Hotel and the Tudor Rose are thus all twentieth-century buildings.

Pond Cottage Lane in West Wickham leads to the permanent caravan site of Crittendene, which occupies the land once belonging to Pond House and is now owned by the Crittendens who live on the adjacent property.

High Broom Wood

Increasingly over the last 30 years there has been a tendency to open up local woodland to the public and at the same time reduce its management, with the result that old trees uprooted by gales are left leaning against others at crazy angles and woodland herbs have disappeared. The erosion of the bluebells in Kelsey Park once the fences were removed is an example, as is the disappearance of both townhall clock (*Adoxa moschatellina*) and woodruff (*Galium odoratum*) from Spring Park Woods and the near extinction of the common dog violet (*Viola riviniana*) from Harvington.

Fortunately *A. moschatellina* is still flourishing in High Broom Wood, its little terminal flower head with four green 'clock faces' looking out in different directions with a fifth staring up into the sky.

In 2002 flowers bloomed very early and by 23 March the bluebells and yellow archangel (*Lamiastrum galeobdolon argentatum*) had already begun to open. They were preceded by masses of lesser celandine (*Ranunculus ficaria*), covering the ground on either side of the river with patches of wood anemones (*Anemone nemorosa*), in the less-trodden places and a strong growth of marsh marigolds (*Caltha palustris*) in the marshy areas, including a clump on the edge of the river bank. At two sites, well spaced apart, the uncommon golden saxifrage (*Chrysosplenium oppositifolium*), also appropriately named lady's cushion and buttered eggs, formed patches at the edge of the river.

Less common were wood sorrel (*Oxalis acetosella*), with its attractive light green leaves, dogs' mercury (*Mercurialis perennis*) and some lavender-pink milk-maids (*Cardamine pratensis*).

The only really common weed was wavy bittercress (*Cardamine flexuosa*), with white and red deadnettles growing close to the entrances to the wood.

Proximity to housing was evidenced by the dumping of such household rubbish as a sink, settee, metal table frame and a child's easy chair. Garden shrubs had established themselves – the red camellia, the yellow batchelor's buttons (*Kerria japonica*) and the red berries of the spotted laurel (*Aucuba japonica var. maculatum*) were easy to see. There were also daffodils scattered through the wood with the yellow archangel, with its large, silvery leaves, also possibly a naturalised garden escapee.

Garlic mustard (*Alliaria petiolata*) was growing strongly along the edges of the paths and would soon be in flower, with cow parsley or Queen Anne's lace (*Anthriscus sylvestris*) much in evidence throughout the woodland. Cuckoo pint (*Arum maculatum*) was widely distributed, with one patch of the alien *Arum italicum*.

With the warm interval at the end of March, the nettles (*Urtica dioica*), hogweed (*Heracleum spondylium*), dandelion (*Taraxacum officinalis*), ground elder (*Aegopodium podograria*) and goosegrass (*Galium aparine*) were well on their way to taking over once the early woodland flowers had died down but the blues of ground ivy (*Nepeta hederacea*), ivy-leaved speedwell (*Veronica hederifolia*) and the wood forget-me-not (*Myosotis sylvatica*) had started to show, along with the green of alkanet (*Pentaglottis sempervirens*).

At the edge of the woodland on the Monks Orchard side was a spread of common comfrey (*Symphytum officinale*) as March came to a close, as well as some honesty (*Lunaria annua*).

April began with warm weather and bluebells were opening everywhere. The earlier bluebells were *Endymion hispanicus* with the true British bluebell *(E. non scriptus)*, which is also in evidence, later flowering, purple-blue, drooping and of more delicate construction. There were two garden escapees at the South Eden Park Road end of the wood, one the Cornish three-cornered leek (*Allium triquetrum*), so called because of its three-sided stem, and also called the snowbell, the inflorescence being an umbel of white bells drooping to one side. The other was a saxifrage, a plant related to London Pride but from a group of hardy perennials of the genus *Heuchera* with pale yellow flowers. Golden saxifrage, townhall clock, marsh marigolds, wood sorrel, yellow archangel, milkmaids, bluebells, wood anemones and lesser celandine were all at their best here. A week later, ramsons (*Allium ursinum*) were beginning to show at the other end of the wood. Closely related to and superficially resembling *A. triquetum*, its leaves are broad and its flowers are in star-like umbels, the petals lacking the green line on the back. The leaves smell strongly of garlic and can be used in a fish sauce. One has to be careful, however, not to confuse them with white bluebells!

There are many blackcurrant bushes *(Ribes nigra)* in the wood, now in flower and recognised by the aromatic leaves, as well as large patches of herb robert (*Geranium robertianum*). The pendulous sedge (*Carex pendula*) grows in substantial clumps a couple of metres high along the riverside. Each graceful drooping inflorescence is composed of one or two yellow male spikes with four or five brown female spikes below.

By the middle of April greater stitchwort (*Stellaria holostea*) and the small periwinkle (*Vinca minor*) were in flower. The rarely reported shining cranesbill (*Geranium lucidum*) was growing against the fence at the Monks Orchard Road entrance. Its flowers are tiny and pink with unnotched petals and the leaves are glossy.

At the end of April, as the hawthorn (*Crataegus monogyna*) came into flower, the red campion (*Silene dioica*) appeared by the riverside, its pale pink colour suggesting that it was probably a hybrid with the white campion. By now, the English bluebells (*E. non scriptus*) were at their best throughout the wood.

The cuckoo pint was producing its pale-green hooded spathe containing a purple spadix which will later bear a spike of bright orange berries. In the case of *A. italicum* the spadix is yellow. Wood avens, also called herb bennet (*Geum urbanum*) were beginning to produce their yellow flowers, which by June would turn into masses of hooked achenes.

The first of May brought two cup-shaped yellow flowers, one common and the other an unusual find. The creeping buttercups had been building up their leaves for a time but suddenly the clumps were covered with the bright yellow cups of petals with the sepals close up underneath, unlike the bulbous buttercup where the sepals are reflexed. The yellow-flowered strawberry was the other yellow flower, appearing as a mat on the bank near the stepping stones. This originated in India and is rarely found growing wild in the UK. A pink-flowered strawberry grows in St George's churchyard, Beckenham.

The bright blue flowers of another speedwell could be seen at the edges of the paths in early May, more strikingly blue than its earlier cousin. This was Germander speedwell (*Veronica chamaedrys*), identified by the two opposite rows of hairs on the stems.

By the end of May the tree canopy was complete and most of the spring flowers fruiting. Wood avens was flowering all along the paths and some lanky guelder roses (*Viburnum opulus*) were in bloom, although nothing in comparison with those planted in the South Norwood Country Park. There is a noticeable contrast between the two park areas, one Croydon the other Bromley. The SNCP has a regular warden in attendance every day but the barely managed High Broom Wood has only an occasional visit. The litter bin near to the Monk's Orchard Road entrance is rarely emptied and a silver birch fallen across the path there was left obstructing it for too long. When an ash tree split in the SNCP it was removed within 24 hours. The same cannot be said for Harvington, where a tree obstructed the path by the river at the Manor Way entrance for weeks. The policy now in Bromley seems to be to spend money once in ten years or so on a 'refit' and then to leave the parks to look after themselves. Nevertheless, High Broom Wood is an asset, a credit to the borough and a fitting example of what could be applied elsewhere, e.g. St James' Stream in the grounds of Bethlem Royal Hospital.

Four other garden escapees were flowering, one a form of periwinkle with blue-purple star-shaped flowers, (possibly *Vinca major var. oxyloba*) growing at the West Wickham end, the second patches of pink-flowered hardy geraniums, the third St John's Wort (mostly by the river), tutsan (*Hypericum androsaemum*) and the invasive bellflower, *Campanula poscharskyana*. The hard rush (*Juncus inflexus*)

Lucy, Pat Manning's West Highland terrier, on the stepping stones over the River Beck in High Broom Wood.

(*Calystegia silvatica*) climbing up. Bracken (*Pteridium aquilinum*) was also beginning to grow through everywhere with patches of male fern (*Drypteris felix mas*). Japanese knotweed (*Reynoutria japonica*) grew vigorously by the river. By the paths were a few daisies (*Bellis perennis*), some white clover (*Trifolium repens*), hedge mustard (*Sisymbrium officinale*) and patches of chickweed (*Stellaria media*) but oddly there were no thistles in evidence.

The canopy is dominated by old alder trees (*Alnus glutinosa*) that seem to have been coppiced long ago as many grow several trunks from the same place. They are unusually tall and there are birch trees growing equally high among them. These appear to be silver birch (*Betula pendula*) or hybrids and many have come to the end of their lives. A few hybrid oaks (*Quercus sp.*) are there, with horse chestnut (*Aesculus hippocastanum*) and the sweet chestnut (*Castanea sativa*), many trees of which still come into leaf although blown over by the storms of previous years. Field maples (*Acer campestre*), sycamores (*Acer pseudoplatinus*) and a red-leaved maple (*Acer sp.*) are quite common. There are at least two very old trees of false acacia (*Robinia pseudoacacia*) and some willows (probably *Salix nigra*), with a few ash trees (*Fraxinus excelsior*).

The shrub layer is composed of hazel, (*Corylus avellana*), hawthorn (*Crataegus monogyna*), elder (*Sambucus nigra*), a few dog roses (*Rosa canina*) and guelder roses (*Viburnum opulus*), holly (*Ilex aquifolium*), apple (*Malus sp.*), brambles (*Rubus fruticosus agg*), snowberry (*Symphoricarpos rivularia*), butterfly bush (*Buddleia davidii*), garden privet (*Ligustrum ovalifolium*), the occasional barberry (*Berberis vulgaris*) and laurel (*Laurus sp.*).

A few other plants, although they are not as common, have been reported in this area: the dogwood (*Cornus sericea*), *Cotoneaster franchetii*, alder buckthorn (*Frangula alnus*), *Hyacinthus x massartiana*, redcurrant (*Ribes rubrum*), water chickweed (*Myosoton aquaticum*) and the fern *Polystichum setiferum*. Omitted from this survey are the grasses (*Gramineae*) and the majority of the non-flowering plants, although there are several mosses, including the liverwort *Pellia* and fungi present. Conifers are largely absent apart from an occasional yew sapling.

and the white beak sedge (*Rhynchospora alba*) were growing by the river where the graceful fronds of the broad buckler fern (*Dryopteris dilatata*) covered the banks together with some harts-tongue fern (*Phyllitis scolopendrium*).

The growth of flora during late spring was noticeably coarser, with brambles in flower, curled dock (*Rumex crispus*), broadleaved dock (*Rumex obtusifolius*), hedge woundwort (*Stachys sylvatica*), enchanter's nightshade (*Circea lutetiana*), greater burdock (*Arctium lappa*), greater plantain (*Plantago major*) and the willowherbs (*Epilobium hirsutum* and *E. montanum*) all in evidence. The ground is largely covered in ivy (*Hedera helix*) and there is honeysuckle (*Lonicera periclimenum*) in the shrub layer with white bryony (*Bryonia dioica*) and greater bindweed

Mystery Page

Do you recognise these local landmarks?
Turn to page 160 to find out if your answers are correct.

A

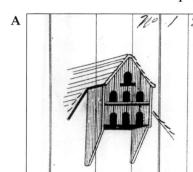

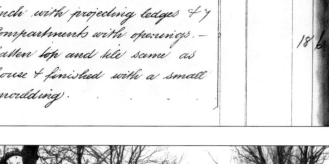

N° 1 *Deal Dovecote as sketch with 1½" shaped ends remainder out of inch with projecting ledges & 7 compartments with openings.— batten top and tile same as house & finished with a small moulding.*

18/6

B

C

D

E

CHAPTER 6

The Churches of Monks Orchard and Eden Park

Far left: St John's Church magazine, 1950. (ES)

Left: The old parish church of St George.

For many centuries Beckenham was served by the parish church of St George's, with records dating back to 1539 and gravestones in the churchyard dating from 1678, with older memorials inside the church. There were only about 1,000 people living in the district in 1800 but the population explosion that followed the sale of land for building and the arrival of the railways led to a corresponding burst of church building. First came St John the Evangelist in Shirley in 1856, St Paul's on the Cator estate in 1864, St Mary's in Shortlands in 1868, the temporary iron church of Christchurch in 1873, Holy Trinity and St Barnabas in 1878 and St James' in 1879. Nonconformist churches included Elm Road Baptist in 1883, the Congregational church in 1888,

Churchfields Road Mission Hall in 1886 and St Augustine's in 1910. Without a doubt the most prominent church in the district has been St John's in Eden Park Avenue, which was not ready for use until 1933. Dating from 1952, there was also St George's in Elstan Way and St Edmund's RC Church, which was dedicated in 1938.

In the parish of St James, St John's Church is the daughter church of Christchurch and was established as an evangelical alternative for those who disliked the rituals of 'high' church. It was designed to serve the housing developments of Eden Park. In 1932 Merlin Grove and Eden Way were still under construction, with Ernest Grove, Ronald Close and Monks Orchard Road hardly begun and Links Way

Laying the foundation-stone of St John's church hall. (M&AD)

Julie Conway comes second as a pedestrian crossing in the fancy dress at St John's, 1962. (AC)

non-existent. Stonepark Avenue was still an unmade road adjoining the footpath of Village Way. Maps of the period show the site of the church as being St John's Field on which stood Eden Hall, demolished in about 1890. The land, then owned by a Mrs Petley and valued at £1,000, was donated for the building of the church and in February 1931 Christchurch voted to start construction, with subsequent congregations donating the necessary money. Sunday afternoon services were held in Mrs Petley's meadows and the corrugated iron mission hall, which had stood near Shaftesbury Road in Croydon Road, was dismantled and re-erected as St John's church hall. The foundation-stone of the new building was laid on St John the Baptist's Day (24 June) 1932 by the Rt Revd E.A. Knox, aged 84. Designed by Pite, Son & Fairweather and built by J. Elliman & Son, the church was dedicated by the bishop exactly one year later. It had cost about £18,500 with over 500 subscribers. As well as the land for the church and vicarage, the Petley family also donated the chancel, the organ and the stained-glass St John the Baptist window. The St John's magazine of July 1950 carried a report of a new window in the chapel, dedicated to Mr and Mrs Petley, which was to replace that totally destroyed in the war. The font was a gift from a family who had lost their first child, Tony Thorpe, at the age of 10 months in 1926. The pulpit came from the builders. On the consecration of the church as a separate entity in 1936 an interesting decision was made over vehicular access, with the southern entrance becoming the way in – now you know who to blame for having to cross the flow of traffic both on the way in and on the way out!

Clearly visible on aerial photographs, the worst damage to the church was caused by a V2 rocket, one of only two to fall on Beckenham, which severely damaged the vicarage and choir vestry and destroyed the church hall. In 1956 war damage compensation contributed to the £14,701 needed to rebuild the hall, the societies that have since used it being almost too numerous to mention. The St John's magazine of April 1956 (price 4d.), announced the expected opening of the new hall on 7 June and mentioned the Campaigners' upcoming jobs week and cruise on the Broads, while the Sunday school planned to go to Chessington Zoo by coach (4s.9d. including zoo and circus) and the Women's Meeting were off to Bognor for the day.

In John Somerville Meikle's *The Spreading Chestnut Tree* is an account of St John's between 1932 and 1982 and certainly many of our contributors fondly remember their local church.

St James' Church in Elmers End

Services began in Elmers End when Catherine Marsh, sister-in-law of the Revd Chalmers, rector of the parish church, held services there from 1855 in a labourer's cottage. In 1865 a small iron church was erected opposite Goddard Road and approached by a rustic bridge over the stream flowing beside the road from Upper Elmers End.

With the donation in 1879 of a plot of land by Mr W.S. Forster and the collection of £700, a committee was formed to raise funds from local landowners to build a permanent church. From 1873 the rector of St George's had been William Cator of the influential Beckenham Cators, whose appeals to fund the new church were well received. Architect Sir Alex Rose Stenning supplied plans for builder Mr John Cox and at a cost of £3,000 both church and school were planned. Robert Borrowman, who subsequently wrote *Beckenham Past and Present*, was one of the three trustees.

The first stone was laid by Lewis Loyd of Monks Orchard on 3 August 1879 and by November Bishop Tufnell had dedicated the nave, with the Revd Alfred Barber as priest. The chancel was added in 1888 and the church consecrated on 19 January 1889. The school opened in October 1880 and of the 900 population of Elmers End, accommodated 91 boys and girls and 49 infants, with fees of 3d. for the first child and 2d. for each sibling. Six months later HM Inspectors reported excellent teaching and by 1922 the school was becoming crowded. Then, with the creation in November 1924 of St James' as a new parish, its buildings were needed for the parsonage. The Rochester Diocesan Board removed the school from its list from 1 June 1930, when it was taken over by Marian Vian.

The parish of St James' stretches from Queen's Road to Aylesford Avenue and from Stanhope Grove to Dorset Road on the other side of the railway line.

Peggy Foster was a tireless supporter of St James' and a deaconess from 1951 to 1966. While she was a member of staff at Langley Park School for Girls, Father Brassell would often visit to discuss social matters such as marriage and abortion.

Percy Jones

On the reredos in St James' Church is a painting by A.K. Lawrence, RA. Called 'The Resurrection', it shows the Lord, attended by two Archangels, rising from the grave towards a small bright cloud in the extreme top centre. The background, a Kent landscape, symbolises local devotion to the Resurrection. This painting was donated in memory of lay reader Percy Jones, and there is a bronze plate on the Communion step which reads: 'To the glory of God, in loving memory of Percy Jones, lay reader of this church, died January 4 1953.'

St John's of Shirley

The origin of St John's was the Shirley Chapel, a simple rectangular building consecrated in 1836 to

The lych-gate at St John's, provided by Lewis Loyd.

The old wooden St George's Church in Elstan Way, now used as the church hall. (NT)

serve the growing population of hamlets Stroud Green and Upper and Lower Shirley. The chapel was built from porous bricks and uncomfortably damp, as well as being too small for the congregation, and in 1847 the Archdeacon instructed the Revd Matthew Farrer to build a new church. This, however, was only achieved with the zeal and co-operation of Lewis Loyd when he became resident in Addington parish and accepted the post of churchwarden, holding meetings in 1854 at his mansion, Wickham Park, to settle the details. Lewis and the Earl of Eldon, of Shirley House, donated £1,000 each and Gilbert Scott was asked to design a church costing £3,600. The foundation-stone was laid that same year by the Archbishop of Canterbury, the balance of

money required coming from all over Croydon. Consecration of the church, dedicated to St John the Evangelist, took place on 3 July 1856. Sadly, in this same year, Matthew Farrer's second wife died, leaving him with two young sons and a daughter. His first wife had died with their infant child in 1844, a year after their marriage. He remained vicar until 1879, when he retired to manage the Yorkshire estates of his elder brother, and on his death in 1889 was buried beside his wife and fourth son at the south-east corner of the churchyard.

Money for the running of the church was always a problem, its main source of income being from pew rents but most of its congregation were poor. However Lewis Loyd could always be depended

The Brownies and Guides of St George the Martyr. (M&AD)

Above: *Monks Orchard TWG on an outing to Crystal Palace Park.* (MOTG)

Left: *Hazel Croissant in her Easter bonnet, c.1992, when the TWG had just started to use St George's church hall.* (M&AD)

upon to contribute to church funds and in 1873 gave a lych-gate to the church. The Revd William Wilks took over in 1880 and at his own expense persuaded the Croydon Gas Co. to extend its gas mains to light the church, making evening services possible. With the church becoming steadily more popular, Lewis Loyd, in addition to choir stalls, had an organ installed in a chamber on the south side. Undamaged during the Second World War, the old Lewis and Compton organ survived for over 100 years until replaced in 1992 by a Danis Frobenius organ, at a cost of £150,000.

The influence of the Revd Wilks cannot be under-estimated. Before the introduction of the welfare state it was the Church which cared for the poor and Revd Wilks started numerous clubs, including the Coal Club, the Shoe Club, the Clothing Club, the Choir Boys' Clothing Club, the Slate Club, the Cricket Club and the Children's Church Guild. Lewis Loyd was the President of the Working Men's Club, which he opened on 25 April 1886.

The Revd Wilks is permanently remembered in the name of Wilks Gardens, off Orchard Avenue – particularly apt as he had a great love of gardening and, from wild poppies, developed the Shirley poppy, whose colours vary from bright red to white

Anne Gammon's Medau dance group takes time off for Christmas lunch at St George's hall, 2002.
Left to right, back row: *Joan, Anne, Brenda, Pat, Jean, Mary, Audrey;*
middle row: *Mary, Evelyn, Hazel;* front row: *Pat, Marjorie, Anne.*

with all shades of pink in between, with a white centre in place of the black of the wild flower. The mace carried by the mayors of Croydon bears a Shirley poppy motif. Vicar of St John's for 35 years, on his retirement the Revd Wilks bought seven acres of ground adjoining the vicarage and planted shrubs from all over the world. He built a house which he called 'The Wilderness', where he died some 10 years later.

Lord Ashburton had provided three acres of land for the churchyard, with Lord Eldon extending it by another three acres in 1907, and with many well-to-do Croydon families buried here, there is not another church in the vicinity with so many impressive memorials. Like other local churches, it was badly damaged during the Second World War, when more doodlebugs fell on Croydon than on any other London borough. St John's unlucky day was 25 July 1944, when a doodlebug fell at 2.20p.m. in Spring Park Road. While the church roof was badly damaged and all the windows blown out, the school was demolished, being rebuilt in 1953. When it opened its doors in June 1954, parents were putting children as young as one year old on the waiting list for admission!

St George the Martyr in Elstan Way

As early as 1924 it became apparent that a new place of worship would be required for the developing Monks Orchard estate. The Revd Wilk's successor, the Revd George Jones of St John's, with the help of Arthur Lloyd, acquired the site of the present church in Elstan Way. In 1937 the wooden hall used by so many societies today was built at a cost of £1,750 and became the first church under the Revd Harold Welles. On the sale of All Hallows in Lombard Street, £12,000 was reserved for a permanent building and the present church and vicarage were built in 1952 with the Revd Bromley Walker the first incumbent of the new parish.

Situated among the housing developments of the old Ham Farm beside the surviving farm cottages, St George's church hall is, at the time of writing, a striking centre of church-based and community activities, with the children's crèche, Mothers' Union, St George's club, whist drives, Rainbows, Brownies, Medau dancing, Andy Pandy club, Harmony dance club, child health clinic, police surgeries, Pop-in and, since 1992, the Townswomen's Guild, which used to meet in the Monks Orchard Primary School. Guides, Beavers, Cubs and Scouts are held in the Scout hut, a gift from Mr J.L. Wild in 1937. The 2003 church fête, organised by Karen and Glyn Jones, raised an astonishing £1,450.

St Edmund's

The striking Roman Catholic Church of St Edmund's in Village Way had much more humble beginnings. Mary McInally tells the story of how St Edmund's came about in her book about the Beckenham School, *Minshull House*:

In 1916, my parents moved to what was then a small road off the main street, called Village Way. There was one detached house at the village end, a bungalow in the far opposite corner and six small terraced houses in between. There was woodland at the top of the road and a small farm next to the Pavilion cinema in the High Street. St Edmund's Church and hall were housed in two adjoining pebble-dashed buildings beside some wasteland opposite the farm. The floors of the temporary church were bare wood on which were rows of stained pine benches and kneelers. The organist [my father] had a small stool to sit on and it collapsed one day as he sat on it during Father Donovan's sermon! Regular whist drives, jumble sales and summer fêtes held to raise money were so successful that the new church was completed in 1938 on the green opposite the temporary buildings. It was fitted with a Hammond organ, plus 'Stations of the Cross' by Eric Gill and Jacob Epstein's 'Virgin Mary and Child' above the front entrance doors. It fits well with the modern Gothic design of the church although Archbishop Peter Amigo who blessed the new building did not appreciate it.

Langley Farm, from a drawing by Mrs Lancelot Holland in 1828. (NL)

The Good Samaritan memorial window was installed in memory of Mary's father.

Meanwhile the woodland and farm were sold to developers. Trees were felled, ground was levelled and Irish labourers were employed to build houses all the way up Village Way.

By 1936 it was ready to become the busy through-road that it is today, with St Edmund's Church occupying a prime position just off the High Street.

Upstairs and Downstairs with the Hollands

In the past, Beckenham society typified the concept of upstairs and downstairs and there is no better example of this than two families called Holland in the early 1800s.

The 'upstairs' family was that of Lancelot Holland and his wife Charlotte Mary Peters. In 1828, as their family grew and grew, they moved from a very comfortable London home to Langley Farm off South Eden Park Road. The last of their 15 children was Eleanor Mary, born in 1831, and it is from her writings that we find out with absolute certainty about the life that they all lived.

Father had only one brother, Uncle Henry, who lived with Aunt Caroline the spinster sister. He was a great man in our youth and so handsome. He had a noble head with lovely silvery locks at the back and such lovely dark eyes. He was rich and excessively benevolent and invented a fund to assist men imprisoned for debt, also helping in hospitals. Uncle Henry lived to be 80 and Aunt Caroline lived on alone until she died at 85. Our mother, before marriage, was the eblonisante Miss Peters and had reddish gold hair, brilliant complexion and pretty teeth.

We inherit tastes for landscape gardening from great-grandfather Lancelot Capability Brown and for architecture from grandfather Henry Holland. After dinner at 6.30p.m., dressed in low bodices and with bare arms, we went out with our shawls and wandered about the valley and new kitchen garden. Just one acre

with roses, all standards in rows, a broad walk with all kinds of flowers on each side, masses of honeysuckles, a path of pink acacia and the currant bushes, raspberries, strawberries, cherries, apples and plums in the kitchen garden.

By contrast, the 'downstairs' family was that of William and Martha Holland who, at least from the time of the 1851 census, lived in the middle of Beckenham in Kelsey cottages. Neither was native to Beckenham, Martha Street being from Harrow in Middlesex and William from Lewes in East Sussex, but they married in Beckenham in 1833 and all their children, starting with Thomas Christmas (possibly Christian) in about 1839, were baptised at St George's. Only Thomas was destined to carry on the family name as William, Catherine and Rebecca remained unmarried and Henry died in an accident in Beckenham in 1862. On the evening of Friday 10 February, Henry, aged 16, was out playing with the boys when Andrew Maynard, the son of one of Squire Lea Wilson's gardeners, came and interfered with their game. Henry started a fight with Andrew which ended in a stabbing, Henry being taken to the George, where his progress was satisfactory, and then transferred to Guy's Hospital. On Monday 3 March, however, he died and Andrew was charged at Maidstone Assizes with manslaughter. Henry was buried in St George's churchyard on 7 March.

As a young man, Thomas married Emily Jane of Kingston, the couple and their baby, Edward, at first living with his parents, William and Martha. Ten years later, in 1871, they had moved to one of the Cator Cottages in Croydon Road, on the way to Elmers End and they had lost little Edward (who died aged six in September 1866) and had three more boys – Thomas Henry, George and James John. They were soon to benefit from the Birkbeck housing estate, built from 1879 for the labourers and workers of the big estates. By 1881 Thomas was living in Arthur Road (later Churchfields Road), with five daughters and another son, Frederick.

CHAPTER 7

Steps on the Way
to Bromley Borough

The Beckenham coat of arms complete with its Tudor supporters (from Bromley Museum archives) and inset the pre-Charter Arms before the supporters were added in 1935. The plaque is stored in Bromley Museum.

Dr James Henry Bennett receives his freeman award in the council chamber of Beckenham town hall. Note the coat of arms over the fireplace and the mace on its stand. (CW)

There have been seven forms of local government in Beckenham. Parish business was the responsibility of the Common Law Vestry until the Public Health Act of 1872, when it passed into the hands of the Rural Sanitary Authority – water-borne diseases such as cholera were rife in the village. Further changes came thick and fast, the Parochial Committee being followed by the Local Board from 1880 until 1894, when the High Street was decked with flags and bunting wishing 'Success to the Local Board' and 'Prosperity to Beckenham'.

Great celebrations heralded the advent of the Urban District Council that resulted from a new Local Government Act. From that time on, Beckenham worked towards becoming a borough in its own right. It amalgamated with West Wickham and prepared for its charter by building the town hall in Church Avenue on the site of the rectory, which

had been designed by Robert Adam in 1788 – there is an Adam fireplace, saved from the rectory, in the mayor's parlour at the Civic Centre at Stockwell Close. The Duke of Kent opened the town hall in 1932, the UDC having obtained a grant of Arms (shield and crest) in 1931 to which Tudor supporters were added in 1935, the year of the silver jubilee of George V, as the UDC became the new Borough of Beckenham. It was granted a Borough Charter with Sir Josiah Stamp GCB, GBE as charter mayor.

After the presentation of the charter in Croydon Road Recreation-Ground (otherwise known as Croydon Rec), the main event of the day was the parade of decorated vehicles in two sections, Beckenham and West Wickham, with the first assembling at Ravenscroft Road and the second at Monks Orchard Road. They met at the war memorial, turned up Rectory Road and then processed through the High Street on their way to the recreation-ground, taking about three hours. There were ten classes, that of historical tableaux including the stagecoach carrying Dr Samuel Johnson on a visit to

Left: *Alan and Robert Duncan on the Syme &
Duncan float.* (M&AD)

Below: *Business floats passing the Home &
Colonial store in Beckenham High Street
during the 1937 coronation celebrations.*
(M&AD)

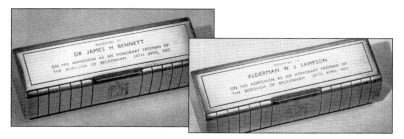

Left: *The bronze caskets holding the
freeman scrolls of Dr James Henry
Bennett and Alderman William
Joseph Sampson.* (CW)

Below: *The admission of Winston
Churchill as freeman of Beckenham.*
(FB)

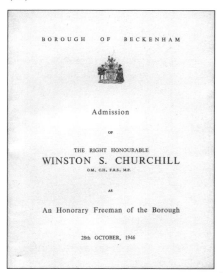

*Sir Winston Churchill examines his award of freeman of the Borough
of Beckenham.* (FB)

Left: *The mayor's entourage leaves St George's Church after the civic christening of Felicity Edden.* (FB)

Far left below: *Dr Edden's polling card for the Eden Park ward.* (FB)

Below left: *Dr Edden of Eden Park Avenue.* (JF)

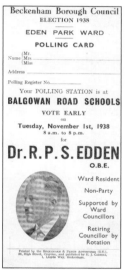

John Cator at Beckenham Place. Children aged between 10 and 16 could enter their decorated cycles, with decorated motor or horse-drawn vehicles, both private and trade, providing other classes.

The flags were out again in 1937 to celebrate the coronation of George VI, and in 1953 four-times mayor, Alderman Sampson, led the procession for the coronation of Elizabeth II. In 1939 many plans came to fruition, such as the erection of new buildings including the main Beckenham Post Office (near the war memorial), Beckenham central library and the West Wickham fire station in Glebe Way; the long-awaited Odeon cinema at Elmers End was built on the site of a picturesque old cottage, once used for the film *Blossoms*; the Duchess of Gloucester opened the extension to Beckenham Hospital; the hall of St John's Church in Eden Park Avenue was planned and, at the end of the year, the Beckenham and Penge Maternity Home (later the Stonepark Maternity Home) opened in Stone Park Avenue. The first baby born there, on Christmas day, was Lesley

Smith and the mayor of Beckenham, Alderman Jeff, presented her with a silver cup.

Except for St John's church hall, all of these buildings welcomed so proudly in 1939, have either been demolished, like the town hall, or are much less used. While Beckenham was still a borough, the honour of freeman was granted to Sir Winston Churchill, Sir Josiah Stamp and Aldermen Dr James Henry Bennett, James Crease and William Joseph Sampson. Among the words spoken when the resolution was passed to honour Churchill were the following:

When the danger was greatest and there seemed little if any ground for hope that we could possibly survive the ordeal, then it was that Mr Churchill constantly rallied and supported us and the rest of the nation by his words and strength of purpose. By his staunchness, determination and confidence, however dark the prospect, he gave us hope and encouragement, inspiring us to carry on to meet our ordeal with courage and patience and to unite in doing what little we could in the common cause of liberty.

Designed by wartime Civil Defence staff officer Mr Sindall, the scroll was sealed in a bronze casket made by Butler-Jones (Nameplates) Ltd, a Beckenham foundry, and presented to Churchill at his home at Chartwell, Westerham, on Monday 28 October 1946. The delegation, introduced by the Rt Hon. Harold MacMillan, MP for Bromley, included the incumbent and three former mayors. In his speech acknowledging the honour, Mr Churchill said:

Beckenham is not far from my home in the heart of beautiful Kent. It stands in the well-known track of 'Bomb Alley' and I fear that many marks of those ordeals still remain among you.

Wartime statistics reveal that Beckenham suffered

Menu card from the 1945 disbandment dinner of Beckenham Civil Defence, showing the explosives that fell on Beckenham during the war. (JF)

1,201 alerts, a crashed enemy aircraft, 973 HE bombs (of which 143 were unexploded), 13 parachute mines with two unexploded, at least 9,000 incendiaries, 73 flying bombs and five V2s. There were 351 people killed (including the charter mayor), 602 grievously injured and 1,151 less so. At least 20,000 properties were destroyed or seriously damaged. In 1947, one of a limited number of lace panels made by Dobsons and M. Browne & Co. Ltd of Nottingham and depicting the Battle of Britain was given to both Sir Winston Churchill and to Beckenham. When Beckenham ceased to be a borough, its panel went to the Royal Air Force Station at Biggin Hill and when that closed in 1992 both panel and case were refurbished and put on public display at Bromley Civic Centre.

One of the former mayors present at Mr Churchill's ceremony was Dr R.P.S. Edden, who had his house in Eden Park Avenue built on a double site to accommodate his surgery. His daughter Felicity, born that year, had the honour of a civic christening at St George's Church. Known as 'Doc', Dr Edden received many letters of regret on his retirement from the council in 1953, though his family, his practice and numerous other interests continued to keep him busy.

Coming to Eden Park in 1934, he was elected by the Residents' Association as their first chairman and was nominated as Independent candidate for the ward in the council elections, culminating in his election as mayor for 1937/8. He was a keen cricketer, a past president and supporter of Beckenham Town FC, an active member of Beckenham Rotary Club (of which he was president from 1940–42) and for many years, from its inauguration, president of Beckenham Bowling Club. During the war he ran the mobility service to provide fast medical help when and wherever needed and was among the first six of Beckenham's mayors whose names were given to the blocks of flats at the corner of Brackley and Southend

Dr Bennett, first mayor of Beckenham. (CW)

Dr Bennett in his locomobile with daughter Myrtle – the lack of numberplates dates the vehicle to pre-1903. (CW)

Roads – Stamp, Bennett, Parker, Edden, Healey and Jeff. On 22 March 1953, to commemorate the coronation, he was among the 13 Beckenham mayors and three representatives who each planted an oak tree beside the Petley house in Harvington – trees which now form the mayoral avenue running from the children's play area to the woodland – known fondly to Sheila Black, who walks her dog Joy there, as 'The Mall'.

Dr James Bennett, the first reserve to charter mayor Sir Josiah Stamp, was elected first mayor of Beckenham in November 1935, when he presented the silver chain and gold enamelled badge to the new council. He ran his practice in the house where his youngest granddaughter, Carol Walklin (née Jeffries), was born and which now holds the Little Theatre. Dr Bennett then moved across the road to Corner Ways, eventually selling the practice to Edward Shipsey, whose brother Maurice was grandfather of Edward, the last baby born at Stonepark Maternity Home. Carol, who lives today in Thornton Dene, has many memorabilia of her grandfather, the most striking of which is a silver salver bearing the signatures of councillors in office in 1955, when the honour of freeman was granted to both Dr Bennett and Alderman Sampson. Carol also has a heavy bronze casket, designed by Mr Robin Day and Mr Yabsley of the Beckenham Art School and similar to that presented to Sir Winston Churchill. The scroll it contained is now framed and hangs on the wall. Dr Bennett served Beckenham for 25 years from his election as member for Copers Cope in 1920. He held numerous posts and presided as chairman of the library committee at the formal opening of Beckenham library on 4 March 1939, his little granddaughter Carol presenting flowers to mayoress Mrs Healey and to Mrs Bennett, her own grandmother! For 40 years Dr Bennett had a keen interest in

Beckenham Hospital and in 1914–18 served at Balgowan, site of the military hospital. He would be pleased to know that his great-granddaughter, Jane Walklin, is, at the time of writing, a successful film editor who has worked for Yorkshire TV on programmes such as 'Heartbeat' and 'Lost for Words' with the late Thora Hird. In 1992, under the name Nell Bennett, Carol produced *All the Year Round*, an entertaining illustrated allotment diary recalling incidents from her childhood in the heart of Beckenham.

Alderman Sampson, born in Bristol in 1894, came to Beckenham in 1930 and served the Beckenham local authority for 21 years from 1934. He became an alderman in 1941 and was mayor for three years during the war. He represented the council on numerous bodies and was one of the earliest wardens to enrol, in 1937 becoming the town's chief warden. He became mayor for the fourth time in coronation year and when he died in April 1959 his funeral was conducted with full civic honours. Sadly his daughter, Margaret Lightfoot, was killed while walking her dog in Epping Forest in 1975.

Town Clerk Charles Eric Staddon, from 1930 until his death in 1952, played a vital part in the success of Beckenham Borough. His daughter Margaret fondly remembers the councillors and aldermen of those days, and her best friend at St Christopher's was Carol Walklin's sister, Daphne Jeffries!

Alderman William Duncan of Beckenham firm Syme & Duncan was mayor in 1955/56. As well as many photographs of notable local events, his family also has his jabot, a bronze ash tray and his alderman's chair, passed on when Beckenham was absorbed by the London Borough of Bromley.

Pride and delight in Beckenham as a borough lasted only 30 years and there was little celebration

Inset right: *The lace jabot.* (M&AD)

Below: *Alderman's chair of William Duncan.* (M&AD)

William Duncan visited his wife's memorial seat, outside the town hall, on his 90th birthday. (M&AD)

Right: *The mace of the Borough of Beckenham and the insignia of the mayor and mayoress.* (FB)

Above right: *The Adam fireplace in the mayor's parlour at the Civic Centre.*

Above: *A welcome cuppa at the prize-giving at Beckenham Technical School in 1955.*

Right: *A board from Bromley Museum showing the mayors of Beckenham from 1935 to 1960.*

BOROUGH OF BECKENHAM
1935
CHARTER MAYOR:
SIR JOSIAH C. STAMP. G.C.B. G.B.E.

CHARTER TOWN CLERK:
C. ERIC STADDON

YEAR	MAYOR
1935-1936	ALDERMAN DR. J. H. BENNETT
1936-1937	ALDERMAN R. T. PARKER
1937-1938	COUNCILLOR DR. R. P. S. EDDEN O.B.E.
1938-1939	ALDERMAN F. HEALEY J.P.
1939-1940	ALDERMAN R. W. JEFF
1940-1941	COUNCILLOR W. J. SAMPSON
1941-1942	ALDERMAN W. J. SAMPSON
1942-1943	ALDERMAN W. J. SAMPSON
1943-1944	ALDERMAN C. A. CAMPBELL
1944-1945	COUNCILLOR R. S. JACKSON
1945-1946	ALDERMAN C. G. BROOK
1946-1947	COUNCILLOR J. H. ATKINS
1947-MAY 1949	COUNCILLOR T. B. BOYD
1949-1950	COUNCILLOR T. W. MALLETT
1950-1951	COUNCILLOR E. C. DIXON
1951-1952	COUNCILLOR C. P. CHRISTIE
1952-1953	COUNCILLOR G. C. W. WHITE
1953-1954	ALDERMAN W. J. SAMPSON
1954-1955	COUNCILLOR C. B. CURTIS.M.B.E
1955-1956	COUNCILLOR W. DUNCAN
1956-1957	COUNCILLOR D. R. KNOX-JOHNSTON
1957-1958	COUNCILLOR H. H. BROOK BROWN
1958-1959	COUNCILLOR KATHLEEN A. MOORE
1959-1960	COUNCILLOR W. S. ROBBINS

in 1965 when it became a satellite of Bromley, although there was a farewell dinner at the public hall on Wednesday 23 March 1965 at which the mayor, Councillor Alfred Johnson, presided, answering to the toast 'The Borough of Beckenham', proposed by Dr Edden. Sir Josiah Stamp's address when he took up office had suggested that Beckenham would remain a borough for a century or more, which at the time have must seemed forever. The number of Freemen of Beckenham doubled before the changeover, with awards in 1964 to Aldermen Parkin, Brook, Atkins and Boyd Boyd and Richard Jackson. The 27 Bromley freemen created before 1997 included, in 1987, Mrs Sheila Stead MBE and Dame Cicely Saunders DBE.

Along with Petts Wood, Orpington, Penge and Chislehurst, Beckenham made up the biggest London borough in four and a half authorities, Sidcup having left Chislehurst to join Bexley. Henry Parkin, who lasted throughout Beckenham's life as a borough, continued to serve the new Bromley Borough for a further 20 years. Beckenham was fortunate in that gifted accountant Tom Sowerby, who had much county experience dealing with thousands of pounds rather than the hundreds in Beckenham's accounts, had become treasurer in 1963 in readiness for the change. He valued the sterling qualities of Beckenham's councillors and stayed in the new borough until 1977. In his day he was a keen cricketer and as a member of Beckenham Cricket Club would open the bowling with Derek Underwood at the other end. He retired to Beckenham to enjoy the parks and tree-lined roads and to watch Kent play at their new ground in Copers Cope Road. Other notables were former mayor James Atkins, Chairman of the Education Committee, Town Clerk Charles Eric Staddon and Borough Engineer James Dove. The last decision made by Beckenham Council in 1965 was to approve the building of West Wickham swimming baths in defiance of the new London Borough of Bromley Council. Beckenham members present included Mayor Alderman Alfred Johnson, Deputy Mayor Councillor Max Williams, Town Clerk Webster Storr and Borough Treasurer Tom Sowerby. Anyone who enjoys swimming at West Wickham Baths should remember they have the old Beckenham Council to thank!

The borough arms, introduced in 1965.

SERVIRE · POPULO

Above: *The last meeting of Beckenham Council, 1965.* (M&AD)

Right: *Programme for the farewell dinner for the Borough of Beckenham, 1965.* (FB)

Borough of Beckenham

MEMBERS' AND PAST MEMBERS' FAREWELL DINNER

WEDNESDAY, 31st MARCH, 1965

THE PUBLIC HALL,

Bromley Road, Beckenham

The Worshipful The Mayor
Councillor Alfred T. Johnson, J.P.
Presiding

Usually the London Borough of Bromley mayor wears Bromley's chain of office but sometimes he/she wears the Beckenham chain; one such occasion being to honour Carey Blyton, nephew of Enid Blyton, when Labour mayor John Holbrook wore the chain on 14 March 2002. Surviving Beckenham insignia are kept at the Civic Centre with some relics preserved at Orpington Museum, but most of the property of Beckenham Borough was dispersed among interested residents and relatives. It is a little-known fact that the mace used at all official occasions is that of Beckenham, with the coat of arms replaced with that of Bromley. Old Beckenham has been keeping an eye on proceedings all along!

A Marks & Spencer's store and car park has replaced Beckenham's municipal buildings and the town's shops have been converted to eating places and estate agents with not a butcher, fishmonger or green-grocer among them. The first Beckenham Grammar School, later Beckenham Technical School and finally The Studio on the site of the old Clock House may be the next historic building to go. Beckenham Cottage Hospital (which became the Beckenham Hospital when it was extended in 1939) will be preserved

merely as a shell and even the Three Tuns is under threat. Where has our town of Beckenham gone?

Bromley was awarded its Charter in 1903 when Sir Thomas Dewey was Charter Mayor, its first Mayor in 1903/04 being Frank Griffiths. Orpington became a UDC in 1934 and was granted arms showing the River Cray in the centre of a shield edged with a green band representing the green belt and two red mural crowns representing urban development.

Given five years to get used to the idea, it was still a bitter pill for Beckenham and West Wickham, Penge, Orpington and Petts Wood, Chislehurst and Bromley when they were forced, in 1965, to relinquish their individuality and combine into a single London borough represented by a cinquefoil.

✦ CHAPTER 8 ✦

Personalities

Julie Andrews

It is with the greatest of pleasure that we lay claim to Julie as a resident, even if it was only briefly during the war at No. 15 Cromwell Road with her mother Barbara and stepfather Ted Andrews. During this time she attended Woodbrook School and was fondly remembered by headmistress Miss Mead for her 'voice like an angel'. It is said that the first time her soaring four-octave voice was heard in public was in a Beckenham air-raid shelter.

Hugh Bean CBE

Of all the popular figures of whom Beckenham may be proud, there can be none more truly of the town than Hugh Bean. Born in Croydon Road, Beckenham, he started school at Balgowan and went on to Marian Vian in the days of Kit Bailey. His family enjoyed music and his mother and his sister Elsie were both proficient at the piano. With his father teaching him the rudiments of the violin when he was only five, however, it seems inevitable that the instrument was to form the basis of his career. At nine, on the recommendation of Herbert Kinsey, adjudicator of the Croydon Festival, he became a pupil of Albert Sammons, with whom he studied for almost 20 years.

During the war, he did not leave Beckenham, attending the Beckenham and Penge Grammar School throughout and like many children during that period had some close shaves when cycling between home and school.

The music master at the grammar school was Australian musician Hubert Clifford with John Couling the leader of the orchestra. The school always came first or second in the Westminster Schools competition and later Hugh and John played together for two years in the BBC Symphony Orchestra. Nancy Wiseman, much-loved music teacher at Beckenham County School for Girls, led the violas in the grammar school's summer alfresco concerts. The gifted children of the late Elise Beeton and Peter Handy were well known to Hugh, their daughter Thelma later becoming leader of the Liverpool Philharmonic Orchestra.

Conscription into the Grenadier Guards gave Hugh the chance to join their string players at official dinners – after playing in the minstrels' gallery at Windsor Castle he encountered King George VI and on another occasion was overjoyed to be one of the

musicians at the presentation of the Graham Sutherland portrait to Sir Winston Churchill.

In 1963 Hugh was leader of the Philharmonic Orchestra and in the same year married Mary Harrow, at that time on the orchestra staff. They moved into Stone Park Avenue where, with the enthusiastic help of Hugh's father from across the road, the level back garden was ideal for setting up a steam railway. With the birth of their daughter Fiona, the family was complete.

Associated with the Royal College of Music from the age of nine, by July 2004 Hugh would have held the office of Professor of Violin for 50 years. His pianist for 38 years was David Parkhouse.

Although leader of the Philharmonia, BBC Symphony and London Symphony Orchestras in turn, Hugh was in great demand as a soloist and as a player of chamber music, both abroad and all over Great Britain, although he was always based in Beckenham. Among his many recordings are the Elgar Concerto with the Royal Liverpool Philharmonic for EMI and, famously, Vaughan

Hugh Bean, aged five, playing the violin in the garden at Hampden Road. (HB)

Above: *Hugh Bean with the Royal Liverpool Philharmonic Orchestra.* (HB)

Left: *And baby makes five!* Left to right: *Mary, Mrs Bean with Fiona, Mr Bean and Hugh.* (HB)

Below left: *Engine-driver Hugh gets under way.* (HB)

Williams' 'Lark Ascending' with Sir Adrian Boult. His extensive tours have taken him to North and South America, Europe, Scandinavia and China, as well as the Middle and Far East.

Appointed FRCM in 1968, he was awarded the Cobbett Gold Medal for chamber music in 1969 and the CBE in 1970.

Hugh died suddenly on Boxing Day, 2003. His talent and jovial personality will be long and proudly remembered.

David Bowie at Croydon Road Recreation-Ground

We owe to our forebears the existence of Croydon Road Recreation-Ground ('Croydon Rec'), a patch of green parkland close to the High Street, where celebrations have been carried out year after year. It is now watched over from a tiny hut near the tennis-courts by the 'Friends of Croydon Rec' to ensure the park is not encroached upon by building developments. Of all the worthy occasions enjoyed there, perhaps none was more successful than when David Bowie played in the bandstand.

The day of 16 August 1969 dawned exceptionally

David Bowie at Croydon Rec. (DB)

fine for the free festival at the Croydon Rec. The compère was David Bowie, yet to become a superstar, who usually appeared on Sundays at the Three Tuns in what became known as the Beckenham Arts Lab. To a crowd of about 3,000 Bowie played solo many of the tunes that later appeared on his 'Space Oddity' album. His friend David Bebbington, a professional photographer working for the Ministry of Defence, took many photographs including the one shown on page 143 and was also one of the puppeteers for the Brian Cole and Barbara Moore Puppet Show.

Other local groups to perform were Comus, Gun Hill, Gas Works, Miscarriage, Bridget St John, Nita and Dave Jones, Kamirah, Giles and Abdul and the Strawbs.

The various money-raising stalls included a barbecue, candyfloss, fortune telling and tarot readings, ceramics, herb and poster stalls and aluminium rings from Dave Grozier and Pete Logan. Angela Bowie-to-be sold hamburgers cooked in a wheelbarrow. Another friend and one of the organisers, Mary Finnigan, declared the festival a great success especially as 'all the visitors were well behaved'!

Peter Duncan

Although now resident in Wandsworth with wife Annie and his son and three daughters, adventurous action man Peter Duncan was brought up in Beckenham and attended Balgowan and Hawes Down schools. After a decade of acting on stage, film and TV, he joined Sarah Greene and Simon Groom on the 'Blue Peter' team in 1980, viewers noticing a change in presentation as Peter cleaned Big Ben from a bosun's chair suspended 97 metres above the street. He also took part on 29 March 1981 in the first-ever London Marathon, in which he was placed 1,868 out of 6,418 with a time of 3 hours, 11 minutes, 42 seconds. He ran in four more London Marathons without beating this first time.

In 1984 he filmed the first series of 'Duncan Dares', getting the best of beds of nails, tarantulas and snakes with remarkable skill, fitness and daring. After five years he left Blue Peter to renew his acting career, directing and starring in the musical *Barnum* in Ilfracombe, Devon. Training for six months before taking on this testing role, he has played it several times, most recently in 1999. He has taken on numerous roles and was nominated for the Olivier Award for Best Actor in a Musical when he played Denry Machin in *The Card* at the Regent's Park Theatre. He is also a familiar face on TV, where he has appeared in such productions as 'Sons and Lovers', 'Warship', 'King Cinder' and 'The Big Race'. In 2004 he appeared with his family on Channel 5 in 'Chinese Breakaway', a follow-up to CBBC's Travel Bug, which explored South America and the Himalayas. He also went on an African safari.

Peter Duncan. (PD)

Peter is from a theatrical family that has a long association with pantomimes such as *Robin Hood*, *Cinderella* and *Aladdin* and Peter has played Captain Hook in *Peter Pan*. His parents, Alan and Pattie Gale, ran a show in the north every year and his sister, Julia Gale, has appeared in 'Grange Hill' and 'Hot Gossip'. For the next five years Peter is to be Britain's Ninth Chief Scout.

Artist Tim Feltham

Tim produced his first conscious piece of art – squared paper firmly coloured black – at Eden Park School. After attending Oak Lodge, followed by a period with Ravenswood's art master Mr Frampton, Tim studied at Croydon College of Art for five years. His website (www.galeriechienecosse.co.uk), with its exciting use of colour, shows how far Tim has travelled since those early days at infant school.

If you have visited the Churchill Theatre in the last 20 years you have certainly seen Tim's work – he is part of the crew which paints sets for shows such as *Babes in the Wood*, *Jack and the Beanstalk* and *Inside the Firm* and he also produced the banners advertising a visit from Roland Rat as well as performances of *La Folie*, *Dick Whittington* and *Snow White*. He was

A favourite pet painted by Tim Feltham. (TF)

commissioned to do an Elvis display in The Glades and, for his own amusement and delight, draws caricatures of dogs – hence the name of his website. He paints portraits of children and animals and welcomes commissions for family and other pictures.

Katie Lawler of Langley Park

One of a family of four, with brother Robert and sisters Karen and Kelly, Katie is a performer truly representative of Beckenham. Why of Langley Park? All the children attended Langley Park schools after Balgowan and Katie owes everything to the encouragement she gained there, especially from head of drama Bridget (Bridge) Doherty. Early successes for Katie included *Sweet Charity* and *Cabaret*, not forgetting the fashion show displaying clothes from The Glades in Bromley, and she went on to take part in the Sunday afternoon show on Capital Radio with Andy Peters of 'Blue Peter' fame.

When her twin sister Karen considered applying for 'Big Brother' on TV's Channel 4, she passed the complicated application forms over to Katie. A holiday in Dubai and kick boxing at Amida in Stanhope Grove supplied material for the video required for the application and the result was of such a professional standard that she was accepted to appear on the programme. Selected from 9,166 entries where boys outnumbered the girls 11 to 9, Katie has been the only female winner from the 21 countries so far taking part. All the family was there on the triumphant night she won.

She says it was a wonderful experience and that she had the time of her life! When asked why her daughter won, Mrs Lawler said Katie was adaptable, down to earth and fun to be with – especially with her talent for mimicking accents. Katie's two sets of grandparents as well as her parents, two sisters, one brother, small nephew and Charlie the Westie are all extremely proud of her hard-won success and not in the least envious. One fact of note from Jean Ritchie's book *Inside Big Brother* is that the site of the 'Big Brother' house at Elstree Studios was originally the huge concrete reservoir used for filming the bouncing bombs in *The Dam Busters*.

Katie won a year's contract to appear on the breakfast show 'RI:SE' and became used to having a car call at 3a.m. to take her to the studio. At the time of writing she lives on the new Waterside estate at Park Langley, *OK* magazine of Wednesday 12 November 2003 featuring her apartment.

We shall watch Katie's progress keenly and hope that her dreams of becoming well known in radio come true.

Bob Monkhouse OBE

'Personally, I don't think there's intelligent life on other planets. Why should other planets be any different from this one?'

A master of the one-liner, Bob was born in Beckenham on 1 June 1928 and sadly, ever-smiling and quick-witted, died on 29 December 2003 at Eggington in Bedfordshire.

As a youngster Bob was devoted to his grandfather, a custard powder tycoon of Clerkenwell firm Monk & Glass (Monkhouse and Glasscock). When it was acquired in 1958 by General Foods Corporation, which included Birds Custard, the jolly monk with his custard bowl disappeared from the shops. Frederick Glasscock was smitten with the legend of King Arthur and built King Arthur's Great Halls at Tintagel in 1929–33. He died on a cruise in July 1936 and was buried at sea. Grandfather Monkhouse died when Bob was nine and the shock and disappointment caused a tendency to a nervous stammer that remained with Bob throughout his life.

After attending Miss Norah Woodham's St George's School at No. 14 Albemarle Road, he went on to the Grange preparatory school at No. 25 Wickham Road, where the headmaster was Mr Beater – a lovely name for a headteacher who provided boxing and physical training for his pupils! What a trial for nine-year-old nine-stone Bob! He then went to Dulwich College, where he met the two people perhaps most influential in his life, cartoonist, collector and writer Denis Gifford (1927–2000) and his future script-writing partner, Denis Goodwin. Goodwin and Monkhouse did not get together until Denis, who was selling radios at Gamages, heard Bob wisecracking on the radio and traced him through the RAF. Together they wrote material for as many as seven radio shows a week featuring stars such as Ted Ray, Tommy Handley, Bob Hope, Frank Sinatra, Jerry Lewis and Dean Martin.

Pat Mannings' first memory of Bob is at the Elm Road church youth club when he was about 15 and already showing perfect timing and talent as a stand-up comedian, working with David Munro and twins Tom and Pat Sears. He toiled away as a cartoonist, leaving his efforts in Gifford's desk for his approval. Bob and Denis edited comic magazines and the Dulwich College student magazine. Many of the jokes in *The Beano* and *The Dandy* were theirs. They went on tour with the West Bees concert party, giving charity performances with Denis as the comedian and Bob the straight man.

The halls of Elm Road Baptist Church continued to be a centre for local talent. In the early 1950s composer Carey Blyton, nephew of Enid Blyton, made his first public appearance there. In the same concert was John Mann, better known as Snowy White in *Dick Barton, Special Agent*. Performing with Carey were friends from the Beckenham and Penge Grammar School who went on to form the Beckenham Salon, giving professional concerts involving performers such as Hugh Bean, baritone Jack Frost, harpist Enid Quiney and tenor Rene

Katie Lawler's class at Langley Park School, 1996. Left to right, back row: Geraldine O'Mahoney, Hannah West, Kelly Bond, Lindsay Crowther, Becki Payne, Alice Hamer, Laura Day, Natalia Pietrzyk, Jenny Green, Carly Hagan; middle row: *Jane Shelley, Miss Colloff (teacher), Tina Brown, Heather Eustace, Cara Lombard, Sasha Cherry, Akita Sawyer, Katie Lawler, Laura Fisher;* front row: *Claire Richards, Sarah Bignell, Sarah Tregent, Charlotte Vickers, Mrs Turner (head of year), Kate Holcome, Elise Bragoli, Sarah Urqhart.* (KL)

Katie relaxes after the mini marathon, 1991. (KL)

Katie and Charlie the Westie, 2002. (KL)

Soames. Writer David Munro met Bob Monkhouse at the Elm Road youth club and the pair became good friends, associating with others from the Salon, including composer Geoffrey Russell Smith and Russell's wife Mollie. David married Phyllis, niece of Alderman James Crease, and Phyllis remembers meeting Pat Coombes (a pupil at the Beckenham County School) when they visited Bob and Elizabeth in Crossways Road.

By the age of 18, when called up for National Service in the RAF, Bob had already made £20,000. His parents did not approve. His radio debut in 1948 was followed by his marriage at Caxton Hall, Westminster, in November 1949, to WAAF Elizabeth Thompson. Unhappily there began a lifelong separation from his father, although Bob was reconciled with his mother shortly before her death. He cared greatly for his spastic son Gary and had another son, Simon. His adopted daughter Abigail however, along with his second wife, Jackie Harding, his secretary, whom he married in 1973, are the only family to survive him.

Bob appeared in 12 films, notably *Carry On Sergeant* in 1958 and *The Dentist in the Chair*. His TV debut in the 1950s with 'Fast and Loose' was followed by 'Candid Camera', 'Mad Movies' and 'For Love or Money'. He compèred the London Palladium, which led in 1967 his hosting games show 'The Golden Shot' followed by such shows as 'Celebrity Squares', 'Family Fortunes', 'Bob's Full House' and 'Opportunity Knocks'. On the West End stage he starred in Cole Porter's *Aladdin*, Neil Simon's *Come Blow Your Horn* and *The Boys from Syracuse* by Rodgers & Hart.

Within his profession he was recognised as one of the best cabaret acts and was a top after-dinner speaker, named as such in 1988 by the Guild of Professional Toastmasters. He was the subject of 'This is Your Life' in 1983 and was honoured in 1986 for his charity work as an officer of the Most Venerable Order of the Hospital of St John of Jerusalem. He received the OBE in 1993 and was again named Best After-dinner Speaker. His autobiography, *Crying with Laughter*, went straight into the bestseller list in 1993 and a second volume, *Bob Monkhouse Over the Limit*, came out in 1998. He was always prepared to help up-and-coming comedians such as Frank Skinner and Stephen Fry and kept up with changes in the media. For example he presented the first lottery shows and the lunchtime programme 'Wipeout'. In 1999, Denis Gifford and Bob collaborated on a two-part radio show, 'A Hundred Laughs for a Ha'penny', a history of comic papers. Appearing on 'Parkinson' only six weeks before his death Bob was still cracking jokes about his own medical condition.

There were hidden depths to Bob: he had valuable collections of matchbooks, comic strips and films and was also a connoisseur of wines and whiskies. On his death he was praised by Mike Yarwood, Ian

Hislop, Max Bygraves, Nicholas Parsons, Sir Norman Wisdom, Des O'Connor and Ken Dodd, who called him 'a king among comedians'.

Until he married, Bob lived with his parents, Wilfred and Dorothy Monkhouse, and his brother John, who was five years older, at No. 168 Bromley Road. According to his biography he was christened in Beckenham as Robert Alan. Both his father and his brother were chartered accountants; John married and had two children, eventually retiring to Sussex. He was reunited with his brother in 1993 when he wrote to congratulate Bob on his OBE.

While we regret his passing, there will always be much for us all to remember of Bob Monkhouse – his generosity, his brilliant talent and his earnest desire to succeed in his chosen field.

John Surtees: The Only Man to Win World Titles on Two and Four Wheels

Born in 1934 at Westerham, John moved as a baby with his family to the Eden Park Parade, where his father, Jack, ran a motorcycle business and raced a motorcycle and sidecar combination. Jack Surtees with son John, and Stan Hailwood, with his son Mike, were the top grass-track riders of their day. Ron Whittenham remembers the grass circuit for motorcycle racing at Layham's Farm, where he went to watch crack riders, including Jack Surtees on his combination.

When war broke out, Graham Walker, father of Murray Walker, persuaded Jack to join the Army despite his being over age, his job then being to help organise the workshops at Catterick

Right: *John Surtees is the victor.* (JSU)

Below: *John Surtees, guest of honour at the anniversary of Monks Orchard School.* (VW)

and to train DR riders. The motorcycle shop had to go and the family moved to a house in Shirley, where they were all bombed out! Jack took them to Catterick until 1943, when he managed to get a council-house in Mardell Road opposite Monks Orchard School, and so John came to attend the primary school and was asked years later to attend its golden jubilee celebrations. From there he went to Ashburton, where the deputy head, Ivan Frederick (Nick) Neech, became well aware of his pupil's talents. According to Tony Johns, it was always possible to pick out John Surtees on the track by his superior riding style, line and angle.

Before going on to do an apprenticeship with the Vincent HRD company, John helped his father as a mechanic in the shop that Jack opened at Forest Hill after the war.

His first race in 1949 was on a 500cc Excelsior B14 when he was still underage! His world motorcycle championships were all on a MV Augusta. In 1956 he won on a 500cc but from 1958–60 he won on both 350cc and 500cc bikes.

In 1958 John established the motorcycle shop on the Bell Parade in West Wickham, where he sold all the major marques until signing for Ferrari in 1963. By 1964 he had switched to four wheels and won the Formula 1 world title driving a Ferrari. He also won numerous Formula 2 events and was involved in a near-fatal crash at Mosport, Ontario.

By 1970, John was building the Surtees Formula 5000 cars that won both the British and American Championships. In 1972 he personally won the Imola Italy Gold Cup and Japanese Grand Prix with a Surtees T510 but then announced his retirement from racing because of the pressures of management. We are all very proud of him and of that shop on the Bell Parade!

Tom William Thornton (1857–1933)

It would be difficult to find a man who loved Beckenham more than Tom Thornton – or T.W., as he was known to his friends. Perhaps his greatest achievement that has had a knock-on effect for the future was the part that he played in saving Kelsey Park from residential development. With members of the council seemingly more concerned with financial gain than conservation of the Kelsey woodland and park, T.W.'s lanternslide lectures won the day as letters against the project poured into the council. On 30 May 1913 the park was opened to the public in perpetuity.

Those of us with an interest in genealogy or local history find the Beckenham directories, published by Thornton's *Beckenham Journal* from 1884 until 1939, a valuable resource of house names, streets, businesses, schools, churches and residents.

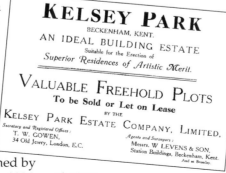

KELSEY PARK
BECKENHAM, KENT.
AN IDEAL BUILDING ESTATE
Suitable for the Erection of
Superior Residences of Artistic Merit.

VALUABLE FREEHOLD PLOTS
To be Sold or Let on Lease
BY THE
KELSEY PARK ESTATE COMPANY, LIMITED.
Secretary and Registered Offices :
T. W. GOWEN,
34 Old Jewry, London, E.C.
Agents and Surveyors :
Messrs. W LEVENS & SON,
Station Buildings, Beckenham, Kent.
And at Bromley.

William Malyon, a prominent member of the district known as Alexandra Cottages, had started the *Beckenham Journal* in September 1876, and nearly five years later had disappeared back to the City and his printing business in Fore Street, at which point the *Beckenham Journal* was published under new management. In June 1881 the new editor was T.W. and the circulation was 2,000. The Thorntons continued the paper until 1955 when they sold out to the *Kentish Times*, which also bought Thornton's shop which was later sold, although its name was retained until 2003. All that remains today is the plaque erected by Eric Inman about the 1902 balloon flight.

Although Tom attended Christchurch rather than St George's, he maintained a keen interest in the graveyard's upkeep. He secured the services of Queen Victoria's specialist gardener when most of the ancient yews had to be replaced by young trees. The restoration of the thirteenth-century lych-gate in 1924 was carried out as a memorial to his two sons, who were killed in the First World War. We have Tom Thornton to thank for the crocuses and other spring flowers naturalised among the gravestones. He also sent fresh turf from his garden to replenish the grass in the churchyard, a feature sadly neglected today. He created gardens all over Beckenham – not only at his house in Kelsey Square but also at the rectory and behind the Constitutional Club. The Beckenham Horticultural Society was one of Tom's most successful ventures, involving not only his great love of flowers and gardens but also his unrivalled organisational abilities.

When he died in 1933, it was thought that Thornton's Corner would remain in perpetuity but now, some 70 years later, the unimaginable has happened and the last shop has closed. At T.W.'s funeral the staff of Thornton Ltd lined the path from the lych-gate to the church along with members of Cator Lodge Freemasons and rows of wreaths. The very unusual compliment of a peal of muffled bells accompanied the crowds inside and outside the church for this most respected citizen. Among the mourners was Tom Copeland, brother-in-law of the deceased (Tom Copeland and Tom Thornton had married the Freeman sisters). Tom Thornton's granddaughter, Valerie Sheldon (née Thornton) and Tom Copeland's great-nephew Tony Johns are second cousins.

The Thornton dynasty came to an unexpectedly early end. T.W. and his wife had four sons and four daughters but Stanley and Hedley were killed in the First World War. Only the youngest child, Victor, married but he had two daughters and when he died in 1963 the name Thornton died with him. His sisters were Constance, Gertrude, Dorothy and Edith and his

The coffee table with silver tray inscribed: 'To William Thornton with hearty congratulations from his many Beckenham friends as a token of sincere esteem for his public spirited interest in the welfare of the town. On the attainment of 50 years association as proprietor of the Beckenham Journal *and his seventieth year presented with other gifts by the subscribers at a reception at the Public Hall on 14 December 1926.' The table also has a panel reading: 'Case made from part of the 12 century lych gate* [from St George's] *at Beckenham restored in 1925 in memory of Hedley and Stanley Thornton who gave their lives in the Great War. The beading is from the old yew trees in the churchyard.'* (VS)

surviving brother, Frank, was a notable singer in his day. Victor attended the Beckenham Technical School (until recently The Studio) and was well known as a Shakespearean actor and producer. He was the editor of the *Beckenham Journal* from the Second World War and carried on his father's tradition of putting Beckenham first. He not only persuaded the Council to close the High Street for a fair on 6 June 1953 to celebrate the Queen's coronation but also put on an unforgettable performance of *The Merry Wives of Windsor* in a replica Elizabethan playhouse beside the tulip tree in Kelsey Park. Sadly, the tulip tree has also gone.

Frank (Dot) Morris (1932–2002)

Frank, better known in football circles as Dot or Dotty Morris, is one of Beckenham Town FC's legends. His nickname came from his promotion as a youngster to a team of older boys, in which he was much smaller than the others. He was probably the best player ever to wear a Beckenham Town shirt. He signed for Crystal Palace, for whom he played over

70 games, and then moved on to the Southern League and Tunbridge Wells United FC. When his playing career was over, he returned to Beckenham Town as coach, later serving on the committee with his wife, Shirley.

Frank was also a gifted boxer and was both schoolboy champion of Great Britain and ABA champion. He represented Great Britain as an amateur boxer and combined a tremendous combative spirit in the ring with a gentle nature outside it. He is indeed sadly missed.

William Joyce

Perhaps it is a surprise to all of us to be reminded that William Joyce, better known as Lord Haw Haw, lived for a time in Upper Elmers End Road. His daughter, Heather Iandolo, has provided her own personal view of her famous father, who fled to Germany and taunted Britain with propaganda broadcasts during the Second World War: 'My father never killed anyone. He only made speeches. He was wicked, I suppose, but he was not as evil as some.'

CHAPTER 9

The Fight for Bethlem's Metropolitan Open Land

The view across farmland at what used to be Park Farm, in 2003. (BE)

There is no woodland in Beckenham to equal the range, age and magnificence of the trees in the Bethlem grounds. This includes surveys of High Broom Wood, Beckenham Place Park (now of course Lewisham but formerly Beckenham), Harvington, Kelsey Park, Crease Park and the South Norwood Country Park (now Croydon but latterly Beckenham). At the time of writing, encroachment of the few remaining havens for wildlife and, incidentally, our own enjoyment includes the following: loss of Beckenham Technical School's playing-fields at the back of the leisure centre to housing on Turners Meadow; the extensive private housing development on the late Burroughs Wellcome estate that threatens the nature reserve of the East Beck; and the sale of Eden Park School at No. 204 Upper Elmers End Road, the site of the nineteenth-century house, Holly Lodge, for the building of Asprey Mews. There is also the myriad of closes and gardens built in the grounds of Victorian houses throughout the borough. No wonder our small population of garden birds is decreasing with the loss of their nesting sites and food sources, while the urban fox is becoming a pest. As woodland sites such as Harvington and Bethlem are left poorly managed, the casual onlooker sees them as derelict places fit for nothing but building on

and covering with concrete, with the prospect of more ratepayers at the end of it. This seems to be unimaginative and a very sad end for the acres of open land passed on to us by those who toiled there through the ages. Surely such development as the NHS deems necessary in the Bethlem parkland can be restricted to areas already built on. This is our last chance to keep some truly wild land in our midst – we either take the opportunity or risk losing the land to housing.

The Birds of Bethlem Royal Hospital Grounds

Dave Dack, warden of the South Norwood Country Park at Elmers End, contributed the following account of the birds that he identified in the Bethlem grounds:

I am a bird-watcher with 30 years' experience in the field, covering Britain, Europe, the Middle East, West Africa, East Africa, the West Indies, North America and Central America.

I have a wide experience of conducting bird surveys both at home and abroad as well as leading groups to various locations. I have been asked to undertake a survey of the birds around Bethlem Royal Hospital, an area with much potential but, due to the nature of the site, one that has never been covered by many bird-watchers. On a total of 24 occasions between June and the end of September 2002 I visited the site to assess it. Below is a list of my observations:

List of species (55)
Sparrowhawk (Accipiter nisus)
Kestrel (Falco tinnunculus) M
Hobby (Falco subbuteo)
Pheasant (Phasianus colchicus)
Black-headed Gull (Larus ridibundus) M
Common Gull (Larus canus) M
Herring Gull (Larus argentatus)
Lesser Black-backed Gull (Larus fuscus) M
Wood Pigeon (Columba palumbus)
Stock Dove (Columba oenas)
Collared Dove (Streptopelia decaocto)
Turtle Dove (Streptopelia turtur) R
Cuckoo (Cuculus canorus) M
Rose-ringed Parakeet (Psittacula krameri)
Tawny Owl (Strix aluco)
Swift (Apus apus)
Green Woodpecker (Picus viridis) M
Great Spotted Woodpecker (Dendrocopos major)
Skylark (Alauda arvensis) R
Sand Martin (Riparia riparia) M
House Martin (Delichon urbica) M
Swallow (Hirundo rustica) M
Meadow Pipit (Anthus pratensis) M
Pied Wagtail (Motacilla alba)
Wren (Troglodytes troglodytes)
Dunnock (Prunella modularis) M
Robin (Erithacus rubecula)
Stonechat (Saxicola torquata) M
Blackbird (Turdus merula)
Song Thrush (Turdus philomelos) R
Mistle Thrush (Turdus viscivorus) M
Lesser Whitethroat (Sylvia curruca)
Whitethroat (Sylvia communis)
Garden Warbler (Sylvia borin)
Blackcap (Sylvia atricapilla)
Chiffchaff (Phylloscopus collybita)
Willow Warbler (Phylloscopus trochilus) M
Spotted Flycatcher (Muscicapa striata) R
Goldcrest (Regulus regulus) M
Long-tailed Tit (Aegithalos caudatus)
Blue Tit (Parus caeruleus)
Great Tit (Parus major)
Nuthatch (Sitta europaea)
Treecreeper (Certhia familiaris)
Jay (Garrulus glandarius)
Magpie (Pica pica)
Jackdaw (Corvus monedula)
Carrion Crow (Corvus corone)
Starling (Sturnus vulgaris) R
House Sparrow (Passer domesticus) R
Chaffinch (Fringilla coelebs)

Greenfinch (Carduelis chloris)
Goldfinch (Carduelis carduelis)
Linnet (Carduelis cannabina) R
Redpoll (Carduelis flammea) M

M: Medium conservation concern
R: High conservation concern

No doubt if all seasons of the year were surveyed a higher species count would be recorded. All of the above species were noted as being in territory during the summer months and the majority would have been expected to have bred on site.

Conclusion of Bird Survey
The area is an important haven for birds, both breeding and migrating.

It contains a selection of habitats, e.g. mature woodlands, open fields, hedgerows and secluded areas that are vitally important as nesting and feeding grounds.

Any development proposals would have a disastrous effect on the value of the area to its wildlife.

Trees in the Bethlem Grounds

A general survey of the trees at Bethlem excluding more recent planting (2004) round the hospital buildings revealed 40 established species in 2002.

The woodland is notable for the dominance of the pedunculate oak in all stages of growth from the smallest sapling to very old trees that must have been part of the ancient woodland of the area. Although the predominant feature of the woodland is its maturity, the trees are in fine condition and not leaning or felled by the strong winds, as is the case elsewhere in the borough.

Most of the hedges are unmanaged and there are relict hedges of a few species, typically the pedunculate oak plus ash, hawthorn, elder and some elm saplings, which to seem to have been left from the old woodland and appear as rims round the fields used as pasture. It is worth remarking in passing on the fine-leaved nature of the pasture grasses, where the coarser grasses are absent and thistles and ragwort are rare.

In this general half-day survey, field maple, dogwood and blackthorn were not seen, such is the dominance of the English oak on this site.

Although the ornamental lakes of the mansions Wickham Park and Monks Orchard were filled in during the 1940s for the safety of the hospital inmates, there is still a river, the St James' Stream, running through the parkland. Today it is hidden by the overgrowth of brambles but it could be opened up to make a riverside walk from Shirley to Upper Elmers End. Unfortunately this would not be possible while the hospital provides for unstable patients. It can be seen temporarily in its culvert at the side of Asprey Mews before it passes under the road to flow to Elmers End where it joins the Chaffinch.

Mammals of the parkland include foxes as part of a wild ecosystem, able to survive without resource to dustbins and fast-food waste. They can be seen playing in the fields and basking in the sun. Although the fox Nipper and her cubs each year visit a bungalow in Orchard Way overlooking the estate, she has reared them in the park. Badgers regularly use an ancient sett and there has been a colony of long-eared bats as well as pipistrelles near the old walled garden.

The Campaign to Save the Protected Land of the Bethlem Royal Hospital

The Bethlem Royal Hospital has been in our community at its present (2004) site in Monks Orchard Road since 1930. The 240-acre site is covered by the legislation protecting Metropolitan Open Land and Green Belt areas.

Since the South London & Maudsley NHS Trust (SLaM) took over the running of the hospital in the mid-1990s, many applications have been submitted to build on the protected land and, despite residents' objections, two very large buildings have been constructed. Residents were also upset when their objections failed to prevent the erection of a tall telephone mast in the grounds.

Early in 2002, SLaM made an application for another new building on the protected land. This time it was for a Medium Secure Unit (MSU), a building larger than anything else in the area and surrounded by an 18ft-high security fence, giving it the appearance of a prison and clearly visible from the Wickham Road.

This 89-bed MSU is to provide accommodation for the treatment of patients with psychiatric problems, the majority of whom will have committed serious criminal offences, such secure accommodation also being deemed necessary for other patients as a result of incidents in other mental healthcare facilities. Some of the patients will have been transferred from Broadmoor or other high-security hospitals. Part of their treatment allows unescorted leave into the community.

In 2000, a similar application from SLaM to develop the Cane Hill Hospital site with an MSU raised thousands of objections from concerned residents. Croydon Council refused this application with the main objections being 'inappropriate development on MOL/Green Belt' and 'Fear of Crime'.

At a meeting at the Bethlem Royal Hospital on 18 March 2002, SLaM was present to discuss their latest application with members from Monks Orchard Residents' Association (MORA), West Wickham RA (WWRA) and Spring Park RA (SPRA). One question posed was, 'When is the final date for objections to be in by?' SLaM answered, 'In two days' time.'

That was the green light for what Bromley Council described as the biggest campaign, with more objections than any application in the council's history. Almost 7,000 written objections were sent, in addition to representations from West Beckenham RA, West Wickham RA, Wickham Common RA, Eden Park RA, Monks Orchard RA, Park Langley RA, Langley Park RA, Copers Cope RA, The Friends of Kelsey Park and many local schools.

It was discovered that further applications, submitted by SLaM at this time, were for the re-designation of almost half the Bethlem grounds as a Major Developed Site (MDS) and also to downgrade the conservation areas within the grounds. Should these applications be successful, the effect would be to weaken the protection of extensive mature woodland and the open space of the grounds and allow more development.

The Campaign Against Bethlem Building Expansion (CABBE)

CABBE was formed in March 2002, when a group of

October 2002 survey, 40 tree species found			
alder	elder	lime	privet
apple	elm	London plane	scots pine
ash	hawthorn	maple (Norway)	silver birch
beech	hazel	maple (red leaved)	spindle
black poplar hybrids	holly	maple	sweet chestnut
box	hornbeam	monkey puzzle	sycamore
cedar	holm oak	pedunculate oak	wayfaring tree
cherry	horse chestnut	petraea oak hybrids	black willow
copper beech	laurel	tulip tree	goat willow
dog rose	Lawsons cypress	turkey oak	yew

Protest march in West Wickham High Street, 18 May 2002.

The surviving balustrades of Monks Orchard mansion.

concerned local residents got together to oppose the planning application by the South London & Maudsley NHS Trust (SLaM), to build an 89-bed Medium Secure Unit (MSU) at the Bethlem Royal Hospital, Monks Orchard Road, Beckenham. This being their latest application as part of the ongoing expansion plans for the site.

We made it clear from the outset that **we were not** against the Bethlem Hospital, the patients or the staff, only the massive expansion programme proposed by SLaM, which is too much for this or any other community to absorb.

CABBE was accepted as representing the local community against this application.

The Bethlem site is owned by the Corporation of London and leased to SLaM for a 'peppercorn rent'. The site covers 240 acres and is designated Metropolitan Open Land (MOL), which is afforded the same protection as Green Belt.

All over the country, people oppose the indiscriminate development of MOL/Green Belt and this was to be no exception. Once developed, these areas of natural beauty, which provide a habitat for a multitude of flora and fauna, are lost for ever.

The CABBE team spent many hours researching, organising meetings and marches and co-ordinating leaflet distributions. The public needed the facts about what was proposed, rather than simply the information put out by SLaM.

In July 2002, the Bromley Development Control Committee sat in public, with the Great Hall at the Civic Centre packed to its 600 capacity and many more people outside. The application was soundly refused. The chairman of the Development Control Committee, Councillor Tony Wilkinson, said, 'We could not grant planning permission because the site is part of Metropolitan Open Land and the proposal constituted inappropriate development.'

Regardless of that decision, however, and of the planning regulations and fears of local residents, SLaM were determined to get what they wanted in whatever way was necessary. In April 2003, a public inquiry by the government's planning inspectorate was held, which lasted for seven days. Unbelievably, the government inspector decided to allow the application, giving his reasoning in a report published in June 2003.

One of SLaM's claims had been that there were 'no alternative sites'. In the four years to 2003, over £1.5bn had been realised through sales of NHS land and property, including land owned by SLaM and appropriate for MSU development, one example being the site of the South London Women's Hospital near Clapham Common, sold to Tesco and [at the time of writing] as yet undeveloped because their plans were refused by Lambeth Council. A further £900m worth was to be sold in the following two years.

The future of the Bethlem Royal Hospital site remains uncertain, with SLaM in residence and

having achieved Major Developed Site (MDS) status, but only for the area covered by the existing hospital buildings, while the conservation areas remain intact. Their management of the existing 29-bed MSU remains questionable and security at the Bethlem site remains lax. The damage SLaM has done by refusing to be sufficiently open and honest will be long lasting. The records show that previous governors of the Bethlem did not treat this community with such disrespect.

Laurence Wright (CABBE), March 2004.

The South London and Maudsley NHS Trust Bethlem Bulletin, 2002

Let us hope that the NHS Trust keeps to the sentiments expressed in their bulletin, as follows:

It is not the case that we would like to develop new units all over the site. In total Bethlem has over 240 acres. Roughly two-thirds of this area contains areas of nature conservation interest, including woodland that is over 1,000 years old. There is absolutely no question of us proposing any future development on this part of the site, nor would we want to since our staff and patients value the pleasant environment at Bethlem as much as other people who live in the local area. Even if we did want to, the strict rules on planning mean we wouldn't be allowed to.

We agree with local residents that the value of the Bethlem site is outstanding in terms of the beauty of the landscape. This is why we have commissioned an ecological survey of the site. This will enable us to develop a long-term plan to ensure the maintenance of the environment, including the areas of nature conservation.

Bob Akers, Monks Orchard Residents' Association

The association was established in 1923 to represent the interests of members. The grounds of the Bethlem Royal Hospital form the southern border of Monks Orchard and the green and wooded land is a treasured amenity. The news that an application had been made by the South London and Maudsley Trust to build a Medium Secure Unit on the site created considerable unrest. Those living adjacent to the site had [already] experienced their gardens being invaded by absconding patients and there was some fear, especially among those families with young children. There was anger at the loss of valuable open space when other more appropriate brownfield sites were available. The members of Monks Orchard Residents' Association realised that it could not fight alone and decided to unite with CABBE in resisting the proposal. This Association will work tirelessly to resist any further building expansion on the site.

In Conclusion: Concern about the Bethlem Parkland

It can be seen in these pages that the Monks Orchard estate has a long history, which can be traced accurately over the last 250 years. Prior to this we know that the fields were laid out in the Middle Ages and we can go back to 1661 to find reference to fields named Monks Mead, Monks Orchard Field and Monks Orchard Wood. Munke was the name of an Addington family that at one time owned land in Beckenham and West Wickham.

In the eighteenth century, the population of Beckenham numbered about 1,000 and there were three principal landowners, the Burrell family of Kelsey owning the land in question. In the Bromley Local Studies Library is a document dated 1791–06 in which Beckenham is described as 'beautifully varied by alternate elevations and depressions interspersed with magnificent seats and extensive woods.'

The White Lodge near the White Hart on the main road into West Wickham is the southern lodge of the estate. There was a similar North Lodge at Upper Elmers End near where the late Eden Park School, formerly Holly Lodge, was demolished in November 2002. Neighbouring roads are called Lodge Gardens and Holly Crescent.

Park Farm occupied 235 acres, including Monks Orchard Wood running diagonally across the northern edge of the farm, this at the time being the county boundary between Surrey and Kent. The farm buildings were situated at the south-east corner near to where the Dower House is at the time of writing. According to the Rocque map the farm dates from 1762, when it was known as West Shirley Farm. A track led off to the King's Arms next to the White Hart. In the Burrell 1820 sale, Park Farm was sold to John Maberley, who also bought the adjoining Ham Farm. When he died in about 1833, public-spirited banker Samuel Jones Loyd MP bought the property.

Samuel developed Park Farm by building new stables and outhouses inscribed with his name and the date 1843, which may be the date of the lodges. His mansion was named Wickham Park beside which he had planted a Lebanon cedar and a tulip tree in his walled garden. Part of the high wall and many magnificent mature trees are still there today by the Dower House. To the south of the house is a meadow containing fine oak trees with some regeneration by oak and ash saplings that should be allowed to progress into an oak woodland. At least this would serve to extend the narrow corridors of woodland left to wildlife moving from the thin strip of High Broom Wood by the River Beck and the South Norwood Country Park further west at Elmers End.

In about 1854 Samuel Loyd disposed of Wickham Park to his cousin Lewis Loyd junr, who built a new mansion to the north of the big lake, which he had developed into an ornamental feature with a wide horseshoe-shaped waterfall in a series of steps. The watercourse, which came from the lake and possibly rises at Miller's pond, flows out under Upper Elmers End Road. Passing near to the Elmer Lodge pub, it meets the Chaffinch near St James' Church and is known as St James' Stream. The river is seriously overgrown where it passes along the east side of the meadow. Traces of a waterfall can be seen near to where garden balustrades of the mansion remain. Completed in 1854, this mansion was called Monks Orchard. The previous Samuel Loyd mansion was later called the Dower House, although this seems to have been a smaller building on the same site.

The land on which Lewis Loyd built his mansion was in Kent and was part of Eden Park Farm, situated at the end of Stanhope Grove. The mansion passed to a nephew, who moved to Wiltshire in 1911 after which there were various lettings until the big auction sale of 1920. This included Ham Farm, of which only the road name Ham View remains, Eden Park Farm, of which nothing remains, and the White Hart at West Wickham. Park Farm did not sell until 1924 when the Bethlem Royal Hospital took it up.

The land now part of the Bethlem Royal Hospital grounds is ancient farmland, a remnant of the extensively farmed and wooded estates of Langley and Kelsey. There is nothing else left in Beckenham of this nature. The South Norwood Country Park has gone to Croydon, its boundaries always under threat, in exchange for the Bethlem parkland that is now in Beckenham. Beckenham Place Park is now entirely in Lewisham, as is the John Cator mansion of 1773.

Beckenham dates from Saxon times, known once as Beohha's settlement, which has been translated as 'village on the stream'. It was once a place of rivers but now these waterways appear only briefly to the public eye because they have been directed underground. They can, of course, be seen on the obsolete Beckenham arms as two wavy lines representing the Beck and perhaps the Chaffinch. However, those arms were in use for just 30 years – the span of Beckenham's life as a borough (1935–65). Now the area is part of the London Borough of Bromley.

Last Word from Ian Muir and Pat Manning

If an area of outstanding mature natural beauty can be sacrificed to allow brownfield sites to be handed over to supermarket developers, and the constant erosion of the MOL/Green Belt continues at the current rate, then there will be little or no MOL/Green Belt in our children's lifetime. Future generations, like current and past generations, will be able to argue credibly that a little bit can be taken here and a little bit taken there.

The old Beckenham 'with a situation as delightful as it is salubrious' is now reflected only in its road names and in popular books of picture postcards. At the time of writing, Beckenham is distinguished only by the poverty of its Christmas lights!

Troy the bearded collie bounds free through Harvington Woods in 1980.

Ye scatter'd birds that faintly sing
The reliques o' the vernal queire.
Ye woods that shed on a' the winds
The honors o' the aged year.

Subscribers

Christina F. Abbott, Beckenham,
    Kent/attended Eden Park School
The Abbott Family (Jack, Jean, Rebecca,
    Amanda and Christina), Beckenham
Marjorie and Bob Akers, Monks Orchard,
    London
John Amos, West Wickham, Kent
Celia Andrews (née Walker), Eden Park,
    Sevenoaks
Eric C. Arnold, Eden Way, Beckenham,
    Kent
Norman Aylen (Ron), Eden Park
Alan and Jean Barber, Shirley
Mrs J. Barnard
Mr David Bartholomew, Eden Park Garden
    Centre
Paul Bartholomew, previously of Eden Park
Mr Tony Bartholomew, Eden Park Garden
    Centre
Gordon and Betty Bealby, Eden Way,
    Beckenham
Rebecca Bealby, Market Rasen, Lincolnshire
Jean B. Bedford, Eden Park
Patricia A. Bennett, Kings Lynn, Norfolk
David N. Bentley, New Malden, Surrey
Janet Berlin (née Couchman), London
Mrs S. Black, Eden Park, Beckenham
Peter and Sheila Blackburn, Elmers End
Elizabeth A. Bligh, Eden Park, Kent
Pam and Peter Bowden, Manor
    House/Eden Park and Monks Orchard
Alan Boyden, Glanfield Road
Brenda Brent
Mr Kely Brockhouse, Kempton Walk,
    Shirley
Ray Burden
Carol and Roy Campbell, Merlin Grove,
    Beckenham
M.J. and L.M. Campbell, Eden Park, Kent

John Camping, Lloyds Way, Beckenham
Ms G.M. Challenger-Francis, Eden Park
Joy Chapman (née Smith), Eastbourne
Deborah and Ken Chappell, West Wickham
The Chinese Garage, Beckenham
Anthony and Gillian Clayton, Roland
    Close, Beckenham
Anthony F. Codling, late of Ernest Grove,
    and Janet C. Codling (née Cordy), late of
    Eden Park Avenue, Beckenham
Marjorie Cole, Shirley, Croydon
Hilary Cook (née Whybrow), Eden Park,
    Beckenham
Sue K. Cook, Eden Way, Beckenham
Geoff Cooper, Shirley, Croydon
Peter Cooper and Dr Sheila E.L. Mawaziny,
    Shirley, Croydon
Mr John C. Cordy, Eden Park Avenue,
    Beckenham
Hazel Croissant, Shirley
David Crowe, Beckenham
Mrs Louise E. Cummings, Beckenham
S. and J. Deal, Eden Park
The Dellers, Eden Way
Mr D.R. Dibben FICE, FIMECH, MCIWEM,
    Eden Park
S.J. Dibbs, Shirley, Croydon
M. Patricia Dix, Eden Park, Beckenham
Christine E. Dolman (née Stenning), South
    Eden Park Road, Beckenham
Gill Donaldson, Wokingham
Michael J. Donovan, Eden Park,
    Beckenham
Neil and Barbara Dow, Beckenham
Peter and Sylviana Driscoll
Bert and Joan Durling, Eden Park
M.G. Edden and Felicity Edden, Eden Park
    Avenue
Edenham High School, Croydon

Jayne Edwards, Monks Orchard, Shirley, Surrey
Mr Derek N. Eldridge, Eden Way
Mr Keith Eldridge, Folkstone, Kent
David and Jill Emerson, Shirley, Croydon
S.J. Emmons, London
Pamela J. Evans, Shortlands, Bromley
Jane Fabb, Upper Elmers End, Beckenham
Mr and Mrs Maurice Feltham, Beckenham, Kent
S.M. Figgett, Eden Park, Beckenham
Hazel Flitter (née Sparrow), Beckenham
Michael B. Flynn, Monks Orchard
John Anthony Ford, Eden Park
Tim Fox and Family, Eden Way
C.H. Franks, Maidstone, Kent
John W. French, ex Eden Park Avenue
Kenneth Geary, Elmers End, Kent
Joan E.E. Gibbs, Eden Park, London
Elizabeth Gibson, West Wickham, Kent
Rosalind M. Goodworth (née Waller), Eden Park
Pamela Grant, Shirley, Croydon
Debra Greenslade, Eden Park
Jean P. Greenwood, Eden Park, Beckenham, Kent
Jacqueline Grice (née Stenning), South Eden Park Road, Beckenham
Celia Grugeon, Eden Park
B. and D. Gulliver, Eden Park, Beckenham
Lisa and Richard Guy, Beckenham
Joyce Hammond, Tonbridge
The Hart Family, Eden Park, Beckenham
Ritchie Hepburn, 'Edenstone'
Robert Hepburn, Prefabs, Eden Park
Harry Hill, Beckenham, Kent
Pauline Histed, Durban
Dale Holland, Ash Tree Way, Shirley
Joan Holland, Beckenham
M. Holland, Beckenham, Kent
Allen W. Horsley, Beckenham, Kent
Mark D. Hudson, Shirley, Croydon
Charles Hutchings, Monks Orchard
Lesley Huxtable (née Tanner), Monks Orchard
Dr Eric Inman, Beckenham
Marjorie Jack

Barry Jackson, Shirley, Croydon
M.C. Jackson, Eden Park, London
Janet Jeffery, Oakfield Gardens, Beckenham
A.C. Johns, Pett, Nr Hastings
Nicholas and Deborah Johns, Monks Orchard Road, Beckenham
Peter Johnstone, Shirley
P. and R. Kelley, Eden Way
Carole Keyte, West Wickham, Kent
Janet and Margaret Lambert, Longfield, Kent
Des, Sylvia, Kelly, Katie, Karen, Robert Lawler and Charlie the Westie. Beckenham, Kent
Sue and Brian Lehmann, Shirley, Croydon
Ann Lillyman, Eden Park, Beckenham
Valerie Lillyman, Eden Park, Beckenham
Mr Neil Lloyd, Keston, Kent
Graham Lock, Eden Park Avenue, Beckenham
Maureen Lotto, Eden Park, London
Iain and Kaylee Lovie, Barts Close, Eden Park
Mr Alwyne E. Loyd, Teddington, Middlesex
Peter H. Loyd
Masters of Beckenham Ltd, Upper Elmers End Road, Beckenham
Mary McInally, Epsom, Surrey
Ian and Ann McLeod, West Wickham, Kent
Peter D. Miles, Croydon, Surrey
Barbara Mills, Eden Park
The Minster Family (in memory of), Aviemore Way, Eden Park
Mr and Mrs S.J. Morphew, Maidstone, Kent
Shirley Morris
Late I.F. (Nick) Neech, Kingfisheries, Beckenham
Donald R.J. Newman, Woodmere Avenue, Shirley
Audrey Nicholls, Pembury, Kent
John Nightingale, Beckenham, Kent
Tony O'Hanlon, Eden Way, Beckenham
Bryan R. Ough, Aylesford Avenue, Beckenham (since 1934)
Peter H. Oxlade
Robert P. Pack, Eden Park, London
John Padmore, Monks Orchard, Beckenham

Yvonne Paffard, Eden Way, Beckenham
Elaine Payne (née Bryant), Monks Orchard
The Payne Family, South Eden Park
    Road/formerly St David's House
Diana M. Pick, Merlin Grove, Beckenham
The Piper Family, Eden Road, Elmers End
Barbara Plummer, Beckenham
Mr Raymond D. Pope, Eden Park
Miss Helen Randall, Beckenham,
    West Wickham
Jonathan Redman, Beckenham, Kent
Joan and Peter Rees, West Wickham
Mark W. Robertson, Monks Orchard Road,
    Beckenham
E. John Savage, Shirley, Croydon
Mr Alan M. Sealy, Pine Avenue, West
    Wickham, London
Frederick W. Shadbolt, Eden Park
Shirley Sharp, Tunbridge Wells, Kent
C.C.A. and S.M.A. Shaw, West Wickham
Jenny S. Simpson, Abbots Way
Eric H. Smith, Beckenham, Kent
Eric and Jeanne Smith (née Levett),
    Tonbridge
Jan Snazell, Eden Way, Beckenham
Mrs Gillian Soar (née Taylor), formerly of
    South Eden Park Road
John and Pauline Spence, Shirley
Kevin Spooner, Eden Park
Janet Starr (née Evison)
Janet Stenning (née Smith), Monks Orchard
Mrs Sheila Stephen, Reading
David and Liz Stoneham

Betty and Maurice Swift, Monks Orchard
    and Eden Park
Sheila Swift, Monks Orchard
Charles H.R. Taylor, Eden Park Avenue,
    Beckenham, Kent
Mr C. Temple
Stephen J. Thompson, Shirley, Surrey
Miss S. and Mr P. Toull, Eden Park,
    Beckenham
John Vale, Aylesford Avenue, Beckenham
Olive L.E. Varney, Eden Park, Beckenham
Clive Walker, Beckenham, Kent
Roy Walker, West Wickham
John F.W. Walling, Newton Abbot, Devon
Iris E. Ward, Beckenham
G.N.C. Ward CBE, Kenley, Surrey
Pamela Wardell (née Holland), Hasfield,
    Gloucestershire
Cliff and Veronica Watkins, Beckenham
Miss C.J. Watmough, Langley Park School
    for Girls
Ken and Mary Webb, Eden Park
Miss G.M. Webber, Andreck Court,
    Beckenham
Donald Welfare, Shirley, Croydon, Surrey
Mr P.H. and Mrs F.V. Whale, Eden Way
Tony Wheatcroft, Beckenham, Kent
Mr Brian Whittaker, Beckenham, Kent
Sheila Whittingham, Tonbridge
Mrs Rose Williams, Altyre Way, Beckenham
Tobias and Charlotte Williams, Monks
    Orchard
Peter M. Wooler, Eden Park, Beckenham

Answers to the Mystery Page

A The plans of the dovecot on the White Hart, West Wickham.
B One of the Japanese-style lanterns from the 1920s, now in a garden in Hayes Way.
C The 1953 mayoral avenue planted by 13 Beckenham mayors and three of their representatives in Harvington.
D The Edward VIII pillar box in Eden Way, one of three in Bromley. The other two are in St Mary's Avenue and at the junction of Brackley Road and Southend Road.
E The Tudor-style chimney-pots of the Harvington Lodge.

There are now over 120 titles in the Community History Series.

For a full listing of these and other Halsgrove publications, please visit www.halsgrove.co.uk or telephone 01884 243 242.